New Labor History

Worker Identity and Experience in Russia, 1840–1918

NEW LABOR HISTORY

WORKER IDENTITY AND EXPERIENCE IN RUSSIA, 1840–1918

EDITED BY
MICHAEL MELANCON
& ALICE K. PATE

BLOOMINGTON, INDIANA, 2002

SLAVICA

First published in 2002.
Each article copyright © 2002 by its author. All rights reserved.

Library of Congress Cataloging-in-Publication Data

New labor history : worker identity and experience in Russia, 1840-1918 / editors Michael Melancon and Alice K. Pate.
  p. cm.
  Includes bibliographical references and index.
  ISBN: 0-89357-303-5
    1. Working class--Russia--History--19th century--Congresses. 2. Labor movement--Russia--History--19th century--Congresses. 3. Russia--Social conditions--1801-1917--Congresses. I. Melancon, Michael S., 1940- II. Pate, Alice K., 1957-

HD8526 .N48 2002
305.5'62'094709034--dc21

2002026928

Slavica Publishers
Indiana University
2611 E. 10th St.
Bloomington, IN 47408-2603
USA

[Tel.] 1-812-856-4186
[Toll-free] 1-877-SLAVICA
[Fax] 1-812-856-4187
[Email] slavica@indiana.edu
[www] http://www.slavica.com/

Special thanks to Tom and B.

Contents

Michael Melancon and Alice K. Pate
   Introduction 1

Boris B. Gorshkov
   Factory Children: An Overview of Child Industrial Labor
   and Laws in Imperial Russia, 1840-1914 9

Page Herrlinger
   Orthodoxy and the Experience of Factory Life
   in St. Petersburg, 1881-1905 35

Sergei L. Firsov
   Workers and the Orthodox Church
   in Early Twentieth Century Russia 65

Nikolai V. Mikhailov
   The Collective Psychology of Russian Workers and Workplace:
   Self-Organization in the early Twentieth Century 77

Alice K. Pate
   The Liquidationist Controversy: Russian Social Democracy
   and the Quest for Unity 95

Mark D. Steinberg
   Proletarian Knowledges of Self: Worker-Poets
   in Fin-de-Siècle Russia 123

William G. Rosenberg
   Some Observations on the Question of "Hegemonic Discourse":
   Language and Experience in the Scripting of Labor Roles 161

Michael Melancon
   "Into the Hands of the Factory Committees": The Petrograd
   Factory Committee Movement and Discourses, February to
   June 1917 177

Michael C. Hickey
   Big Strike in a Small City: The Smolensk Metalworkers' Strike
   and Dynamics of Labor Conflict in 1917 207

Michael Melancon and Alice K. Pate
   Afterword 233

Index 241

Contributors

Sergei L. Firsov is professor in the Philosophy Department at St. Petersburg University, Russia. He has published three books, *Pravoslavnaiia tserkov' i gosudarstvo v poslednee desiatiletie suchestvovaniia samoderzhaviia v Rossii* (St. Petersburg, 1996); *Vremya v sud'be: Sviateishii Sergei, patriarkh moskovskii i vseia rusi* (St. Petersburg, 1999); *Russkaiia tserkov' nakanune peremen (konets 1890–1918 gg.)* (Moscow, 2002).

Boris Gorshkov is a Ph.D. candidate at Auburn University. His forthcoming dissertation is entitled "Russian Factory Children: Child Industrial Labor in Imperial Russia 1780–1917." He is author of "Serfs on the Move" *Kritika* 1 (Fall 2000): 627–56; and "Serfdom in Eastern Europe," in *Encyclopedia of European Social History*, ed. Peter N. Stearns, 6 vols. (New York, 2001) 2: 379–388.

Page Herrlinger is Assistant Professor of History at Bowdoin College. She is currently completing a manuscript, "Class, Piety, and Politics: Workers, Orthodoxy, and the Problem of Religious Identity in Russia, 1881 to 1914," based upon her dissertation.

Michael Hickey is author of more than a dozen articles on the 1917 Revolution in Smolensk Province, and is the editor (with E. V. Kodin) of *Smolenshchina na stranitsakh amerikanskoi instoricheskoi literatura* (Smolensk, 2000). He is currently completing a monograph on the history of Smolensk's Jewish population.

Michael Melancon is Associate Professor of History at Auburn University and has published *Socialist Revolutionaries and the Russian Anti-war Movement, 1914–1917* (Columbus, OH, 1991) and numerous articles. He has completed a manuscript, "Anatomy of a Massacre: the Lena Gold Fields Shooting and the Crisis of Late Imperial Russian Society."

Nikolai V. Mikhailov finished his dissertation "Peterburgskii Sovet bezrabotnykh i rabochee dvizhenie v 1906–1907 gg." in 1995. Currently he is senior researcher with St. Petersburg Institute of Russian History of Russian Academy of Sciences, a specialist in regional and local history of the Russian workers' movement at the beginning of the twentieth century. He has published *Sovet bezrabotnykh i rabochie Peterburga v 1906–1907 gg.* (Moscow-St. Petersburg, 1998); *Lakhta: piat'vekov istorii: 1500–2000* (Moscow-St. Petersburg, 2001).

Alice K. Pate is Associate Professor of History at Columbus State University. Her article, "Workers and Obshchestvennost': St. Petersburg 1906–14" will soon appear in *Revolutionary Russia*. She has completed a manuscript "Liquidationism and the Quest for Unity: Russian Social Democracy and the St. Petersburg Metalworkers' Union 1906-1914." Currently, Pate is beginning work on a mongraph "Workers and Civil Society in Late Imperial Russia."

William G. Rosenberg is Alfred G. Meyer Collegiate Professor of History at the Univesity of Michigan. He is the editor, with Edward Acton and Vladimir Chernaiev, of *Critical Companion to the Russian Revolution, 1914–1921* (Bloomington, IN 1997) and the author of many other other studies.

Mark D. Steinberg is an Associate Professor of History and Director of the Russian and East European Center at the University of Illinois. He is the author of *Moral Communities: The Culture of Class Relations in the Russian Printing Industry, 1867–1907* (1992), *The Fall of the Romanovs: Political Dreams and Personal Struggles in a Time of Revolution* (Berkeley, 1995), *Voices of Revolution, 1917* (New Haven, CT, 2001), and of the forthcoming *Proletarian Imagination: Self, Modernity, and the Sacred in Russia, 1910–1925*.

Introduction

The 1917 Russian Revolutions were among the pivotal events in modern history, a fact not altered by the disappearance of the Communist state. Scholars continue to study the American, French, Chinese, Latin American, English, and other revolutions precisely because they perceive these events as crucial to our understanding of recent history. The editors offer this volume, which arises from the Allan K. Wildman Group for the Study of Russian Workers and Society, in that spirit.[1] Although existing historiography of the Russian Revolutions and its historical bases is informative and suggestive, it is neither exhaustive nor definitive. The essays of this collection, authored by Russian and American historians, offer approaches to the study of labor history designed to supplement and deepen our knowledge of the workers' role in late tsarist and revolutionary history. They do so by using previously unavailable sources and employing methodologies that escape the confines of Cold War ideologies. The essays cover the period from 1840 to 1917 and examine worker experience both at the center and on the peripheries. They include contributions by well-established historians who have helped shape our current understanding of Russian labor history, as well as essays by scholars who are now beginning to make a mark on the field. The collection revisits familiar themes such as socialist activism but with fresh interpretations. At the same time, it explores new, or at least less familiar, subjects such as rank and file worker aspirations, worker psychology and identity, child labor, and worker religion. Several articles examine the role of language as it prefigures and reflects social needs and identities. The collection

---

[1] Allan K. Wildman, Professor of Russian History at Ohio State University, edited *Russian Review* and studied workers, soldiers and peasants in revolutionary Russia. In 1997, several scholars acquainted in various capacities with his work and outlook organized the Study Group in order to promote a continued examination of the workers' movement. The group organizes panels and paper presentations at national and regional academic conferences.

is sensitive to the category of workers as complex, conscious entities. It deliberately eschews the imposition upon worker experience of ideology external to workers' daily lives. In pre-1917 Russia, as elsewhere, workers came into contact with several competing ideologies, adapted aspects of these ideologies to their own use, and, with their help, developed a sense of self, place, and future in the modernizing world. Workers were not, however, defined by these ideologies, much less by any one of them. Nor is it possible to comprehend worker experience through the lens of any particular ideology. This volume's perspective, with its portrayal of the Russian Empire's workers as self-determining actors, has potential use for the field of labor history in general. It suggests an alternative to the existing historiography that has focused heavily on elite attitudes and has bound the history of the workers' and revolutionary movements to a narrative about the Bolsheviks' rise to power.

Traditionally, practitioners of Russian labor history have perhaps linked their subject too closely to contemporary events in the Soviet Union and Russia. In the 1920s, Soviet historians first attempted a systematic study of worker experience. Shaped by the ideological priorities of the new government, the resulting highly politicized studies emphasized the radicalization of workers and their subsequent turn to the Bolshevik party. The authors used as evidence a growing collection of worker memoirs published in the Soviet Union and statistical research that demonstrated economic exploitation. By the 1930s, Soviet historiography had begun to emphasize the high level of Russian workers' political consciousness, which, in their view, found its best reflection in the ideology of the Bolshevik faction of the Russian Social Democratic Workers' Party. In response to the quite tendentious Soviet interpretation, Western historians of the post-1917 decades, deprived of access to Soviet archives and therefore overly reliant on the accounts of Russian émigrés, focused heavily on high politics and the elite socialist leadership. For different reasons and with different results, many of these scholars were hardly more objective than their Soviet counterparts.[2] They tended to stress the incompetence of the tsarist government, the ability of the Bolsheviks to manipulate the

---

[2] See Leonard Schapiro, *Origin of the Communist Autocracy, Political Opposition in the Soviet State, First Phase, 1917–1922* (London, 1955, 1971); Zbigniew Brzezinski and Carl J. Friedrich *Totalitarianism, Dictatorship and Autocracy* (Cambridge, MA, 1956); Robert Daniels, *Conscience of the Revolution: Communist Opposition in Soviet Russia* (Cambridge, MA, 1960); George F. Kennan, *Russia and the West under Lenin and Stalin* (New York, 1961); Adam Ulam, *Bolsheviks: The Intellectual and Political History of the Triumph of Communism in Russia* (New York, 1965); Robert Conquest, *V. I. Lenin* (New York, 1972).

workers, the supposed weakness of labor organizations, and the conflict between the intelligentsia and the workers within the socialist parties. Out of this complex of sometimes questionable approaches and evaluations, they presented the February Revolution as a spontaneous uprising and the October Revolution as a coup without social or political support. With the advent of social history in the 1960s and 1970s, historians in the west (often labeled "revisionist"), began to reexamine the role of the workers in the revolutionary movement.[3] In the end, many came to agree with Soviet historians that the tsarist government's failures radicalized the workers, who also found themselves alienated from the liberals who likewise failed to achieve significant social or political reform. In this famous version, even before the outbreak of World War I increasing worker radicalization made probable a radical revolution that, with the full support of the toilers, would (and, in this version, did) bring the Bolsheviks to power.[4] Ironically, when the cold war ended, the pre-1960s historiography found new credibility in some circles.[5] More importantly for serious students of contemporary Russia, at the same time, publishing opportunities began to disappear just as new research based upon previously unavailable archival sources revealed real shortcomings in the "revisionist" model. Furthermore, many of the former revisionists left labor history altogether, leaving many questions unanswered and even unasked. This volume's contributions, which we will now summarize,

---

[3]Allan K. Wildman, *Making of a Workers' Revolution: Russian Social Democracy, 1891–1903* (Chicago, 1967); A. Rabinowitch, *Prelude to Revolution* (Bloomington, IN, 1968); David Lane, *Roots of Russian Communism: A Social and Historical Study of Russian Social Democracy, 1898–1907* (Assen, Netherlands, 1969); Reginald E. Zelnik, *Labor and Society in Tsarist Russia: Factory Workers of St. Petersburg* (Stanford, 1971); Ralph Carter Elwood, *Russian Social Democracy in the Underground: A Study of the RSDRP in the Ukraine 1907–14* (Assen, Netherlands 1974); A. Rabinowitch, *Bolsheviks come to Power: the Revolution of 1917 in Petrograd* (New York, 1976); Robert E. Johnson, *Peasant and Proletarian Working Class of Moscow in the Late Nineteenth Century* (New Brunswick, NJ, 1979); Dianne Koenker, *Moscow Workers and the 1917 Revolution* (Princeton, 1981); Laura Engelstein, *Moscow 1905: Working Class Organization and Political Conflict* (Stanford, CA, 1982); David Mandel, *Petrograd Workers and the Fall of the Old Regime: From the February Revolution to the July Days* (London, 1983); Steve A. Smith, *Red Petrograd: Revolution in the Factories, 1917–1918* (Cambridge, 1983); Rose L. Glickman, *Russian Factory Women: Workplace and Society, 1880–1914* (Berkeley, 1984); Gerald D. Surh, *1905 in St. Petersburg: Labor Society and Revolution* (Stanford, 1989).

[4]Leopold Haimson, "The Problem of Social Stability in Urban Russia, 1905–1917," *Slavic Review* 4 (December 1964), and 1 (March 1965).

[5]Richard Pipes *Russian Revolution, 1899–1919* (London, 1990); Martin Malia, *Soviet Tragedy: A History of Socialism in Russia, 1917–1991* (New York, 1994); O. Figes, *A People's Tragedy: The Russian Revolution 1891–1924* (London, 1996).

seek to reopen the debate and stimulate interest in the history of the Russian worker.

Existing studies of nineteenth-century labor have commented only in passing on child labor. Boris B. Gorshkov's article is the first attempt since Gessen's Russian language studies of the 1920s to consider the pervasiveness of child factory labor in Russia. The author illustrates that children played a great role in the development of the economy and industries in Russia and in the formation of the industrial labor force. According to archival evidence, during the mid-nineteenth century children accounted for fifteen–twenty percent of the work force in certain industries. These children were often, but not always, employed as unskilled laborers for auxiliary operations. With the development of the capitalist economy during the late nineteenth century, the reliance on child laborers became even greater or, put another way, their exploitation deepened. The article considers the general dynamics of child labor, including the social composition of child workers, their numbers, workday and wages. While exploring attempts of the tsarist government to regulate children's employment, it also sheds light on the process of imperial lawmaking.

Even though worker's spirituality has received some attention from scholars, the actual spiritual lives of workers in relation to Russian Orthodoxy or other organized religions have largely escaped analysis. The articles by Page Herrlinger and S. L. Firsov explore the phenomenon of worker religion, although from different viewpoints. Herrlinger analyzes worker and priest memoirs, as well as contemporary religious articles, in a new examination of religious Orthodoxy and religious life. She describes the attempts by the church hierarchy to return workers to traditional Orthodoxy. With rich examples drawn from worker experience, the article explores the urban challenge to spirituality. Herrlinger examines the discourses of religious leaders to reveal the social context of changing church and worker roles. She agrees that factory life altered beliefs and practices among workers but also suggests ways in which Orthodoxy survived in the worker milieu. Contrary to Herrlinger, Firsov adheres to more traditional views by arguing that most workers indeed rejected traditional forms of spirituality and therefore became indifferent to religion and the Church. Even so, Firsov recounts efforts by the church hierarchy to defend Orthodoxy from the growing impact of socialism on urban workers and to protect them from "moral collapse." In a new analysis of worker voices, he also analyzes efforts of worker religious groups at the local level to reassert spiritual values. Their failure to bring devoted workers back to the Church resulted from the inability of the Church hierarchy to redefine organized religion in a way that addressed urban workers' needs. He concludes that Church efforts to reassert religious authority through traditional channels failed. Nevertheless, Firsov notes a sincere devotion to religious beliefs, however defined, among many workers.

N. V. Mikhailov, Alice Pate, and Mark Steinberg suggest new interpretations of worker mentalities in the decades immediately prior to the revolution. Mikhailov seeks to escape Soviet-era historiography's artificial creation of worker-peasant oppositions by examining the links between peasant and worker mentalities. Peasant collectives such as the village commune and, even more so, the peasant family served as the basis for worker self-organization in factories and cities. As recently arrived peasant-workers attempted to overcome the uncertainties of urban life, they constructed regional brotherhoods (*zemliachestva*), production and work cooperatives (*arteli*), and cadres of factory and shift leaders in order to express and defend their perceived collective interests. The article discusses this phenomenon not in terms of peasant attempts to recreate village life in the city but in terms of peasant collective psychology as it developed strategies for urban survival. Exposure to city and factory life was transforming, but workers with their roots in the village adapted to the new conditions (were transformed) in ways conditioned by village-oriented mentalities and practices. In a positive sense, the bases for urban worker collectivism and politicization lay in peasant mores and psychologies. The article thus neatly obviates worker-peasant antinomies and, perhaps more importantly, implies that worker activism and consciousness reflected something quite different from the commonly-portrayed passive receipt of values and impulses from political elites.

Pate's contribution, which directly addresses socialist activism among workers, continues and broadens this theme. She uses new data and analysis to re-address and re-evaluate an old question, that is, the Liquidationist and anti-Liquidationist movements within Russian Social Democracy. Pate argues that after the 1905–07 revolution the émigré leaders, both Menshevik- and Bolshevik-oriented, adhered to views and discourses that reflected already outmoded programs and practices. Within the post-1907 workers' movement, workers and socialist activists, including many Social Democrats, espoused an array of legal and illegal activities and de-emphasized factional and even party labels in favor of an inclusive and multi-voiced approach. Within the Social Democratic leadership, Menshevik and Bolshevik leaders maneuvered to identify language that would position them to best occupy leading positions in the internal movement, with "unity" (which might be defined either as Social Democratic or socialist unity) being the key term in the discursive struggle. By 1912–14 Lenin managed to carve out a set of terms that won for the Bolsheviks a temporarily superior position in many workers' eyes as supporters of "unity," even though many Menshevik positions and outlooks were closer to predominant worker attitudes. Tragically the battle of words among émigré leaders sacrificed the chance to build a new inclusive worker-oriented party.

Steinberg continues this discursive exposition by providing careful analysis of worker self-imaging through a study of worker poetry and prose from 1905–17. He finds that workers demanded recognition of themselves as human beings with specific intrinsic rights. This individual consciousness had the potential to strengthen worker resistance and class action. Many worker authors criticized the vices and cultural backwardness of their peers, especially worker superstition and passivity. The "universality of suffering" in worker experience, though degrading and humiliating, resulted not in despair but action. Steinberg warns that the resulting action could champion either the collective or the individual hero. Individual suffering led to the assertion of resistance to the "intolerable injustice" in late tsarist Russia. In fact, Steinberg concludes, the worker-author as actor presented a "dangerous discourse" by the time of the Revolution of 1917.

Three articles explore labor history during 1917. Discussing the period from February to July 1917, William Rosenberg examines hegemonic discourse in Russian historiography. He focuses on the manner in which discourse creates roles rather than on how it creates identities. The article considers the relationship of social context and behavior to experience in a careful examination of two sets of texts—the Plekhanov Commission in April 1917 and the protocols of the conference of Factory Inspectors in June 1917. According to the Plekhanov Commission, workers could not act on their own to win political and economic advancement. The Conference of Factory Inspectors protocols reversed this by assigning an activist role to Russian workers. Rosenberg's examination of these two texts shows that discourse and real life experience are not radically disconnected. Michael Melancon reclaims factory committee discourse for the workers' movement by re-evaluating worker outlooks as reflected in those discourses. In order to keep factories functioning and to assert worker aspirations for control over industrial production, factory committee activists worked out a program and attendant terminologies. Through careful analysis of voting patterns, committee members, and resolutions, Melancon argues that from the inception of the February Revolution the factory committee movement worked out an assertive non-factional approach to workers' problems. Factory committee discourses and the activists who framed them were, respectively, non-partisan and multi-party. Melancon concludes that later in the year the "Bolsheviks allied themselves to an already well-developed popular movement" and gained political advantages from doing so, a success that should not be confused with organizational and discursive hegemony. Rather, the factory committee discourses mirrored both long-term worker aspirations and actual practice during the first months of the revolution.

Michael Hickey examines the role of a provincial city's largest 1917 strike in the working out of revolutionary events. Although his article's approach is primarily narrative, it operates through juxtapositions and counterpositions of several understandings of the revolution, that is, through revolutionary discourses. Throughout much of the year, all sides in the labor-state-entrepreneur triangle interpreted their actions and aspirations in terms of the welfare of the revolution. Sharpening national conflict, however, gradually undercut the positions of the entrepreneurs and the moderate socialists (as Provisional Government spokespersons) and consolidated support for the leftists, defined here as Bolsheviks, leftist SRs, and other radicals. In this context the two major sides in the dispute—the workers and their union representatives on the one hand and the entrepreneurs on the other—deployed the language of class conflict: the rights of labor versus the rights of private property. By an odd twist of fate, when during 1918 workers again struck for economic reasons, the former union leader, then a Bolshevik, now a Communist functionary, joined the entrepreneurs in criticizing the workers' demands, even using the same statist language as the moderate socialists of the previous year. *Plus ça change*, the author seems to say, except that, the author notes at the end, the Bolsheviks in power really were different in how they responded to worker unrest on their watch. The piece's merit is that it constitutes a succinct local résumé of almost intractable general revolutionary problematics.

This collection operates under a radically different set of assumptions than many previous studies of the Russian working class. The pieces—individually and collectively—avoid assigning a universal or special role to Russian factory workers and related laborers. The collection's approach rather seeks to understand the aspirations and motivations, and therefore actions, of a dynamic segment of late tsarist society. This dynamism, conceived of practically rather than ideologically, is displayed in the dual senses of the workers' great role in the growth of the economy and their crucial role in the revolutionary movement and revolutions. The authors here imply no invidious comparisons between the urban proletariat and other societal groups. Although the Soviet period does not come within this collection's scope, one need only ponder the verbal strategies and programs of the Soviet state and the Communist Party, with their constant references to the proletariat and industrialization, to comprehend the practical and symbolic significance of the workers. The collection's editors and contributors are asserting that without understanding labor history, as well as the history of other major societal groups, we will never arrive at genuinely usable interpretations of the early twentieth century's fateful events.

We would like to acknowledge the other members of the Allan K. Wildman Group—Deborah Pearl, Dave Pretty, Henry Reichman, Phil Skaggs, Jerry Surh, Isabel Tirado, and Reggie Zelnik—who participated in the discussions and debates that led to this collection. We are particularly indebted to Reginald Zelnik for bringing to our attention the Firsov and Mikhailov articles, not to mention his insightful remarks and constant encouragement. In the absence of Allan Wildman, Reggie became the group's *éminence grise*. We also want to express our gratitude to Jerry Suhr and Oksana Federova for sacrificing their valuable time to translate the Russian language pieces. Allan Wildman, to whom this volume is dedicated, always maintained openness to and, indeed, enthusiasm for new approaches. At the same time, he staunchly rejected the merely conjunctural as well as the conjectural. No one working with him could ever visualize history, or any of its episodes, as a closed book. The editors and authors of this volume hope to encourage new and established scholars to view Russia labor and revolutionary experience with the same zest that we believe Allan would continue to display.

Factory Children: An Overview of Child Industrial Labor and Laws in Imperial Russia, 1840–1914[*]

Boris B. Gorshkov

> In childhood's golden times,
> Everyone lives happily
> Effortless and lighthearted
> With fun and joy.
> Only we don't get to run and play
> In the golden fields:
> All day the factory's wheels
> We turn, and turn, and turn...
>
> N. A. Nekrasov, "Children's Cry"[1]

Introduction

In nineteenth-century Russia, as in any industrializing country of the period, industries employed children. Children played an enormous role in the development of the Russian industrial economy and in the formation of the industrial labor force. Some were urban children of the cities' poor or inmates of foundling homes. Most were rural residents and came to industrial areas with their parents or were recruited in the countryside by employers. Throughout the country, industries exploited children,

---

[*] An early version of this article was delivered at the AAASS national convention in Denver, Colorado, 10 Novenber 2000. I would like to thank Professor Glennys J. Young of the University of Washington and Professor Reginald E. Zelnik of the University of California at Berkeley for their helpful suggestions. Special thanks go to Professor Lindy Biggs whose industrial revolution class inspired my interest in this subject. I am also grateful to Professor Michael Melancon for intellectual encouragement and support.

[1] N. A. Nekrasov, *Sobranie sochinenii v vos'mi tomakh*, 8 vols. (Moscow, 1965), 1:359.

M. Melancon, A. Pate, *New Labor History*, Bloomington, IN: Slavica, 2002

usually as unskilled laborers for various auxiliary tasks. In the textile industry, children assisted adult workers by carrying bobbins, cleaning equipment, and even working as spinners and weavers. In sugar plants they scaled boilers. In mines children fueled lamps and carried equipment. A late nineteenth-century observer wrote: "[I]nside mines where the atmosphere is suffused with the smell of gasoline used for lamps, which causes headache and nausea, one can see an entire chain of small boys, moving around the gasoline lamps wiping and fueling them."[2] Also, as in the textile industry, children sometimes performed regular tasks normally done by adult workers. In the mid-nineteenth century the average number of children employed in industries accounted for about fifteen percent of all industrial workers. With the rapid development of the capitalist economy during the following decades, the reliance on child labor became even greater. The labor of children was remunerated at one third the lowest rate of the adult male worker and the workday lasted for twelve or more hours. Deprived of their childhood, factory children learned early on all the responsibilities and grievances of adult life. They shared with their parents all burdens and became an important element in family survival strategies. The literary works of Nikolai Nekrasov, Anton Chekhov, Maxim Gorky, and other great writers of the era captured the harsh realities of child industrial labor.[3]

The historiography of industrializing England, France, Germany, and North America has produced a wide array of sometimes controversial studies about child factory labor.[4] They range from accounts that, on

---

[2] Cited in K. A. Pazhitnov, *Polozhenie rabochego klassa v Rossii*, 2 vols. (Petrograd, 1923), 2:28.

[3] Child factory labor is reflected in A. Chekhov's story "Spat' khochetsia"; in Maxim Gorky's novels *Mat'*, *V liudiakh*, and other works; in E. Nechiaev's poem "Gudok"; in the novels of A. Kuprin (*V nedrakh zemli*); L. Serafimovich (*Pod prazdnik*); and in the works of many other poets and writers of the time.

[4] For discussion of child labor in general, see *Child Labor: A Word History Companion*, Sandy Hobbs et al., eds. (Santa Barbara, 1999). On child labor in Europe, see Dialehti Vuniza and Heiner Schaffer, *Kinderarbeit in Europa* (Dusseldorf, 1992). On child labor in England, see Pamela Horn, *The Victorian and Edwardian Schoolchild* (Gloucester, UK, 1989); Clark Nardinelli, *Child Labor and the Industrial Revolution* (Bloomington and Indianapolis, 1990); *Children's Work and Welfare, 1780–1890*, Pamela Horn, ed. (Cambridge, UK, and New York, 1995) and Carolyn Tuttle, *Hard at Work in Factories and Mines: The Economics of Child Labor during the British Industrial Revolution* (Boulder, 1999). On child labor in France, see Colin Heywood, *Childhood in Nineteenth-Century France: Work, Health, and Education among the Classes Populaires* (Cambridge, UK, and New York, 1988) and Lee Shai Weissbach, *Child Labor Reform in Nineteenth-Century France: Assuring the Future Harvest* (Baton Rouge, 1989).

the one hand, portray child factory labor as the worst evil wrought by nineteenth-century capitalist modernization and view children as its victims[5] to, on the other hand, studies that emphasize the Industrial Revolution's positive implications for children's lives. The latter tendency is well reflected in Clark Nardinelli's influential work which suggested that the exploitation of children did not originate in the Industrial Revolution. Indeed, according to Nardinelli, the new job options created by industrialization and the competitive labor market offered children opportunities to escape the even heavier exploitation at home in cottage industry or in agriculture.[6] The employment of children in late nineteenth-century Russian factories, an issue no less significant and compelling than in other industrializing countries of the time, remains largely unexplored. Vladimir Gessen's two 1927 monographs, with the period's well-known historiographical limitations, are even now the major Russian-language studies of the topic.[7] Although some English-language histories of labor in Russia mention the issue of children's industrial employment, the subject has not as yet received specific attention.[8]

This article will provide a general overview of child industrial labor in Russia from the 1840s until the outbreak of World War I. The major questions it will attempt to answer are: what were the extent and dynamics of child labor in the era's factories? What made child labor attractive to industries? What were the social composition of child workers, their workday, and wages and working conditions? How did factory labor affect the health of children? What impact did children's employment have

---

[5] For this interpretation, see Raymond Fuller, "Child Labor" in E. R. A. Seligman, ed., *Encyclopedia of Social Sciences* (New York, 1930) and E. P. Thompson, *The Making of the English Working Class* (Harmondsworth, UK, 1963).

[6] Nardinelli, *Child Labor*, 98. Nardinelli's argument has been questioned by two economic historians of Cambridge University who argued that the Industrial Revolution led to exploitation of child workers. See Sara Horrell and Jane Humphries, "'The Exploitation of Little Children': Child Labor and the Family Economy in the Industrial Revolution" in *Explorations of Economic History* 32 (1995): 485–516.

[7] V. Iu. Gessen, *Trud detei i podrostkov v Rossii. Ot XVII veka go Oktiabr'skoi Revoliutsii* (Moscow and Leningrad, 1927) and idem, *Istoriia zakonodatel'stva o trude rabochei molodezhi v Rossii* (Leningrad, 1927).

[8] The persistence of child labor in imperial Russia's factories is noted in the works of Reginald E. Zelnik. In his early study of tsarist-era labor and society, Zelnik analyzes the legislative efforts the tsarist government devoted to constraining children's employment in industries; *Labor and Society in Tsarist Russia: The Factory Workers of St. Peterburg* (Stanford, 1971). His book *Law and Disorder on the Narova River* describes the conditions of working children in a large cotton mill; *Law and Disorder on the Narova River: The Kreenholm Strike of 1872* (Berkeley, 1995), 26, 72, 132, 169, 174, 228–229.

on contemporary attitudes toward and debates about the issue and how did these debates affect tsarist social legislation? In more general terms, this study simply seeks to explore a little known subject of Imperial Russia's labor history. A major thesis of this study is that during the late nineteenth century the intensive industrial employment of children, with resulting exploitation and decline of health, produced a transformation of attitudes about child labor from initial broad acceptance to condemnation. The growing state and public concern about working children helped form new approaches to the issue that resulted in serious legislative regulation of children's employment, education, and welfare. All these developments provided an important foundation for general social legislation in Russia during the early twentieth century.

Origins of Child Industrial Labor

As elsewhere, child labor in late nineteenth-century Russia did not originate with industrialization but rather had existed well before modernized factories began to appear on Russia's pre-industrial landscape. For centuries the use of child labor in production had been an accepted and common practice, essential for the survival of almost every family. From time immemorial, children had worked in agriculture, as well as in cottage and all other types of domestic industry. Additionally, child labor had been used in most state and manorial factories and in the mining industry throughout the seventeenth and eighteenth centuries.

Various eighteenth-century travelers captured in their descriptions the widespread use of child labor. When he visited the Demidov Nizhne-Tagil'sk metallurgical works during 1739–43, the German geographer Gmelin noted that in the wire shop children from "age ten to fifteen performed most tasks not worse than adult [workers]." In the Nev'iansk mill the geographer observed how seven-year-old boys made copper cups and various kitchen ware. In some workshops, claimed Gmelin, the number of children exceeded that of adult workers.[9] Another German traveler who visited the Ural's mines and metallurgical works in the 1780s wrote that "[it] was nice to see that young ten- to twelve-year-old children work in the blacksmith shop and receive a salary" on a par with adult workers.[10] An account from the Altai region's mines and metallurgical works stated that "beginning in the early spring, employers recruited children [for work] in the mines and factories." Centers of this recruitment were the cities of Zmeinogorsk and Salair, from where children were sent out

---

[9]Pazhitnov, *Polozhenie*, 1:56.
[10]Ibid.

to various mines and factories of the region. In Zmeinogorsk about 800 boys were recruited each year. During the spring and summer they engaged in sorting and other "easy" tasks, whereas during winter they were supposed to attend school.[11]

Historians of child labor in Europe note that the use of child labor in the production process probably reflected the lower classes' traditional beliefs about and practices of child-rearing and education.[12] The same was true for Russia. In families of most social strata, particularly in families of the peasantry and lower urban orders, initiation of children into some kind of work "appropriate to their strength and ability" was perceived as a form of education aimed at preparing children for adult responsibilities. The wide popular acceptance of child labor is well reflected in an old custom of calling juveniles according to the labor task they performed. For example, young boys engaged in helping to plough or harrow were often called *pakholki* or *boronovolki* (plough-boys or harrow-boys).[13] Nonetheless, in addition to its educational side, the acceptance of child labor signified the extent to which impoverished lower-class families in pre-industrial Russia depended for economic survival on the labor contribution of all family members, including children and elders.

The tsarist state concurred in the view that children's involvement in domestic industry, agriculture, or any other productive labor served as an education and apprenticeship for adult occupations. By the beginning of the nineteenth century, the apprenticeship of children had long been a legally established practice. With the purpose of having children "learn a craft" and "gain a professional education," the state sanctioned sending hundreds of urban and rural children, including the inmates of foundling homes, to state and manorial factories. For example, in 1804 the Imperial Senate issued a decree that sent twelve- to fifteen-year-old orphans and other poor children of St. Petersburg to the Aleksandrovsk textile mill "to learn textile making."[14] This was one of many decrees about apprenticeship issued during the late eighteenth and early nineteenth centuries. Apprenticeship of poor children was also aimed at combating poverty among urban lower classes. One such decree stated that children of Moscow and Riazan' who "wander on the streets begging" are

---

[11] Ibid., 57.

[12] For discussion see Weisbach, ch. 1.

[13] T. A. Bernshtam, *Molodezh' v obriadovoi zhizni russkoi obshchiny XIX–nachala XX v.* (Leningrad, 1988), 25, 122.

[14] *Polnoe sobranie zakonov Rossiiskoi Imperii*, 1st series, 1649–1824 (hereafter *PSZ* 1) (St. Petersburg, 1830), no. 21368.

to be sent into apprenticeship in the cities' factories until they attain their majority. The important status given to apprenticeship is suggested by the fact that admission was often carried out on a selective basis. Many state provisions about apprenticeship maintained that only those children could be accepted who displayed the ability to learn and "had not shown any [tendency toward] bad behavior."[15]

Similarly, the government provided the state and manorial factories and mines with a legal basis for using the labor of workers' children "according to the children's age, gender, and strength."[16] This practice is well illustrated by the following example. In 1811, a state official inspecting the Krasnosel'skaia mill, found it "unacceptable" that the mill workers' children under fifteen years of age did not work "at all." This resulted in the issuance of a special Senate decree for this mill that obliged the mill workers' children to gain employment by twelve years of age.[17] (Even prior to the 1861 abolition of serfdom, however, children's employment in these enterprises had declined as a result of the general decline of unfree labor.[18])

In general, according to the laws, the employment and apprenticeship of children was to be carried out with the agreement of the child's parents or, if none existed, with the agreement of local courts or juvenile authorities. Employers, in turn, were obliged to support the children "according to their social estate" and upon the completion of the apprenticeship to pay each child a certain amount of money (sometimes twenty-five rubles). For example, in the Pavlovsk wool and Ekaterinoslav leather mills, the administration was supposed to pay their employed children in money and in kind, the latter of which meant food consisting of various cereal crops.[19] After the completion of the apprentice program, further work in factories depended on the mutual agreement of the two parties (children and factory administration).[20]

The reality, however, often proved to be different from the law's words. Alongside apprenticeship, or even instead of it, many enterprises em-

---

[15] M. Balabanov, *Ocherki po istorii rabochego klassa v Rossii*, 2 parts (Kiev, 1924), 1:27.

[16] *PSZ* 1, nos. 22099, 27438.

[17] M. I. Tugan-Baranovsky, *Russian Factory in the Nineteenth Century*, trans. Arthur and Claora S. Levin (Homewood, 1970), 138.

[18] For discussion of state and manorial factories, see *Rabochee dvizhenie v Rossii v XIX veke. Tom I, 1800-1860: Volneniia krepostnykh i vol'nonaemnykh rabochikh* ed. A. M. Pankratova (Moscow, 1950), 7-107; Boris B. Gorshkov, "Serfs on the Move: Peasant Seasonal Migration in Pre-Reform Russia," *Kritika* 1 (Fall 2000): 627–656.

[19] *PSZ* 1, nos. 22099, 27438.

[20] Ibid., no. 21368.

ployed children for long hours as regular workers. For example, in 1842–43 at the Voskresensk cotton mill a large number of serf children sent to the enterprise "to learn the spinning industry" instead conducted auxiliary work, as was testified to by the factory workers when a strike broke out. The employer insisted that "the children live in a quiet building, have healthy food, and perform work suitable to their age." The provincial government officials found, however, that the children, who "still needed parental care," worked day and night from fourteen to sixteen hours a day.[21] Also, as noted, it was not unusual for employers to assign children to perform "ordinary" adult work.[22] Children's wages, however, were lower than those of adult workers, even when they performed the same kind and volume of work. For example, in the Altai region mines and metallurgical works, children under the age of fifteen received six rubles a year and from fifteen to seventeen—twelve rubles, plus a daily award of two–three kopeks, much lower than the wages of adult workers.[23] Regardless, these children provided an important part of family income since most lower-class families depended absolutely on each member's economic contributions.

During the early 1800s, the Russian government introduced the first timid steps to regulate children's employment. These early initiatives were limited to certain industries and even to single factories. For one very early example, in the late 1810s the Minister of the Interior, O. P. Kozodavlev, proposed to outlaw the labor of workers' wives and children in state factories. His single voice, however, was not enough to ban this practice because, as noted, most state officials still viewed child labor as a form of education and apprenticeship.[24] In the 1830s, the finance minister Count E. F. Kankrin urged employers not to utilize their juvenile workers for laborious tasks and to limit their workday.[25] He issued circular letters to the employers requiring them, among other things, to "provide welfare, not exhaust [their workers] with laborious work, and take into account the gender and age of each [worker]."[26] On 7 August 1845, the government prohibited work between midnight and 6 A.M. for children under twelve years of age.[27] The state placed the responsibility for implementation

---

[21] Gessen, *Istoriia zakonodatel'stva*, 50.
[22] Pazhitnov, *Polozhenie*, 1:56.
[23] P. Brandenburgskii, "Zheleznye zavody v Tul'skom, Kashirskom i Aleksinskom uezdakh v XVII stoletii" in *Oruzheinyi Sbornik*, books 1–4 (St. Petersburg, 1875).
[24] Tugan-Baranovsky, 141.
[25] Ibid.
[26] Gessen, *Trud*, 34.
[27] *PSZ* 1, no. 19262.

upon local officials and, unfortunately, applied no penalties for violations, a factor that in Russia and elsewhere ensured non-compliance.[28] These partial measures were the government's belated reaction to disturbances among state and manorial workers at a time when such unrest was on the increase. Their lack of uniformity and fragmentary nature suggests that the earliest tsarist child labor decrees were sheerly reactive to specific situations and did not reflect a desire on the part of the government to eliminate or seriously regulate child labor.

Thus well before industrialization child labor had been a widespread traditional and legalized practice, welcomed by most social classes and supported by state laws. Because children's involvement in productive labor had been an accepted custom and because of the valuable contribution of children's wages to family income, parents were willing to send their offspring to factories when they emerged. Simultaneously, from the onset of industrialization manufacturers viewed children as more adaptable than adults to the new factory regime and, moreover, better able to learn to work with the new machinery and technology. The conjuncture of these factors made children an important source of labor for late nineteenth-century Russian industrialization.

Children in Industries

Notable changes in the Russian economy occurred during the first half of the nineteenth century. By the middle of the century, a new capitalist mode of production began to challenge traditional manufacturing forms. Manorial and state factories showed the first signs of decline, whereas free market enterprise began to expand. The textile industry experienced the most remarkable development. The mechanization of the industry during the 1840s marked an early stage of Russia's industrialization.[29] The rapid development of the new capitalist forms of production provoked an important change in the employment system. In contrast to state and manorial factories that used unfree labor and unlike domestic manufacturing that relied on the labor of family members, new capitalist enterprises employed free contracted workers. By the 1850s contracted labor became the dominant type of industrial employment.[30] The accelerating

---

[28] Tugan-Baranovsky, 139.

[29] For discussion of Russian industrialization, see William Blackwell, *The Beginnings of Russian Industrialization, 1800–1860* (Princeton, 1968) and Olga Crisp, *Studies in the Russian Economy before 1914* (New York, 1976). For discussion of the textile industry, see P. A. Khromov, *Ocherki ekonomiki tekstil'noi promyshlennosti SSSR* (Moscow and Leningrad, 1946).

[30] For discussion of labor force, see A. G. Rashin, *Formirovanie rabochego klassa*

tempo and intensification of the capitalist economy during the second half of the century coupled with mechanization and technological innovation created a massive demand for semi-skilled and unskilled industrial labor. This was complemented by the rapid population growth and changes in the rural economy after the 1861 reform that led millions of rural residents, adults and children, to seek industrial employment. According to A. G. Rashin, the number of industrial workers grew from 706,000 in 1865 to 1,432,000 in 1890. In 1879–85 about thirty-three percent of Moscow province's factory workers began their employment under the age of twelve and 31 percent between the ages of twelve and fourteen.[31]

It is difficult to estimate accurately the number of children employed in industries. Statistics on child labor during early Russian industrialization are fragmentary for the simple reason that no one conducted systematic surveys of labor. The existing fragmentary data suggest that in the mid-nineteenth century about twelve to fifteen percent of factory and mine workers were children. With the expansion of the capitalist economy during the following decades, the absolute number (if not the percentage) of children working in industries grew dramatically. For example, data on the Altai mines and metallurgical works suggest that in 1842 of the 19,522 workers in the area, "under-aged" workers constituted about twelve percent (2,267).[32] According to figures from Moscow province, by the end of the 1850s the number of child workers reached 10,184 or 15.2 percent of the province's factory workers.[33] About ten years later, in 1871, the number of working children in Moscow province increased to 29,144 and constituted 15.4 percent of the workforce.[34] Existing statistics reveal nothing about the age and gender of working children. The absence of coherent data on child labor suggests the government's lack of concern about the issue at that time.

More detailed statistics on children's employment in industries come from the 1870s and the early 1880s, when various state agencies and public associations began to gather data on child industrial labor. In 1874 the Commission for Technical Education of the Russian Technical Society made an independent inquiry among a number of industrialists to acquire

---

Rossii (Moscow, 1958). See also Gorshkov, "Serfs on the Move," 635 note 32, 639–641.

[31] The figure of industrial workers includes workers of factories, mines and railroads. Cited in P. I. Kabanov, ed., et al., *Ocherki po istorii rossiiskogo proletariata* (Moscow, 1963), 21, 23.

[32] Pazhitnov, *Polozhenie*, 1:58.

[33] Tsentral'nyi istoricheskii arkhiv Moskvy (hereafter TsIAM), f. 17, op. 34, d. 48, l. 244. See also Gorshkov, 644.

[34] Gessen, *Trud*, 46.

information regarding juvenile employment. Most industrialists, however, failed to respond to this inquiry.[35] According to data received by the commission from 135 manufacturers of various provinces of the empire, 3,085 workers (17.8 percent) were children and juveniles from six to eighteen years of age.[36] The number of children employed in the surveyed concerns ranged from six percent of the work force in a rope factory to forty percent in a hat factory. The youngest child worker was a six-year-old boy. Children aged six to nine accounted for 1.4 percent (42) of all working children; ten- to twelve-year-old children—19 percent (574); thirteen to fifteen year olds—37 percent (1154); sixteen- to seventeen-year-old juveniles—27 percent (840), and eighteen-year-old workers—15.6 percent (480). The youngest female workers were two eight-year-old girls. In the reported enterprises female working children accounted for twenty-one percent (649) of the 3085 working children. We should recall, however, that at that time most female working children were employed in various domestic services[37] not covered by statistics. In most factories the work day for children lasted about twelve hours, and in some enterprises it reached fifteen and even seventeen hours (the same as for adult workers). Some local governments also conducted surveys of factory labor. In 1880 a Moscow city commission (organized in 1877) reported that out of 1771 workers in five inspected factories, 176 (9.94 percent) were children under fifteen and 155 (8.75 percent) were fifteen- to eighteen-year-old juveniles.[38] These data, although more detailed than in previous decades, are still fragmentary and must be used along with information from later surveys.

In 1882 the Ministry of Finances department of commerce made inquiries through its local agencies about the employment of children in factories. By August 1883 they received 2,792 responses from entrepreneurs in various parts of the country. Table 1 represents the number of workers and children employed in the reported factories in 1883.[39] Although it is impossible to define the exact number and proportion of children employed in all Russian industries, according to the figures presented in Table 1 some general tendencies can be traced.

---

[35] "Vnutrennee obozrenie," *Vestnik Evropy* 5, no. 10 (1875): 801–826, 824.

[36] E. Andreev, *Rabota maloletnikh v Rossii i v Zapadnoi Evrope* (St. Petersburg, 1884), 43–49.

[37] L. A. Anokhina, M. N. Shmeleva, *Byt gorodskogo naseleniia srednei polosy RSFSR v proshlom i nastoiashchem* (Moscow, 1977), 63.

[38] TsIAM, f. 1780, op. 1, d. 14, ll. 4, 110–112.

[39] Andreev, *Rabota*, 1–160, appendix.

Table 1. Number and Percent of Workers and Children Employed in Various Reported Industries in 1883

Industry	Number of Mills	Number of Workers	Number (%) of Children at Age: under 10	10–12	12–15	Total Number (%) of Children
Fiber processing:						
Cotton spinning	27	14,935	56 (0.4)	406 (2.7)	2,666 (17.9)	3,128 (21.0)
Cotton weaving	40	22,929	99 (0.4)	534 (2.3)	2,087 (9.1)	2,720 (11.8)
Cotton finishing	76	36,279	25 (0.1)	446 (1.2)	3,423 (9.4)	3,894 (10.7)
Other cotton processing mills	31	80,779	68 (0.1)	1,371 (1.7)	7.645 (9.5)	9.084 (11.2)
Linen spinning and weaving	18	22,251	46 (0.2)	738 (3.3)	2,948 (13.6)	3,732 (16.8)
Other linen processing mills	20	1,987	0	2 (0.1)	76 (3.8)	78 (3.9)
Wool washing	16	4,872	128 (2.6)	207 (4.3)	570 (11.7)	905 (18.5)
Wool spinning	22	3,568	3 (0.1)	115 (3.2)	995 (27.9)	1,113 (31.2)
Wool weaving	32	10,092	14 (0.1)	142 (1.4)	659 (6.6)	815 (8.1)
Wool cloth making	103	25,135	44 (0.2)	537 (2.1)	2,417 (9.6)	2,998 (11.9)
Other wool processing mills	10	899	0	0	22 (2.4)	22 (2.4)
Silk weaving	18	4,288	7 (0.2)	53 (1.2)	288 (6.7)	348 (8.1)
Other fiber processing mills	89	9,719	24 (0.2)	167 (1.7)	1,143 (11.8)	1,334 (13.7)
Total fiber processing mills	507	237,733	514 (0.2)	4,718 (2.0)	24,939 (10.5)	30,171 (12.7)
Mining and metal	709	145,053	55 (0.6)	404 (0.3)	7,208 (5.0)	7,667 (5.3)
Food processing	811	105,726	154 (0.2)	848 (0.8)	5,456 (5.16)	6,458 (6.1)
Minerals	209	15,003	142 (1.0)	688 (4.6)	1,767 (11.8)	2,597 (17.3)
Lumber	240	17,649	46 (0.3)	114 (0.6)	933 (5.3)	1,093 (7.9)
Printing, binding	79	3,536	0	17 (0.5)	609 (17.2)	626 (17.7)
Chemicals	142	8,172	0	86 (1.1)	505 (6.7)	591 (7.8)
Other industries	203	7,922	50 (0.6)	66 (0.8)	262 (3.3)	378 (4.8)
Totals	2,900	540,794	961 (0.2)	6,941 (1.3)	41,679 (7.7)	49,581 (9.2)

It is clear that most factories used child labor to one extent or another. The figures suggest that 49,581 (9.2 percent) of the 540,794 factory workers reported on were children of fifteen years of age and under. The overwhelming majority of child laborers (30,171 or 60.9 percent) were employed in textile manufacturing and, in particular, in the cotton industry (18,826 children or 38 percent). Many children were also employed in mines and metallurgical plants (7,667 or 15.5 percent), and in food processing (6,458 or 13.1 percent).

The importance of child labor in the Russian cotton industry is notable and matches the experience of other industrializing nations. According to the data gathered by the Commission for Technical Education in 1874, 22.4 percent of the cotton industry labor force consisted of child and juvenile laborers from six to eighteen years of age. The figures for

1883 presented in Table 1 suggest that children aged fifteen and under accounted for 12.2 percent (18,826) of the industry's workers. Evidence from the British Parliamentary Papers show that in 1874 the workforce in English textile (mostly cotton) factories consisted of 12.5 percent of eight- to twelve-year-old children, 8.4 percent of thirteen- to seventeen-year-old male juveniles, 54.4 percent of women of thirteen years and over, and 24.7 of men of eighteen years and over. The English cotton industry depended more heavily on child workers than other industries.[40] Analogously, in 1865 most of France's child laborers (59.7 percent) were employed in mostly cotton textile mills.[41]

Table 2 . Ages of Child Workers in Workshops of Sokolovskaia Cotton Mill (1882)

Mill's depart-ment	under 10			10–12			12–15			Total			Male	Fem	Tot
	M	F	Tot	M	F	Tot	M	F	Tot	M	F	Tot			
Spinning	1	2	3	6	13	19	90	12	102	97	27	124	342	236	578
Weaving	0	0	0	1	2	3	19	81	100	20	83	103	318	572	890
Printing	0	0	0	3	0	3	46	0	46	49	0	49	976	301	1277
Total	1	2	3	10	15	25	155	93	248	166	110	276	1636	1109	2545

The profiles of child labor in the Russian textile industry are suggested by Table 2, which presents data about children employed in the workshops of A. Baranov's Sokolovskaia cotton mill in 1882.[42] The Sokolovskaia Cotton Mill was located in the Aleksandrovsk district of Vladimir province, the center of Russia's textile production. The mill had several main workshops which included spinning, weaving and finishing workshops, as well as secondary works an iron foundry, metal workshop, brick-yard and peatery. The total mill's work force consisted of 2,221 male and 1,275 female workers, all local peasants. Of the 2,545 main workshops employees, 276 (10.8 percent) were children. According to Table 2, 45 percent of the mill's children (124) worked in the spinning shop. The new mechanized process of spinning associated with the introduction of the self-acting mule created a demand for semi-skilled and unskilled workers to assist spinners. All thirty-two spinners of the shop were male adult workers because the operation of the self-actor required strength. The children

---

[40] Nardinelli, *Child Labor*, 106, Table 5.2.
[41] Weissbach, *Child Labor Reform*, 165, Table 4.
[42] P. A. Peskov, *Fabrichnyi byt Vladimirskoi gubernii: Otchet za 1882–1883 god fabrichnogo inspectora nad zaniatiiami maloletnikh rabochikh Vladimirskogo okruga P. A. Peskova* (St. Petersburg, 1884), see prilozheniia, pp. 3–53 for the Sokolovskaia Mill.

performed various auxiliary operations which included piecing together broken threads (19 children), setting up bobbins (62), sorting (13), and other secondary tasks. In the weaving shop fifty-one child workers of age twelve–fifteen were weavers and fifty-two children—secondary workers. Of the 276 factory children, only eighty-three (30.1 percent) were literate and semi-literate. Some children (11.6 percent) attended the mill's school located nearby. The working day in the mill lasted for twelve hours in two six-hour shifts. The working week included 5.5 days. Skilled adult workers received from twenty to 100 paper rubles a month whereas unskilled workers including children made six and a half to fourteen paper rubles a month.[43]

The exhausting industrial environment and long work hours had a tremendous impact on the health of working children whose physical development was not complete. Industrial labor led to the physical decline of many factory children. Unlike work in traditional agriculture and cottage industry, labor in the new mechanized factories subjected children to the rapid pace of machinery and exposed them to dangerous moving belts, shifting parts, intense heat, high noise levels, and hazardous conditions associated with dust and the use of toxic chemical solutions. "Cachectic" and "pale" were terms most contemporary portrayals used to describe child workers. Contemporaries noted that "the dusty and asphyxiating atmosphere of the factory" is "harmful for the child's immature organism."[44] Numerous accounts point out that children in cotton mills suffered from "an alarming array" of health problems. According to a report received by the Commission for Technical Education in 1874 "in cotton spinning factories children suffer from anaemia. The hands of children who clean machinery are irritated with a rash because of mineral oil. Children who work in preparatory shops suffer from soreness of the breathing canals and throat." In a sugar plant "eight- to ten- and sometimes seven-year-old children scaled boilers in extremely harmful conditions... [The children] suffocate with the dust and soot."[45]

In addition to numerous general illnesses brought about by the new industrial environment, children were more prone to work related injuries than adult workers. A St. Petersburg government factory commission set up in 1859 reported that the highest number of work related accidents occurred to children.[46] As noted, the most coherent data on work-

---

[43] Ibid.
[44] Cited in Andreev, *Rabota*, 12.
[45] Peskov, *Fabrichnyi*, 125–136.
[46] Gosudarstvennyi arkhiv Rossiiskoi Federatsii (hereafter GARF), f. 102, op. 42, d.

ing conditions come from the 1870s and early 1880s. The Sokolovskaia Cotton Mill (Vladimir province) provides valuable data on injuries associated with factory employment. During 1881–82 of the 165 registered accidents, eighty-seven (fifty-three percent) occurred among working children, whereas the children accounted for only 10.8 percent of the factory labor force. The number of registered accidents indicates that in the given period, about sixteen percent of children employed at the mill experienced accidents, as opposed to only 2.7 percent of adult workers. Most accidents involved cuts, wounds, broken limbs, and fractures of arms, fingers, and legs which often led to their amputation.[47] The most frequent accidents happened among children who pieced thread and set up bobbins. The latter task was performed mostly by male children (77.7 percent) and was the most dangerous operation. About thirty-seven percent of accidents in the spinning shop were associated with setting up bobbins. According to Moscow government officials, a similar pattern of child injuries existed in Moscow and its province.[48] Alongside the impact of the incomplete physical development noted by many contemporaries,[49] a possible explanation for the high rate of work-related accidents among children can perhaps be found in recent research about neurology and developmental psychology. This research emphasizes the different stages of the development of the human brain in adults and children, which in turn produce different patterns of behavior and responses, for instance, while working with machinery.[50]

The editorial of *Vestnik Evropy* pointed out in 1875 that existing data on child industrial labor already sufficed to promote a legislative effort. "Every passing year," claimed the editor, "threatens the health and even lives of numerous factory children, poor victims of need."[51] In 1878 the Moscow city governor called for energetic legislative measures to cope with industrial injuries among children.[52] Some contemporaries even identified the death rates and declining health among young factory workers with warfare. "The most bloody wars," wrote an observer in 1882, "seem an

---

34 (1), l. 76.

[47] Peskov, *Fabrichnyi*, 125–136; see also Table 6 of prilozheniia, pp. 57–67.

[48] TsIAM, f. 1780, op. 1, d. 3, l. 1a.

[49] Recent studies support the observations. For example, the eye movements of preschool children differ from eye movements of adults in a way that limits children's ability to acquire visual information. See Eileen Kowler, Albert Martins, "Eye Movements of Preschool Children," *Science* New Series 215 (19 February 1982): 997–999.

[50] Louis Sugarman, *Lifespan Development: Concept, Theories and Interventions* (London, 1986).

[51] "Vnutrennee obozrenie," *Vestnik Evropy* 10 (October 1875): 801–826, 824.

[52] TsIAM, f. 1780, op. 1, d. 3, ll. 1a–2.

innocent joke... if compared to these losses of life and health."[53] This bitter expression reflected the growing concern among many statesmen and public figures about the health decline of young generations and its potential consequences for the security and well-being of the empire.

Child Industrial Labor: Public Debates and Legislative Efforts

The appeal for child labor protection laws initiated by concerned state and local bureaucrats produced an important discussion of industrial labor among state officials, industrialists and academicians. During the late 1850s, 1860s and 1870s, the government organized various commissions to inspect labor conditions and review existing factory legislation in order to work out new regulations. Already in 1859 the imperial government set up two commissions, one under the ministry of finances to review the factory and apprenticeship laws, and a second under the St. Petersburg governor to investigate working conditions in that city's industries.[54] Both commissions proposed new restrictions on factory labor. The financial ministry team which consisted of government officials, physicians, educators and industrialists suggested that the employment of children under the age of twelve should be prohibited entirely; that work for twelve- to eighteen-year-old juveniles be limited to ten hours a day; and that work between 8 P.M. and 5 A.M. be prohibited entirely for workers under the age of eighteen. These provisions constituted the legislative proposal which in the early 1860s was sent out to provincial governments and industrialists' associations for review and discussion.[55]

Although many entrepreneurs agreed about limiting the minimum employment age to twelve, the dominant attitude toward the proposed restrictions was negative. When the legislative drafts were discussed in the Manufacturing Council (a corporative association of entrepreneurs and industrialists) and its Moscow branch, most discussants suggested following the example of France and Prussia in limiting the working day to ten hours only for children under sixteen years, but did not endorse the idea of prohibiting night work. They insisted that without the help of children night work could not be conducted successfully by adult workers. Most entrepreneurs assumed that the law would have harmful implications for industry as well as for the children themselves. They emphasized that the law's provisions deprived both factories and workers of the freedom of

---

[53] Cited in D. P. Nikol'skii, "K voprosu o vliianii fabrichnogo truda na fizicheskoe razvitie, boleznennost' i smertnost' rabochego," *Zhurnal Russkogo obshchestva okhraneniia narodnogo zdraviia* 8 (August 1895): 611–637, 630–631.

[54] GARF, f. 102, op. 42, d. 34(1), ll. 76–77; d. 34(2), ll. 25–26.

[55] Andreev, *Rabota*, 5,12.

negotiating a work contract and did not in any way prevent parents from exploiting children at home.[56] Not all employers opposed child labor regulations. A few humanitarian voices among the industrialists supported these restrictions and even suggested banning children's employment in the most harmful industries.[57]

Ironically, during the Council's debates many employers expressed concern about children's families and welfare. For example, the brothers Khludov, Tver' textile entrepreneurs, like most employers from other industrial provinces, stated that "children, having lost the opportunity to earn money in factories, would not be able to contribute to their parents' income... and instead of [working] in a light-filled and healthy factory building would damage their health in the stuffy atmosphere of their homes." Most employers insisted that children were usually assigned work appropriate to their gender and age. Other manufacturers argued that the proposed restrictions of children's employment would decrease the incomes of workers' families and make it impossible for them to give their children a proper education.[58]

Many state and local government bureaucrats revealed their scepticism about the industrialists' concern for children's welfare. In characterizing the oppositionist voices, the Tver' governor noted that "the industrialists were hardly concerned about workers' welfare but only about their own pockets." In his polemic with the manufacturers, he bitterly noted that they "supported the most unethical practices." The governor continued that "it is known that the industrialists do not think about people's welfare and education... They simply exploit [their workers and] their... abilities."[59] Most government officials at the state and, particularly, local level favored labor protection laws. The local governments, with their district police and medical offices, were usually the first ones to hear workers' complaints about working conditions and the health problems associated with them. Many felt that it was the paternalistic obligation of the ruling elite to take care of working children.

Although, the employers' concern about children's families was perhaps aimed at covering their real motivations (to exploit the cheapest labor), their arguments nonetheless reflected the harsh economic realities: most impoverished families needed to send their offspring to the factories.

---

[56] *Trudy komissii uchrezhdennoi dlia peresmotra ustavov fabrichnogo i remeslennogo* (St. Petersburg, 1863), 274–278; Andreev, *Rabota*, 5–6, 12,16.
[57] *Trudy komissii*, 274–275.
[58] Ibid., 274–278.
[59] Ibid., 275.

Many contemporaries doubted that the proposed legislative measures would have any positive general impact on children's lives. They closely associated children's factory employment with poverty, which would be hardly overcome by an introduction of a restrictive law. Many argued that these restrictive measures would not eliminate child labor at home, in agriculture and in cottage industry, where working conditions were often as harsh as in new modernized factories. The governor of Vladimir province even noted that "it is more humane for children and juveniles to work in factories than stay at home."[60]

Employers' opposition to significant regulation of child labor proved too strong to be overcome at this time. In 1865 and 1869, the Moscow section of the Manufacturing Council again discussed the regulation of child labor and found that the minimum employment age of twelve was incompatible with the needs of industries. It suggested reducing the minimum age to eleven years and limiting the working day for employed children to ten hours during the day and eight hours at night. Entrepreneurs insisted that the labor of children in industries was an absolute necessity.[61] Although the government commissions' initiatives were debated over a period of ten years during the 1860s, they remained dead letters. Even so, their key provisions, as well as the debates about them, formed the criteria for later, eventually more successful efforts at factory legislation reform.[62]

The legislative efforts and debates also continued throughout the 1870s but, as we shall see, did not, in this case, remain dead letters. In 1870 the imperial government organized a new commission to review the workers' and domestic servants' employment law and appointed State Council member count P. N. Ignat'ev to head it. The appointment of Ignat'ev, who from February 1872 would chair the Imperial Committee of Ministers, signified the high priority the imperial government gave to labor laws. The Ignat'ev commission debates about labor protection laws provided lively topics for the first council of industrialists, which met in 1870 in St. Petersburg. Although the question of the workday still remained unresolved and, indeed, provoked the most lively discussion, the council also addressed, perhaps for the first time in Russia, broader issues of work, education, and morals of juvenile workers. The opinion of entrepreneurs on the working day and the minimum employment age was divided. Some delegates even suggested a ban on industrial employment

---

[60] Ibid., 278.
[61] TsIAM, f. 2354, op. 1, d. 49, l. 38.
[62] GARF, f. 102, op. 42, d. 34(1), l. 111.

for children under fourteen years of age and educational opportunities and suitable work for fourteen- to sixteen-year-old juveniles. These enlightened individuals also wanted to prohibit employment for all juveniles in "perilous" industries, including rubber and tobacco. Such views came mostly from employers who represented technologically advanced factories that had no significant need for child labor. The entrepreneurs of the central industrial provinces, however, opposed a minimum age for factory employment and a maximum workday, with the motivation that "many enterprises of these provinces [are] relatively technologically backward [and] still require numerous auxiliary workers." Some entrepreneurs appealed to laissez-faire ideas and stated that the regulation of child labor was "an attack on the freedom of industry." Industry, they felt, should stay free from government "regulations, restrictions, and inspections."[63]

As representatives of the reform-minded intelligentsia, educators and physicians, who also participated in the council's debates, supported labor regulations. They countered those who opposed legislation by arguing that "the material benefit from the use of child labor is problematic" even for working families because it reduced workers' monthly wages to minimal rates. Professor Vreden, sounding much like the handful of enlightened entrepreneurs, stated that "the law must ban the employment of children under twelve, limit the workday for children between the ages of twelve and seventeen, and allow this employment only in industries not harmful to children's health."[64]

Consensus also did not arise about the issue of schooling for working children. Some delegates agreed that employers must sponsor factory schools while others were not willing to take responsibility for children's education. They argued that education in factory schools must be paid for other than by employers already burdened by heavy expenses. In his response to this argument, Professor Vreden bitterly stated that if industrialists employ children in a way "that brings them significant profits," they must spend some money on the children's welfare and schooling.[65]

As reflected in the council's debates, some industrialists emphasized improving the morals of workers by utilizing an appeal to Christian morality and religious values. For example, regarding the curriculum for factory schools one delegate suggested that the subjects should be limited

---

[63] *Protokoly i stenograficheskie otchety 1-go Vserossiiskogo S''ezda fabrikantov, zavodchikov i lits interesuiushchikhsia otechestvennoi promyshlennost'iu, v 1870 g.* (St. Petersburg, 1872); Andreev, *Rabota*, 41–42; and Gessen, *Istoriia zakonodatel'stva*, 70.
[64] Cited in Gessen, *Istoriia zakonodatel'stva*, 71.
[65] Ibid.

to theology and Christian morals as "the necessary basis for a disciplined worker." Some delegates even argued that restrictions of child labor would demoralize workers: "one asks what would working families do if children do not work until seventeen? What would women do? It is clear what they would do. These families would fall into drunkenness and poverty."[66] Other delegates were concerned about the development of workers' culture and suggested quite different conceptions of workers' morality. Kaigorodov, for example, noted that the moral health of workers actually lay in "the improvement of [their] material and physical well-being" as the necessary basis for workers' culture. He pointed out that, rather than teaching theology, factory schools should educate young workers in the natural sciences, factory legislation, hygiene, history, and so on.[67]

The ongoing discourse about child labor reform broadened the lawmakers' attitudes towards the issue. New legislative approaches, although still largely unenacted, nevertheless were more comprehensive than earlier ones, a factor that bode well for the future. In 1874 the Ignat'ev commission presented a legislative draft for a "Code on personal employment of workers and servants." Although it preserved much of the previous commissions' ideas on limiting the minimum employment age and the workday, the draft also suggested new approaches to labor regulation. It outlawed the employment of children under the age of twelve and proposed limiting the working day for twelve- to fourteen-year-old children to eight hours, or 4.5 hour during night time per twenty-four hours; and for children of the age of fourteen–eighteen to ten hours during daytime or eight hours at night. The draft obliged employers to provide employed children with education and medical care. Unlike the previous propositions, this draft contained provisions for administrative penalties on employers who transgressed the law.[68] The legislative draft was then reviewed by a specially appointed committee that consisted of representatives from various ministries, from provincial and local governments, and from industrialists and nobles. It was headed by the Minister for State Domains, Count P. A. Valuev.[69] The committee considered all these provisions and suggested limiting the maximum workday for twelve- to fourteen-year-old children to six hours a day and for fourteen- to seventeen-year-old juveniles to eight hours a day and six hours at night.[70]

---

[66]Ibid.
[67]Ibid., 70–71.
[68]Andreev, *Rabota*, 7, 41–88. P. Litvinov-Flavinskii, *Fabrichnoe zakonodatel'stvo i fabrichnaia inspektsiia v Rossii* (St. Petersburg, 1900), 13–28.
[69]GARF, f. 102, op. 42, d. 34(2), l. 25.
[70]Litvinov-Flavinskii, *Fabrichnoe zakonodatel'stvo*, 13.

The Valuev committee requested local and provincial governments and various public organizations to respond to questions about the new legislative proposition. As in most previous cases, the provisions of the draft were not supported by most industrialists. One industrialist argued that the law would lead to "the inevitable elimination of all night work, a significant increase of expenses for factory reorganization, and the rise of wages for adult workers because of the elimination of children from production. Replacement of children with adult workers would lead to the increase of production expenses which will serve the interests of foreign competitors."[71] On the issue of children's health one entrepreneur noted that "the cause of poor health of working children is the extremely bad sanitary conditions of their home environment rather than in factory work itself.... Complaints about exhausting child labor and its exploitation by the employers are groundless because," claimed this industrialist with some hypocrisy, "humane treatment of the weak is a characteristic of the Russian people."[72]

The proposed regulations were also discussed in local rural zemstvos and city dumas (elected rural and city councils). As mentioned, the local governments viewed the issue of child employment differently from most industrialists and mostly supported the reformist ideas. In 1874, the *zemstvo* of Vladimir province, an area with a large number of textile mills, suggested some corrections regarding the provisions on factory schools. It proposed that in factories where the number of workers reached 100, the employers should establish schools for all workers' children (not just for employed children).[73]

The issue of child labor was also discussed in 1874 in the Commission for Technical Education of the Imperial Russian Technical Society. The commission gathered important data about children employed in factories and worked out specific recommendations for imperial law makers. On the issue of school education for juvenile workers, the commission came up with concrete and quite progressive ideas. It suggested that factory schools should be set up no more than four miles apart in all locales where the number of factory and shop workers approached 500 people. Additionally, the commission proposed to introduce a tax on all businesses at the rate of one-half to two percent of the amount spent on workers' annual wages in order to organize these schools and a tax for all workers at the rate of one percent of their salary in order to provide free education.

---

[71] Andreev, *Rabota*, 74.
[72] Cited in Gessen, *Istoriia zakonodatel'stva*, 75–76.
[73] Andreev, *Rabota*, 42–43.

The Commission also suggested that the employment of twelve- to fifteen-year-old children should be utilized only if they attended school at least three hours a day. The commission specified that employers should not require children of the age fifteen–seventeen to attend school, nor should they prevent such children from attending school. The commission proposed requiring that fifteen- to seventeen-year-old workers who had not completed at least two years of public schooling attend factory schools.[74] Similar ideas on the schooling of working children were emphasized when child labor was debated at the Council of Russian Industrialists during 1875. The recommendations of the commission for technical education were also considered by the Society for the Support of Russian Industry and Commerce. The Society agreed about most provisions on working safety and education but suggested a minimum employment age of ten years, pointing out the British and French examples.

Most of these legislative proposals, like the ones of the 1860s, were not approved by the Imperial State Council and therefore did not yet become law.[75] Regardless, the proposals and public debates of the 1860s and 1870s helped construct ideas about children and the nature of their work and ultimately facilitated the later introduction and enforcement of laws limiting and regulating child labor. In addition, the public dialogue and its role in the legislative process signify an unexpected aspect of Imperial Russian law making. The eventual laws on child labor reflected not the solitary autocratic will, nor the sole input of this or that lofty bureaucrat, but arose from a substantive process involving discussion and compromise among various social groups and the state.

Child Labor Protection Laws: Impact on Employment

Finally, in June 1882 the State Council decreed that children under twelve years of age be prohibited from employment in industries. The law established the eight-hour day (in two four-hour shifts) for juveniles from twelve to fifteen, "excluding time for breakfast, lunch, diner, attendance of school, and rest." The new regulation also prohibited children's work between 9 P.M. and 5 A.M. in summer and spring, and between 9 P.M. and 6 A.M. in fall and winter, as well as work on Sundays and holidays. In addition, the law's provisions banned the employment of juveniles in "industries harmful to children's health," as jointly determined by the ministries of finances and interior. In the area of education, the law obliged employers to provide at least three hours a day for school atten-

---

[74] Ibid., 43–64.
[75] GARF, f. 102, op. 42, d. 34(2), l. 26.

dance. This law also introduced Russia's famous Factory Inspectorate. All industrial areas of Russia were divided into districts, each of which had an office of inspectors. The inspectors' first primary task was to supervise the implementation of the new laws about child work and education and, in consultation with the local police, investigate transgressions.[76]

Although the 1882 law fulfilled many of the demands outlined in the previous decades' debates, the legislative initiative to regulate children's employment and welfare by no means ended. For example, already on 12 June 1884, the government introduced a new law about mandatory schooling for all factory child workers.[77] Further legislation (1885) prohibited night work for children under the age of seventeen and for women in the cotton, linen, and wool industries. The Minister for Finances, however, reserved the right, with the agreement of the Minister for the Interior, to extend this legislation to other industries.[78]

The records of the district inspectors, the first of which appeared in 1885, provide detailed accounts of children's industrial employment and welfare. These reports did not reflect child labor in artisan workshops, but do suggest the dynamics of children's employment in industries after the introduction of the 1882 law. Most importantly, the number of children working in industries had decreased. For example, the inspector of the Vladimir district (in Vladimir province), Dr. P. A. Peskov, reported that in 292 factories of the district 6,049 out of 97,756 workers were children. This equaled 6.05 percent, "a figure significantly less than before the introduction of the law." Before 1883 children accounted for 10.38 percent of industrial workers throughout Vladimir province; after 1885 the number of children fell to 3.8 percent of the workforce. According to Dr. Peskov's observations, "with the introduction of the law [many] owners dismissed children from their factories."[79] In Kostroma province, before 1883 there were 1,735 children under fifteen years of age working in the province's industries. After the law was introduced, there remained only 695 children of that age, less than half the previous number. The law also affected the workday for children. Before the new law's introduction, the regular workday lasted from twelve to thirteen hours. After it was introduced, the day approached the norm specified by the law.[80]

---

[76] *Sbornik postanovlenii o maloletnikh rabochikh na zavodakh, fabrikakh i v drugikh promyshlennykh zavedeniiakh* (St. Petersburg, 1885).

[77] Ibid., 6–14.

[78] *Polnoe sobranie zakonov Rossiiskoi Imperii*, 3rd series (hereafter *PSZ* 3), no. 3013.

[79] Peskov, *Fabrichnyi byt*; and idem, *Otchet fabrichnogo inspektora Vladimirskogo okruga P. A. Peskova za 1885 g.* (St. Petersburg, 1886), 25–26.

[80] Gessen, *Zakonodatel'stvo*, 100.

In truth, the immediate post-1883 reduction in the number of child workers did not result entirely from the effective implementation of factory laws. The general economic crisis of the mid-1880s forced many factories, particularly small ones, to close entirely and others to lay off workers, including children. By the end of the 1880s, when the crisis was over and the economy began to recover, the number of juvenile workers increased to 7.7 percent, less than the pre-legislation peak but more than during the crisis.[81]

The reopening of many businesses demanded a rapid expansion of the work force, as a consequence of which the inspection system came under attack from employers on several fronts. For example, in 1887 the Moscow Association for the Support of Russian Industry complained to the finance minister I. A. Vyshnegradskii that the introduction of the factory inspectorate caused many "disagreements and conflicts between inspectors and employers." Industrialists stated that "the law place factories at the mercy of persons [inspectors] who do not know the industry and its needs."[82] Under this pressure from the industrialists, the government engaged in a partial retreat by allowing children to work on Sundays and holidays with the agreement of the inspectors and by increasing the workday to nine hours in those industries where eighteen-hour work in two shifts was practiced.[83]

The legislative effort to further restrict child labor nevertheless continued throughout the 1890s and the early 1900s. In 1892 the government issued a decree that introduced restrictions on child labor in the mining industry. Juveniles under fifteen years of age and women were banned from night work as well as work inside mines. The law specified that night work was work between 9 P.M. and 5 A.M. in spring and summer and between 9 P.M. and 6 A.M. in winter and fall. The working day in the mining industry for juveniles was limited to eight hours. Supervision for the implementation of this decree was laid upon district inspectors and their assistants.[84] In 1905 the government created a commission to revise labor legislation and appointed the finance minister N. V. Kokovtsov, a liberal paternalist, as chairman. The commission consisted of prominent state officials and representatives of various business groups. It invited representatives of local government (*zemstvo* and *duma*), members of the

---

[81] Gessen, *Trud*, 65.
[82] Litvinov-Flavinskii, 314–18.
[83] *PSZ* 3, no. 6741.
[84] Ibid., nos. 8402, 11391. Also see *Svod zakonov Rossiiskoi Imperii* (St. Petersburg, 1893), vol. 7, *Ustav gornyi*, no. 655.

factory inspectorate, university professors, and the working class to offer their opinion about its proposals. Although it is not clear that workers participated in the resulting discussion, business and scholarly groups sent in suggestions. On this basis, the commission produced new labor legislation whose propositions were published in *Torgovo-Promyshlennaia Gazeta* (*Newspaper of Commerce and Industry*). As regards child labor, the new laws retained the 1882 law with the addition of statutes that set a maximum workday of ten hours for fifteen- to seventeen-year-old juveniles and required employers to give them seventeen annual holidays in addition to Sundays.[85]

In reality, child labor regulations were difficult to enforce because they were often evaded by employers and transgressed by children themselves. Children, who mostly came from impoverished working class and peasant families, tried to hire themselves out in order to sustain their own lives and, quite often, to provide support for their parents as well. In order to get employment, under-aged children concealed their real ages and claimed to be older than they were. One contemporary account of child workers in a mine stated that "most of [the children] are hardly even thirteen;... many seem to be eleven. But if you ask one of them 'how old he is?', to your astonishment, he will answer: 'fifteen'. This [occurs] with the knowledge of the mine administration... and it is not in the interest of the boy himself to reveal his true [age]—he can lose the job."[86]

Regardless of violations, the laws on children's work and welfare had a quite positive impact. As mentioned, after the introduction of the first basic law in 1882, the number of child workers employed in industries decreased. In 1884, the 132,000 working children below sixteen years of age accounted for fifteen percent of the industrial work force; in 1889 this figure fell to 7.7 percent. In 1913, working children of twelve to fifteen years of age accounted for only 1.6 percent of industrial workers (fifteen- to seventeen-year-old juveniles constituted 8.9 percent).[87] Artisan workshops and cottage industry aside, it is clear that industrial employment of children below fifteen was disappearing in late tsarist Russia before the outbreak of World War I. In 1916, however, because of the impact of the severe labor shortages during the war, the number of juveniles twelve to seventeen years of age employed in industries increased to twenty-one

---

[85] *Rabochii vopros v komissii V. N. Kokovtsova v 1905 gody* (Moscow, 1926), 41, no. 5.

[86] Cited in Pazhitnov, *Polozhenie*, 2:28.

[87] *Svod otchetov fabrichnykh inspectorov za 1914 g.* (Petrograd, 1915), xxxviii. See also Rashin, *Formirovanie rabochego klassa Rossii*.

percent.[88] Unfortunately, this statistic does not provide a breakdown between age group categories (below fifteen versus fifteen and above).

Conclusion

In conclusion, this study reveals that children played an important role in Russia's industrialization. This role reflected not only the large number of child workers but also pertained to the actual production process, which, according to entrepreneurs' own testimony, they had designed to function with children's input. Although widely accepted in pre-industrial Russia, toward the end of the nineteenth century child labor came under attack. The new industrial environment proved itself dangerous for children's health. This provoked concern and debates about children's factory employment. A considerable transformation of the legislation about the employment and work of children occurred during the late imperial period. The ongoing public debates during the 1860s and 1870s about children's welfare, employment, and work altered the attitudes of legislators toward child labor and childhood. Unlike the early legislation, laws of the 1880s and the following decades became more systematic and comprehensive. They dealt not only with the work day and the minimum employment age, but took a bead upon the working conditions, health, and education of children. Although, the laws lagged and therefore had little immediate impact on the generation of children who experienced early industrialization, when they came their provisions had the potential for improving the well-being of future generations of children in Russia. The laws recognized education as a priority of childhood and as a desirable alternative to factory labor. Finally, and most importantly, industries could no longer regard very young children as a source of labor and had to seek production methods and technologies that would end their dependence on child labor. The discussion of the workers' plight, including child workers, and the subsequent passing of legislation to ease the situation reminds us that the tsarist government was willing to rely on measures of amelioration, along with the coercive ones that we usually emphasize, to cope with the worker question. Arguably, by the end of the period under discussion, these and other laws, including the workers insurance law, had the potential for significantly improving the condition of working children had the outbreak of World War I not defeated all such efforts.

---

[88] Gessen, *Trud*, 64–111.

Orthodoxy and the Experience of Factory Life in St. Petersburg, 1881–1905

Page Herrlinger

Beginning in the mid-nineteenth century, village priests in many parts of Russia routinely complained to the Petersburg diocese about the impious and "immoral" behavior of *otkhodniki* returning from the factories there: "young males very seldom attend church," a typical report observed, "[they] freely and openly break fasts, insufficiently carry out the obligations of confession and communion, show disrespect to their parents and in all relationships, and avoid their pastors."[1] By the end of the century, as the rate of migration to the capital reached some 150,000 peasants each year, clerical concerns deepened with mounting evidence that some factory workers were completely indifferent to the Church and the faith, while others were gravitating towards various forms of non-Orthodox belief, including but not limited to atheistic socialism.[2] By the 1905 revolutionary crisis, these various signs of religious decline led a number of Petersburg clergy to conclude that the urban factory had been forsaken by God; "proximity to urban life, acquaintance with the heathen life of the educated classes, [and] superficial knowledge of new

---

[1] *Otkhodniki* refers to workers who migrated back and forth between the city and the countryside. Rossiiskii gosudarstvennyi istoricheskii arkhiv (hereafter RGIA), f. 796, op. 442, d. 2473, l. 144–44ob. Statements such as these can be found throughout the clerical reports of the 1890s and early twentieth centuries. For additional examples, see RGIA, f. 796, op. 442, d. 1407, ll. 380b–40 and d. 1632, ll. 53ob–54.

[2] According to the census figures cited by Gerald Surh, 156,617 persons were listed as either new residents or as "temporary migrants" in the capital, though of course not all of these worked in the factories (*Peterburg 1900*, vyp. 1, pp. 32–33, 169, as cited by Gerald Surh, *1905 in St. Petersburg* [Stanford, 1989], 15.); "Bezotradniia mysli o mrachnykh storonakh sovremennoi religiozno-nravstvennoi zhizni na sv. Rusi," *Missionerskoe obozrenie* 13 (September 1905): 537–47.

doctrines [have] damaged the worker's faith, alienating him from Christ, and removing Christ from the factories and workshops."[3]

To a certain extent, clergy in virtually every industrialized city in the west voiced similar anxieties about the relationship between the conditions of urban factory life and the religious constitution of workers.[4] Our awareness of the secularizing effects of factory life and patterns of de-Christianization among Russian workers is especially acute, however, thanks to the numerous "deconversion" accounts written by Soviet workers after the Revolution, and to the efforts of Soviet scholars to chart the evolution of an "atheistic tradition" in the last decades of the old regime.[5] In fact, for many years, our sense of worker culture rested on the notion that a religious worker was still more "peasant" than "worker," an assumption that almost completely obscured the extent to which religious practices and beliefs continued to define the experience of working-class life in the pre-revolutionary period.

The autobiography of Semen Kanatchikov is undoubtedly one of our richest sources for understanding the increasing sense of alienation many peasant-workers felt towards the religious identity with which they had been raised.[6] Like most worker memoirs written in the 1920s and 1930s, Kanatchikov's account reveals how the rejection of a rural religious worldview was a critical rite of passage in his transformation from a "backward" peasant into a "conscious" worker. At the same time, however, Kanatchikov's narrative is atypical of the genre in that it freely acknowledges the conflict and struggle inherent in the experience of his "apostasy." While insisting that his experiences in the factory milieu made it impossible for him to maintain his religious identity uncritically, Kanatchikov also confesses that it was not easy for him to break away from the religious ties that bound him to his family, his village, and his

---

[3] *Rabochii vopros* (St. Petersburg, 1905), 15, 20.

[4] For an interesting comparative study, see Hugh McLeod, *Piety and Poverty: Working-Class Religion in Berlin, London, and New York, 1870–1914* (New York, 1996).

[5] See, for example, M. M. Persits, *Ateizm russkogo rabochego* (Moscow, 1965) and L. I. Emeliakh, *Ateisticheskie traditsii russkogo naroda* (Leningrad, 1982).

[6] Semen Kanatchikov, *The Autobiography of a Radical Worker in Tsarist Russia*, trans. and ed. Reginald E. Zelnik (Stanford, 1986). For another example, see Boris Ivanov, *Zapiski rabochego: Povest' iz vospominanii detstva i iunoshestva rabochego-sotsialista* (Moscow, 1919), 48–50. On Kanatchikov, see also Reginald E. Zelnik, "Russian Bebels: An Introduction to the Memoirs of Semen Kanatchikov and Matvei Fisher," *Russian Review* 35 (July 1976): 249–89, and (October 1976): 417–47; and R. L. Hernandez, "The Confessions of Semen Kanatchikov: A Bolshevik Memoir as Spiritual Autobiography," *Russian Review* 60 (January 2001): 13–35.

past. In addition, Kanatchikov suggests that his own "deconversion" experience was by no means universal; in fact, the subtext to his narrative is a discussion of the still essentially Orthodox culture of his co-workers in the factories of St. Petersburg and Moscow. Consequently, his account points less to the inevitability of the worker's turn towards atheism than the vulnerability of rural religious identity in the urban factory environment.[7]

The vulnerability of traditional forms of religious identity in the factory environment is the starting point of this paper. Departing from the dominant secularization narrative, I focus instead on the experiences of Orthodox workers as they struggled to balance the demands of their faith with the realities of urban factory labor. More specifically, I bring together evidence from a rather uncommon mix of clerical reports on working-class laity and more traditional sources on worker *byt* (way of life). I use these to examine changing patterns of behavior and belief among factory workers in Petersburg and, to a lesser extent, Moscow from approximately 1881, when the Church founded its urban mission entitled the Society for Religious and Moral Enlightenment (ORRP), until the 1905 Revolution.[8] Taking into account the growing influence of irreligious ideas and behaviors in the factory milieu, my discussion emphasizes two equally important sets of tensions: first, between urban and rural religious practices and beliefs and, second, between religious and secular (as opposed to atheistic) practices.

Among the questions addressed here are the following: What was the role of ritual in the factory, and in workers' everyday life? Where was the center of workers' religious community? How did workers express their commitment to their faith? To what extent do we find changing notions of sacredness? How successful were the Church's efforts to revitalize Orthodox life and promote religious "enlightenment" among workers? To

---

[7]Reginald E. Zelnik, "'To the Unaccustomed Eye': Religion and Irreligion in the Experience of St. Petersburg Workers in the 1870s," *Russian History* vol. 16, nos. 2–4 (1989): 297–326. See also RGIA, f. 20, op. 13a, d. 40, l. 22.

[8]Some recent works which touch on this topic include: Jeffrey Burds, *Peasant Dreams and Market Politics*, (Pittsburgh, 1998), especially ch. 7 (hereafter cited as *Peasant Dreams*); Simon Dixon, "The Orthodox Church and the Workers of St. Petersburg, 1880–1914," in *European Religion in the Age of the Great Cities, 1830–1930*, ed. Hugh McLeod (London, 1995), 119–141; Deborah Pearl, "Tsar and Religion in Russian Revolutionary Propaganda," *Russian History* 20, nos. 1–4 (1993): 81–107. Even after 1917, Orthodox workers and clergy in both capitals would fight hard against the new Soviet state to preserve their churches, and their right to believe. See, for example, William Husband, "Soviet Atheism and Russian Orthodox Resistance," *Journal of Modern History* 70 (March 1998): 74–107.

what extent did new forms of "urban Orthodoxy" begin to emerge among workers toward the end of the nineteenth century? By providing some preliminary answers to these questions, this paper suggests ways in which Orthodoxy "survived" in the factory environment, not as an archaic remnant of rural practice and belief but as an evolving component of worker identity.

Celebrating Life Through the Sacraments

Well into the Soviet period, the vast majority of workers continued to celebrate the most important transitions in life—birth and death—with the help of the Orthodox Church. A budget study conducted in 1908 indicated that even among young textile workers who had severed all ties with the countryside and appeared to be "atheists," many had given a minimal amount of money to the Church to cover the "mandatory costs" for baptisms and funerals.[9] Many workers, though far from all, requested the services of a priest to celebrate their marriage as well. The way in which workers practiced these sacramental rites was, however, changing in response to the realities of factory life. Especially important was their chronic shortage of free time and savings and the absence of an extended family or religious community to help celebrate. Of course, the extent to which workers experienced these constraints depended in large part on where they worked and where they lived. Taken as a whole, the practice of these sacramental rites among urban workers reflected a significant degree of adaptation and, in some cases, abandonment of traditional forms of worship.

The regimentation of the workday and the notion that time has value in and of itself were probably foreign to recent migrants still accustomed to working to natural rhythms and to marking time by church bells. "Urbanized" workers, who especially suffered from a lack of free time, experienced the pressure all the more intensely when it constrained their ability to participate fully in rituals they considered sacred. Most employers were willing to tolerate religious activities if they did not interfere with the factory schedule, yet few of them left their workers with the time or energy for pursuits not directly related to their work.

---

[9] S. N. Prokopovich, *Biudzhety peterburgskikh rabochikh (po dannym ankety, proizvedennoi XII Sodeistvia Trudy Otdelom Imperatorskago Russkogo Tekhnicheskogo Obshchestva)* (St. Petersburg, 1909), 34. During the early Soviet period, baptism was known as the most common religious "stumbling block" to the de-Christianization of workers. This was apparently true even for party workers, especially females. Elena Osipova-Kabo, *Ocherki rabochego byta. Opyt monograficheskogo issledovaniia domashnego rabochego byta* (Moscow, 1928), vol. 1, 200.

Thus, by the late nineteenth century, although some workers were fortunate enough to benefit from the good will of a paternalistic employer, others found themselves at factories where "conditions are such that religious needs are completely ignored."[10] Even in the event of an emergency situation, factory owners often refused to depart from set work schedules, continuing to "extract labor, give out money, and think they have the right not to look beyond [these tasks]."[11] At the Ekateringof paper factory, for example, a worker's ailing infant died without having been baptized, following the factory's refusal to allow the father time off from work to arrange and attend his child's christening.[12] Workers were so outraged by the administration's violation of their perceived right to practice their faith that they quickly organized to elect a twelve-worker delegation to appeal to the factory inspector.

Since funerals tended to be more elaborate, costly, and less predictable in terms of timing, they were even more difficult for workers to carry out in traditional fashion. Some factories, like Einem and Trekhgornaia, contributed towards the expense of a religious burial for workers and their families, but few were generous with allowances of time to mourn a loved one.[13] Thus, the elaborate, extended cycle of death rituals commonly observed by Orthodox peasants—including memorial services and repasts involving the entire village community on the third, ninth, and fortieth day after death and the reading of the Psalter for forty days—was a challenge not many workers were able to undertake. [14] Consequently, worker funerals in cities, even if conducted by clergy, tended to be greatly simpli-

---

[10] "Pervoe pastyrskoe sobranie stolichnago dukhovenstva," *S.-Peterburgskoi dukhovnyi vestnik* 14 (31 March 1897): 277. See also "Prichiny pechal'nikh sobytii," *Tserknovnyi vestnik* 2 (20 January 1905): col. 67.

[11] S. G. Runkevich, *Studenty-propovedniki: Ocherki Peterburgskoi religiozno-prosvetitel'noi blagotvoritel'nosti* (hereafter *Studenty-propovedniki*) (St. Petersburg, 1892), 10.

[12] *Vestnik rabotnits i rabochikh voloknistykh proizvodtsv* (28 February 1907): 10. A copy can be found in RGIA, f. 150, op. 1, d. 154, l. 14.

[13] It was not uncommon for striking workers to demand that the factory administration contribute to the costs of baptism or funerals and grant unpaid leave of up to two weeks in the case of the death of a worker's relative. Nor was it uncommon for the factory to give in to these demands. See the strike demands at the Emil Tsindel factory in July 1905 in N. Morozov-Vorontsov, *Zamoskvorech'e v 1905 g.: Sbornik vospominanii, dokumentov, i fotografii* (Moscow, 1925), 147–49; About the 1904 strike at the Trekhgornaia Mill, see *Rabochie Trekhgornoi manufaktury* (Moscow, 1930), 18, 221.

[14] Christine D. Worobec, "Death Ritual Among Russian and Ukrainian Peasants: Linkages Between the Living and the Dead," in *Cultures in Flux: Lower-Class Values, Practices, and Resistance in Late Imperial Russia*, Stephen P. Frank and Mark D. Steinberg, eds. (Princeton, 1994), 19.

fied in comparison with those in the village. In fact, a 1909 ethnographic study of funeral practices in Novgorod *guberniia* (province) suggested that simplified urban funeral rites were so prevalent that they had an effect on rural practices, especially in the Central Industrial Region.[15]

Funeral practices among workers also changed as the number of non-Orthodox workers grew. In particular, the frequency of secular, or "red" funerals, performed on behalf of radical, atheist workers in the absence of clergy, increased visibly around 1905. Even funerals presided over by a priest sometimes became forums for political speeches, as radicals took advantage of a rare public gathering of workers.[16] At the same time, there was a tendency to combine traditional forms with newer, secular rites, especially when an Orthodox worker was responsible for arranging the funeral of a relative or friend who no longer considered him or herself religious. For example, when the atheist husband of a Moscow textile worker was shot for participating in a Socialist Revolutionary demonstration in October 1905, she defied the admonitions of the clergy and buried him in a red shirt, out of respect for his revolutionary beliefs, but then insisted that a priest perform the funeral rites, out of respect for her own.[17]

As with funerals, Orthodox wedding celebrations among urban workers were constrained by a lack of time, money, and the support of an extended family. Workers with ties to the village often chose to return home for a traditional marriage ceremony with its parade of festivities including the showing of the bride, the striking of hands, and the blessing of the union. Whether they were pulled back to the village by a sense of tradition, parental pressure, or the desire for a "peasant wife,"[18] workers who decided to wed in the village usually had to beg for a considerable amount of time off from the factory administration. Some chose to marry over the Christmas holiday so as to coordinate their absence with the closing of the factory, but they still risked losing their jobs if their absence became protracted unexpectedly. When Semen Kanatchikov served as best man in the village wedding of a co-worker, the extended ceremony caused the groom, his father, and Kanatchikov, as best man, to be four

---

[15] From *Zhivaia starina*, as cited in Worobec, 25.

[16] Tsentral′nyi istoricheskii arkhiv Moskvy (hereafter TsIAM), f. 203, op. 759, d. 1522, ll. 3–4. On the transformation of populist funerals into "rites of protest," see Tom Trice, "Rites of Protest: Populist Funerals in Imperial St. Petersburg, 1876–1878," *Slavic Review* 60 (Spring 2001): 50–75.

[17] See *Rabochie Trekhgornoi manufaktury*, 211.

[18] Prot. N. Grosdov, "Pravda i vymysel o brake," *Tserkovnyi golos* 9 (25 February 1907): 260.

days late returning to the factory; as a result, Kanatchikov lost his job.[19] The problem of time was especially acute for workers in the capital, since their villages tended to be quite far away.

In part because of these time constraints, increasing numbers of workers chose to marry in the city in an Orthodox ceremony. As Diane Koenker has noted, whereas the marriage rite in the village was overshadowed by an extensive series of customs and events, "in cities the actual nuptials were more central":

> [I]nstead of the rural match-making, dowry, bed-selling, and other standard rituals, the participation of the bridal couple's peers in the city was limited to a post-ceremony celebratory "*bal*" which resembled those given by the urban middle classes more than anything from the village.[20]

As the influence of the village community over the ceremony lessened, so too did the prominence of the more pagan or secular rituals associated with peasant marriage, thus further emphasizing the purely Orthodox aspects of the rite.[21]

Not surprisingly, poverty was another factor influencing marriage. Some employers helped to defray the costs of marriage rites, whereas others did not, making it almost impossible for workers to wed in the Church, especially if they were without support from their families.[22] A textile worker in Moscow province claimed (possibly exaggeratedly) that her wedding cost an astounding 300 rubles, although her husband made only twenty rubles a month and she only ten. After her husband's death a year later, she was left financially and emotionally devastated.[23] Without

---

[19] Kanatchikov, *Autobiography*, 52–53.

[20] Diane P. Koenker, "Urban Families, Working-Class Youth Groups, and the 1917 Revolution in Moscow," in *The Family in Imperial Russia: New Lines of Historical Research*, David L. Ransel, ed. (Urbana, 1978), 291.

[21] G. V. Zhirnova, "Nekotorye problemy i itogi izucheniia svadebnogo rituala v russkom gorode serediny XIX–nachala XX v. (na primere malykh i srednikh gorodov RSFSR)," in *Russkii narodnyi svadebnyi obriad: Issledovaniia i materialy*, K. V. Chistova and T. A. Bernshtam, eds. (Leningrad, 1978), 47.

[22] For example, at the Einem candy factory, the Geis brothers supplemented wages with frequent bonuses, especially at Easter and for weddings and funerals. Morozov-Vorontsov, 191.

[23] O. N. Chaadaeva, *Rabotnitsa na sotsialisticheskoi stroike: Sbornik avtobiografii* (Moscow, 1932), 44; Barbara A. Engel, *Between the Fields and City: Women, Work, and Family in Russia, 1861–1914* (Cambridge, 1996), 160; S. G. Strumilin, *Iz perezhitogo, 1897–1917 gg.* (Moscow, 1957), 102. This trend was also evident in the village. The ethnographer Olga Tian-Shanskaia noted that she knew of several cases of unwed peasants cohabitating after they were unable to come up with the fees demanded by

any savings or access to credit, many workers (especially recent migrants with low literacy rates and skill levels) found it impossible to afford an Orthodox wedding ceremony and opted instead for a "civil marriage."[24] S. G. Strumilin explained that, "in general, economic factors influenced our moral judgments significantly."[25] "I wanted to get married in the Church [*venchat'sia*]," claimed one worker cited by Strumilin, "but the priest wouldn't [perform the marriage] for less than twenty-five rubles, [which was all that I made in a month]."

Workers were often frustrated by the Church bureaucracy in the city as well. As Simon Dixon has noted, the law necessitated that the bride and groom receive documented permission from their parish priests before they married.[26] This was a real challenge for workers who had no parish affiliation in the city and had lost their ties with the village. The problem of documentation was equally difficult in the case of divorce or widowhood. Intent upon a religious union but lacking financial resources and the records from her first marriage, the widowed Moscow weaver A. S. Zaitseva and her fiancé had to search long and hard for a priest; in the end, they resorted to bribing a well-connected factory administrator who arranged for them to be married (for a low fee, without the necessary documents) by a priest in a nearby town.[27] Other less persistent (or less devout) workers who found themselves widowed or in undesired marriages arranged in the village were forced by circumstance to form common-law marriages with new partners of their own choosing. As B. Engel has indicated, reports from the countryside at the turn of the century indicate that married male migrants not infrequently ignored the vows they took in the village and became involved with other women in the city.[28]

By the early twentieth century, the trend towards "civil marriage" observed among poorer, less skilled, less literate workers was also evident among educated, skilled, and more "urbanized" workers who claimed to be indifferent to religion.[29] Some still agreed to a church wedding for the

---

the priest to perform a wedding ceremony. See Olga Semenova Tian-Shanskaia, *Village Life in Late Tsarist Russia*, David Ransel, ed. (Indiana, 1993), 134. See also Dixon, "The Orthodox Church," 134.

[24] Engel, *Between the Fields and City*, 160.

[25] S. G. Strumilin, *Iz perezhitogo, 1897–1917 gg.* (Moscow, 1957), 102.

[26] Dixon, "The Orthodox Church," 134.

[27] *Staraia i Novaia Danilovka: Rasskazy rabochikh fabriki im. M. V. Frunze*, P. S. Ignat'eva, ed. (Moscow, 1940), 99.

[28] As cited in Engel, *Between the Fields and City*, 161.

[29] Koenker, "Urban Families," 291. For a more detailed discussion of the issue of civil marriage in the early Soviet period, see Wendy Goldman, *Women, the State, and Revolution* (Cambridge, 1993), especially pp. 103–109.

sake of their family or intended, however, an increasing number chose to marry in a secular ceremony as a way to defy village tradition and signify independence.[30] In the words of one young male worker (in answer to his bride, who had asked him for a religious ceremony), "I am marrying for myself, not for the village."[31] By 1914, the overall increase in civil marriages among Petersburg workers led some observers to conclude: "workers do not distinguish between [civil or religious marriages], legally sanctioned or not. They get to the root of things [and are unconcerned] with official labels."[32]

At the same time, it would be wrong to associate the rise in civil marriage with workers as a class, since in most cases, the decision to forego a religious ceremony was the male's, with or without the willing consent of his partner. For many women, the choice of whether or not to be married by a priest was not theirs to make. In 1896, for example, a fifteen-year-old peasant migrant from Riazan province at the Trekhgornaia factory married Ivan Sergeevich Saltykov, a shoemaker and the adopted son of an older co-worker who was very fond of her.[33] The marriage was not a love match; the couple had been brought together by the bridegroom's mother, who promised the young weaver a "proper" wedding. Some of the bride's co-workers were invited to join the couple for the ceremony. It began with a ritual walk around the cathedral, St. Basil the Blessed (in the tradition of the peasant ritual of circling the village church three times) and concluded with a celebration at a local inn. In recalling the event, however, Saltykova voiced regret that they had not been married by a priest. "Later on ... we were congratulated on our lawful wedlock. It was explained to me that there was no need to get married in a religious ceremony, that it didn't mean anything; I was stupid, not even sixteen years old." In addition to whatever sense of disappointment young women like Saltykova may have felt about having foregone an Orthodox ceremony, they often suffered insults, criticism, and ridicule from other workers, particularly older women.[34]

Religious differences between bride and groom rarely disappeared after the wedding.[35] "Don't be surprised if you find a few icons and lamps

---

[30] See, for example, *Rabochie Trekhgornoi manufaktury*, 50–51.
[31] Ibid., 235.
[32] N. Tinskii, "Grazhdanskie zheny," *Voprosy strakhovaniia* 10 (March 1914): 17–18. See also L. Kleinbort, "Ocherki rabochei demokratii (stat'ia vtoraia)," *Sovremennyi mir* 5 (1913): 169.
[33] *Rabochie Trekhgornoi manufaktury*, 209.
[34] S. Lapitskaia, *Byt rabochikh Trekhgornoi manufaktury* (Moscow, 1935), 77.
[35] M. Davidovich, *Peterburgskii tekstil'nyi rabochii*, vyp. I (Moscow, 1919), 81.

in the modern worker's room," a popular columnist wrote in 1910, "he himself doesn't believe in it, but he has a wife, who, for the most part, is far less cultured than he. He cannot make a complete break with his past, give his wife a new moral conscience. So he arrives at some kind of mechanistic cohabitation of two worlds."[36] Typical was the case of Vasilii Petrovich Bakhvalov, a literate worker at Trekhgornaia, born in 1886 to peasants in Moscow province.[37] By the time he got married in 1913, he had not attended church for five years, whereas his wife (also a factory worker) continued to go regularly. Although the move away from faith was certainly not the husband's perogative alone, some observers attributed the rise in divorce after 1917 directly to the fact that the men had "broken with the church" and were going instead to the theater, lectures, the cinema, while the women continued to go to church.[38] At the very least, it is clear that religion continued to be a divisive issue in the working-class family before and after the Revolution.

Sundays Around the Factory

Some factories, including those that were owned by the state, had their own churches. At factories such as the Izhorsk ironworks in Kolpino, for example, workers were expected to attend mass in the factory church on Sundays and holidays. The parish clergy was officially part of the administrative staff, participating regularly in the workers' religious life and thereby maintaining relatively close ties with (and a close watch on) their parishioners. Those workers who failed to make it to church risked being reported and fined.[39] As suggested earlier, the model of the paternalistic employer was increasingly rare by the end of the nineteenth century, especially in St. Petersburg. Thus, even as some factory owners continued to build churches or chapels in response to an observed decline in their workers' attendance at mass, most tended to neglect religious life in the factory. Within factories holidays and ceremonies such as annual prayer meetings yielded to the Church's insistence that religious observance occur at officially designated parish churches.[40] Of course,

---

[36] A. Zorin, "Rabochii Mir (Sovremennyia nastroeniia)," *Zhizn' dlia vsekh* 2 (1910): col. 105.

[37] *Rabochie Trekhgornoi manufaktury*, 258.

[38] Kostitsyn, 82. The memoirs of Guliutina and Bushueva discuss similar family conflicts over religious issues in the post-1917 period. See Chaadaeva, *Rabotnitsa*, 74, 149.

[39] S. Zav'ialov, *Istoriia Izhorskogo zavoda* (Moscow, 1934), 61. See also, A. M. Pankratova, ed., *Rabochee dvizhenie v Rossii v XIX veke* (Moscow, 1950), vol. 2, part 2, 596–97.

[40] See, for example, "A. R.," "Molitvennyi dom kuptsa I. V. Alekseeva (Tambovskaia

employers themselves were of varied religious backgrounds, though this fact seems to have had little negative impact on Orthodox practices in their factories. Old Believer and non-Orthodox employers were quite attentive to their Orthodox workers' religious needs, probably because of the Church's constant scrutiny. Contrarily, some Orthodox employers demanded Sunday and holiday work.[41]

For those workers who were forced to look beyond factory walls for a place to worship, finding a parish community that was both accessible and welcoming was not always easy. Towards the end of the nineteenth century, urban parishes were completely overwhelmed by the human tide of workers pouring into the city, especially on holidays.[42] In the 1890s, the Church responded to the growing parish crisis with a wave of new construction in working-class areas. By 1895, it had completed a large cathedral on the Obvodnyi canal near the Warsaw Railroad Station; nicknamed "Varshavka," it soon became a popular center of religious activity for local factory and railroad workers.[43] Additional churches followed, but financial limitations ensured that the demand for new parishes exceeded the Church's ability to construct them.[44] As a result, some working-class neighborhoods in the capital lacked a church that could serve as a center of religious life.[45]

This problem was hardly unique to urban areas, but the realities of working-class life exacerbated the crisis.[46] The seasonal and annual ebb

---

ul., no. 18)," *S.-Peterburgskoi dukhovnyi vestnik* 13/14 (1895): 295; "F. O.," "Po povodu zabastovki fabrichnykh rabochikh v Peterburge," *S.-Peterburgskii dukhovnyi vestnik* 30 (1896): 587–89.

[41] See for example, TsIAM, f. 16, op. 89, d. 29, ll. 15–6; RGIA, f. 22, op. 5, d. 161, ot. 1. st. 1, l. 1. "Obshchestvennaia deiatel'nost' sviashchennika," *Tserkovnyi vestnik* 9 (26 February 1904): col. 260.

[42] "F. O.," "Po povodu zabastovki," 587–89.

[43] By 1905, the ORRP had built six: in the mid-1890s, its main church, the Troitskii cathedral, was completed, along with the Pokrovskaia church on Borovoi street, which was financed largely on donations from the Petersburg industrialists Govard and Zhukov. *S.-Peterburgskii dukhovnyi vestnik* 11 (14 March 1897): 216. Other ORRP churches appeared in the Vyborg district, on Bol'shaia Okhta, and in the outlying village of Aleksandrovskoe.

[44] *Otchet o deiatel'nosti Obshchestva dlia rasprostraneniia religiozno-nravstvennago prosveshcheniia v dukhe Pravoslavnoi Tserkvi za 1906 i 1907 gg.* (St. Petersburg, 1908), 22.

[45] Runkevich, *Studenty-propovedniki*, 13.

[46] "F. O.," "Po povodu zabastovki," 587–89. This was a problem endemic to the empire as a whole. According to Gregory Freeze, by 1904, the ratio of parish priests to parishioners in Russia as a whole was 1:1844. See Gregory L. Freeze, *The Parish Clergy in Nineteenth-Century Russia: Crisis, Reform, Counter-Reform* (Princeton,

and flow of working populations and the tendency of workers to move often within cities cut them off from the stable community of believers they had experienced in the village.[47] While some workers tried to compensate for this lack of a religious center by maintaining ties with their village parish, or by worshipping together with members of their family, *artel'* or factory shop, many of the working Orthodox remained tied to urban parishes in which they felt and were often treated like "guests."[48] Commenting on the capital's Nevskii Gate region, known for its high concentration of workers and shortage of churches, S. N. Runkevich of the Petersburg Spiritual Consistory concluded that, "under such circumstances it is easy to see why the population in this area does not exhibit the religiosity characteristic of the Russian people."[49]

How much the lack of an adequate parish structure influenced the frequency of religious practice is hard to judge. Regardless, clerical reports clearly reflect its detrimental effect on the quality of religious life, especially on holidays when the problem was most acute. Evidence suggests that most urban workers attended church on major holidays, even if they failed to go to mass the rest of the year. "In 1900, [at age 27] I stopped going to church; and if I did go, it was only on Easter and Christmas," wrote a former weaver from Moscow, in a perfunctory manner typical of many worker-memoirists discussing the difficult issue of religious belief in the 1930s.[50] Most workers made their appearance in church during Easter with the express intention of performing their annual obligation of confession and communion. After taking into account the "stress of the [factory worker's] everyday labor, which sometimes does not allow even a minute of free time for fulfilling required religious needs," the Petersburg diocese typically concluded in its annual reports that "the number [of workers] failing to confess without explanation is actually insignificant."[51] This was the case even in the revolutionary year 1905, when urban churches stood emptier than usual on Sundays.

1983), 459–60.

[47] As Vera Shevzov has demonstrated in her study of rural Christianity in Vologda province, "while rural believers identified with the Orthodox faith at large, their primary arena for experiencing that faith was the local ecclesial community." Vera Shevzov, "Popular Orthodoxy in Late Imperial Rural Russia," unpublished Ph.D. dissertation (Yale University, 1994), 720.

[48] RGIA, f. 796, op. 442, d. 2290, ll. 207–208, as cited in Dixon, "The Orthodox Church and the Workers of St. Petersburg, 1880–1914," 131.

[49] Runkevich, *Studenty-propovedniki*, 13.

[50] *Rabochie Trekhgornoi manufaktury v 1905 g.*, 201.

[51] RGIA, f. 796, op. 442, d. 2105, l. 124.

For most workers, preparation for the holy sacrament of confession and communion began with a rather strict routine of fasting.[52] In the city, as in the village, the ritual of fasting was still so universal that eating forbidden foods in public remained an effective way to publicize one's apostasy.[53] In some cases, peasant workers even returned to their parish during Lent in order to fast as part of the rural community. When this was difficult, either because of the distance or a lack of time, they often wrote to their village priest about their attendance at confession and holy communion.[54] After receiving communion, workers then devoted themselves to celebratory feasting: a widespread pattern even on the holiest days was to break fasts with a few friends and many bottles of vodka. A. Shapovalov remembered his father as a typically "pious" man who would routinely return home after fasting and feasting only to hang his head low and then vomit into a dirty bucket, when "from his stomach [would come up] all the vodka he had drunk, along with the Holy Eucharist, 'the body of Christ.'"[55] Although the younger worker found such behavior disturbing, even blasphemous, it seems that his father did not.

Clergy routinely expressed concerns about the negative influence of alcohol on the practice of the faith, and worried about the effects of the parish crisis on the exercise of confessing and communicating. During Lent there would be 700–900 worshippers, exhausted from fasting and the stress of their jobs, waiting *en masse* to confess to a single, overworked priest, who may or may not have known them by name. In 1904, Father E. Kondrat'ev calculated that if each parishioner got just one minute, the whole process would still take fifteen hours; "and what kind of confession would that be?" he asked.[56] Since the required blessing took at least twenty seconds, after which worshippers would say their name, kneel to the ground, and make the sign of the cross, there was usually little time left for the confession of sins, let alone a proper response from the priest. The unfamiliarity between priest and confessor, combined with the brevity of the act, made a meaningful exchange nearly impossible.

---

[52] Kabo, 200; A. Shapovalov, *Po doroge k marksizmu* (Moscow, 1922), 34–35.

[53] See, for example, the case of one stylishly dressed "aristocratic" turner named Kozhevnikov, a member of a socialist *kruzhok*(circle). He was noted by his co-workers for the fact that he did not drink, did not go to church, did not remove his cap or cross himself when passing before the icons, and ate sausage and bread with butter on fast days. Shapovalov, *Po doroge*, 34–35.

[54] *Kostromskie eparkhial'nye vedomosti*, year 8, no. 13 (July 1894): 275–76, as quoted in Burds,*Peasant Dreams*, 190.

[55] Shapovalov, *Po doroge*, 9–10.

[56] Sv. E. Kondrat'ev, "K voprosu o poriadkakh v prikhodskikh khramakh," *Izvestiia po S.-Peterburgskoi eparkhii* 13 (10 July 1910): 3.

Given the demands of their labor and the limitations of parish life in the city, it is not surprising that workers tended to be even more erratic than peasants in their patterns of worship on Sundays and minor holidays.[57] The fluidity of the factory population and the lack of a formal parish registration process made it nearly impossible for the Church to keep reliable statistical records of worker practices. Evidence drawn from clerical reports (including articles in the diocesan press and annual *otchety*), various studies of worker *byt*, and memoirs suggests that many workers did not attend Sunday mass on a regular basis. An ethnographic study of Moscow workers conducted by Elena Kabo in the early 1920s, for example, found that among those male workers who admitted to going to church prior to 1918, almost half (forty-eight percent) said they went to mass on major holidays, while only sixteen percent attended more regularly. Among the women, thirty-eight percent claimed to have gone to church every Sunday, while thirty-eight percent attended only on major holidays.[58] The corresponding figures for Petersburg workers would likely indicate an even stronger pattern of behavior, given the severity of the parish crisis and the relatively strong influence of sectarians and socialists there.

Among workers for whom church-going was not a matter of coercion, those with closer ties to the village tended to go to mass more regularly.[59] For example, Semen Kanatchikov's co-worker, the older pattern-maker "Sushchii," continued to observe all the traditional rites of the Orthodox faith, including attendance at mass, much as he had in the countryside.[60] This pattern of behavior was more typical among older workers, perhaps because their sense of religious identity was already well developed before they left the village. By contrast, younger workers were on the whole very lax about going to church on Sundays and minor holidays. Village priests routinely complained to the Petersburg diocese about the tendency of young *otkhodniki* to abandon regular church attendance.[61] Urban structures such as the *artel'* or the factory shop sometimes functioned as a

---

[57] As Gregory Freeze has pointed out, factors such as the impassibility of roads and the lack of a nearby parish often prevented peasants from going to church. See Gregory L. Freeze, "The Rechristianization of Russia: The Church and Popular Religion, 1750–1850," *Studia Slavic Finlandesia* 7 (1990): 113.

[58] Kabo, 199–200.

[59] Prokopovich, *Biudzhety peterburgskikh rabochikh*, 34.

[60] Kanatchikov, *Autobiography*, 7–13.

[61] RGIA, f. 796, op. 442, d. 2473, l. 144–44ob. Statements such as these can be found throughout the clerical reports of the 1890s and early twentieth centuries. For additional examples, see RGIA, f. 796, op. 442, d. 1407, ll. 380b–40; and d. 1632, ll. 53ob–54.

parallel institution to the village community, with older workers watching over younger ones to ensure that they performed their religious duties. Still, this kind of pressure did not always work, since it was relatively easy to get lost in the shuffle of the "big city."[62] Consequently, the picture on Sundays in factory districts was much the same as the opening scene in Gorky's *Mother*, published in 1907: "on holidays the workers slept until about ten o'clock, then the staid and married people dressed themselves in their best clothes and, after duly scolding the young folks for their indifference to church, went to hear mass."[63] Of course, exceptions were not uncommon, especially among younger workers with close ties to the village and a strong sense of tradition. For example, Van'ka Korovin, like his father before him, was known among his co-workers for his piety: "he never misses a single mass," Kanatchikov wrote, "[he] goes to confession every year, takes Communion, and is very concerned about maintaining the splendor of the neighborhood church."[64]

Along with older workers and recent migrants, women (young and old) were more likely than men to spend their free time at mass. Female memoirists typically chose to describe their regular presence in church as an aesthetic and spiritual escape from everyday life, echoing the argument made in the early 1920s by N. K. Krupskaia.[65] Recalling her life in 1905, a Petersburg tobacco worker wrote, "my whole life was taken up with work at the factory ... [O]ur only day off was Sunday, and on Sundays we had housework or church. That's the way life was for women workers then."[66] A young weaver at Trekhgornaia remembered how she and her female co-workers would rise to the sound of the factory bell on Sunday mornings, rush to mass together, and then return to the factory barracks to drink tea, lacking any other place to pass a few hours of leisure time.[67]

Hesitant after 1917 to admit to strong feelings of piety, female memoirists often recalled that, even in the absence of direct parental or community influence, the pull of tradition and a respect for the past continued to attract them to church. In describing her attitudes towards religion in 1905, a young female tobacco worker from Petersburg explained, "I was less than twenty years old then, I was religious, just as my mother

---

[62] Kanatchikov, *Autobiography*, 7–13.
[63] Maxim Gorky, *Mother*, trans. Isidor Shneider (New York, 1947), 4.
[64] Kanatchikov, *Autobiography*, 53.
[65] N. K. Krupskaia, "Rabotnitsa i religiia," *Kommunistka* 3–5 (1922), reprinted in *Antireligioznaia rabota sredi zhenshchin. Sbornik*, L. Stal', ed. (Moscow, 1926), 12–15.
[66] "Rasskaz rabotnitsy o 9-m ianvaria," *Leningradskaia Pravda* 18 (22 January 1925): 7. See also, Lapitskaia, *Byt rabochikh*, 73.
[67] L. D. Krylova, *Zapiski tkachikhi* (Moscow, 1932), 19.

was religious, [and] everyone around me was religious. I never heard anything said against religion. We were obliged to go to church [and] I 'believed' like everyone else."[68] Others claimed to have gone to church as an expression of respect or love for their older relatives, as in the case of one woman who repeatedly promised her husband that she would stop going to church when her aunt, a very religious elderly spinster (*staraia vekovukha*), died.[69]

Memoirs also suggest that the beauty of the Orthodox mass, especially singing by a choir, encouraged both men and women to attend church. The clergy often criticized the industrialized city as an overwhelmingly noisy place, "where one does not feel as close to God" as in the quiet expanse of the countryside. Yet it seems that the dissonance of the factory environment actually drew workers to church on occasion—not only the devout, but the doubting and the indifferent as well.[70] Olga Shirokova, for example, recalled how much she and other Guzhon workers loved going to church to hear the music, even after they had supposedly stopped observing Orthodox rites. "Where better to spend [Sundays and holidays]?" Shirokova explained, "the church was well-lit and beautiful, there was good singing."[71] "I stopped going to church for prayer a very long time ago," claimed a male factory worker, born to peasants in Moscow province in 1886, "but I'd [still] go often to hear church singing. I really love church singing, and there were very good choirs."[72] Singing was in fact so popular among workers that by the late nineteenth century, choirs comprised mostly of workers and shop assistants were a regular feature of working-class religious life. Several hundred workers participated in the choir organized by the ORRP, which rehearsed as many as five times a week.[73]

Aside from indifference or an absence of faith, numerous factors help explain working-class irregularities in church attendance, not the least of which was the lack of a nearby parish. Another factor was the general lack of free time because of the need to take care of marketing, cleaning, and tending to children. Among the young, a sense of adolescent rebellion, particularly among migrant workers enjoying newfound independence from their parents and village elders, also encouraged some to

---

[68] "Rasskaz rabotnitsy o 9-m ianvaria," 7.
[69] *Rabochie Trekhgornoi manufaktury*, 258.
[70] *Rabochii vopros* (St. Petersburg, 1905), 15, 20.
[71] *Rabochii zavod "Serp i Molot" (b. Guzhon)* (Moscow, 1931), 230–31.
[72] *Rabochie Trekhgornoi manufaktury*, 258.
[73] RGIA, f. 796, op. 442, d. 1737, l. 64ob.

skip church. From the perspective of local clergy, however, the reason that most workers were absent from mass was quite clear: preferring alcohol to liturgy, they spent their Sundays at the local tavern, where they engaged in extensive drinking and "wild merrymaking" instead of prayer.[74]

Noting that it was usually easier to find a tavern than a church in working-class neighborhoods, clergy explained the workers' passion for the tavern by their general ignorance, combined with the stress of their physical labor. "It is no secret," wrote the priest Runkevich in 1892, "that factory workers, exhausted by continuous work, rush to seek out amusement in their free time to make up for the labor that buries them daily, and that holidays, which are days off at factories, turn into days of revelry [*razgul*] for the majority."[75] Another missionary described the workers' situation in very similar terms, some ten years later: "living under the hypnosis of exhausting physical labor all week long, the [factory worker] looks to his only day off not for sensible relaxation and the satisfaction of spiritual interests, but for deafening hypnosis, [for] shaking, senseless revelry, [for] alcoholic stupefication."[76]

Excessive drinking not only pulled workers away from the church but often led to behaviors considered to be impious and immoral, to "defile themselves with bad business," including "debauchery, fighting, and even murder."[77] Excessive use of alcohol was the primary cause of blasphemy among workers.[78] Typical was the case of Nikolai Vydrov, an illiterate peasant working temporarily at a brick factory near St. Petersburg.[79] In 1889, an extraordinarily drunk Vydrov was arrested at a tavern for denying the sacredness of the Holy Virgin and avowing his lack of belief in God and the saints. When confronted by clergy the following day, he claimed to remember nothing of his indiscretion and willingly repented.

---

[74] RGIA, f. 796, op. 442, d. 1737, ll. 71ob–72.

[75] "Prichiny pechal'nykh sobytii," *Tserkovnyi vestnik* 3 (January 1905): col. 66; Runkevich, *Studenty-propovedniki*, 9–10.

[76] "Kumiry sovremennosti," *Tserkovnyi vestnik* 6 (1902): 13.

[77] *S.-Peterburgskii dukhovnyi vestnik* 42 (1895): 966.

[78] Conscious, sober acts of iconoclasm were rare among workers, except in the case of sectarians. See, for example, the list of thirty cases of blasphemy involving peasants and workers in the Moscow circuit court system between 1899 and 1913, from TsIAM, f. 46 ("Kantseliariia moskovskogo ober-politseimeistera"), d. 398, sv. 33, l. 93, as cited by F. Putintsev, "Nekotorye fakty o presledovanii bezbozhnikov pri tsarizme," *Antireligioznik* 6 (1938): 45–49. For examples in St. Petersburg, see RGIA, f. 796, op 442, d. 1913, l. 107–107ob; Tsentral'nyi istoricheskii gosudarstvennyi arkhiv g. S.-Peterburga (hereafter TsGIA SPb), f. 19, op. 81, d. 7, l. 2, and D. I. Skvortsov, *Sovremennoe russkoe sektantsvo* (Moscow, 1905), 82.

[79] TsGIA SPb, f. 19, op. 81, d. 7, ll. 2–13.

Beginning in the late 1890s, the ORRP established the Aleksandr Nevskii Temperance Society (Nevskii Society) in an effort to reverse the tendency among Orthodox workers to seek solace and salvation in the recesses of the tavern. Through a proliferation of "temperance tearooms" throughout Petersburg's working-class districts, the Nevskii Society provided counseling and financial support to individuals with drinking problems. At the same time, it sponsored religious lecture series, published vast amounts of religious literature, set up libraries or reading rooms, organized religious choirs, and led pilgrimages.[80] In line with the ORRP's broader goals, the Nevskii Society offered various avenues of spiritual "enlightenment" and recreation in the hope of promoting moral and spiritually healthy pursuits in the community.

The temperance movement was not universally successful, although it sometimes had a profound effect on workers' practices and perspectives. The experience of the Petersburg worker A. P. Shapovalov, who lived and worked in the Obvodnyi canal region of St. Petersburg in the late 1880s and early 1890s, is particularly revealing in this sense. Shapovalov evidently did not have a real drinking problem, although he had once come near death as the result of an excessive bout of holiday fasting and feasting. He was drawn to the local temperance society as much by a desire to escape the oppressive routines of the factory as a need for sobriety:

> The life I was leading had become singularly exhausting. One day was the same as the next. [Life] had ceased to be satisfying. I felt like a bird in a cage. Life began to seem like a prison, [and] troubled desires appeared in my soul—desires for space [and] fresh air.[81]

While Shapovalov suffered from the long hours and six-day weeks experienced by most factory workers, exhaustion no longer kept him from church. In fact, after becoming part of an extended family of (sober) workers in the Obvodnyi canal region, Shapovalov began to maintain a very strict Orthodox lifestyle: "My friends and I spent all of our free time attending church services [and] reading the Bible and the lives of

---

[80] By 1905, chapters were located at the Putilov factory, on Vasil'evskii Island, in the Petersburg district, on Mitavskii pereulok, in Kronstadt, Oranienbaum, Tsarkoe Selo, Sergiev, and Okhta. Among the other activities undertaken at some of the chapters were inexpensive dining rooms, workshops for the unemployed, weekly readings with wall projections, Christmas tree parties, and after later, schools for children. *Otchet o deiatel'nosti Aleksandr-Nevskogo Obshchestva* (St. Petersburg, 1907), 5.

[81] Shapovalov, *Po doroge*, 26.

the saints. We rigidly observed fasts, and all of our money—the half-kopecks which we were able to spare—was handed over for icons and to the church."[82] On Saturdays, they regularly attended evening church services from six until midnight, and then arose at four the next morning to go to mass once again. On Sunday afternoons, they often relaxed by attending the spiritual lectures (*besedy*) offered by local clergy, and then gathered together informally to discuss religious issues. Soon after joining the movement, Shapovalov became a recruiter, convinced, as he later put it, of the "possibility of realizing the ancient Christian ideal [of a world] free from [wealth] and [poverty]."[83] He found that younger workers, as opposed to the older generation, were particularly receptive to the movement's promise of change.

Shapovalov eventually abandoned Orthodoxy to join with the growing ranks of revolutionaries. Nevertheless, his experience attests to the evolution of a new type of urban believer within the working population. Having committed himself to sobriety and joined an active community of believers, his spiritual routine actually became more intense and diversified than ever before. At the same time, he took advantage of the expanding network of opportunities for "religious enlightenment" offered by the urban missionionaries. As a result, he became more knowledgeable about scripture and more conscious of his Orthodox identity.

The clergy often complained about the workers' woefully inadequate knowledge of Orthodoxy beyond even the simplest prayers. Even so, many workers expressed an active desire to learn more about their faith.[84] Memoirists often recalled how they loved to sit around discussing God and scripture in their free time. It was not uncommon for lively debates to erupt between co-workers and roommates over matters of religious (and irreligious) interpretation.[85] With the spread of literacy by the late 1870s, workers began to read popular religious literature and widely circulated Russian translations of the New Testament.[86] They also began to flock to

---

[82] Ibid., 27.

[83] Ibid., 26.

[84] *S.-Peterburgskoi dukhovnyi vestnik* 42 (1895): 966.

[85] See A. Frolov, *Probuzhdenie tul'skogo rabochego* (Tula, 1925), 22; and *Rabochie Trekhgornoi*, 56. On worker debates over religion, see *A Radical Worker*, 29; A. M. Buiko, *Put' rabochego: Vospominaniia putilovtsa* (Leningrad, 1964), 17; *Staraia i Novaia Danilovka*, 123; *Rabochie Trekhgornoi manufaktury*, 50; and Steinberg, "Workers on the Cross," 217.

[86] On reading habits among workers, see Edmund Heier, *Religious Schism in the Russian Aristocracy 1860–1900: Radstockism and Pashkovism*, (The Hague, 1970), 73; RGIA, f. 1574, op. 2, d. 63, l. 1; Jeffrey Brooks, *When Russia Learned to Read* (Princeton, 1985), 22–34.

Bible studies and prayer meetings, many of which were first organized by Evangelical Christians, and then by Orthodox missionaries.[87] To a certain extent, the passionate interest that many Orthodox workers expressed for reading scripture was a natural extension of their traditional love for religious stories, like the lives of the saints, and of their tendency to read books as a source of instruction, "a means to save one's soul and to improve one's life."[88] But for some, like Shapovalov and his friends, it also reflected a newer and even broader trend among workers as their literacy increased, to become more knowledgeable about the issues that mattered to them.[89]

By the early 1880s, public Bible readings (*chteniia*) and religious lectures (*besedy*) became regular features of working-class religious life.[90] On Sunday afternoons and evenings, factory workers and other members of the working population (including artisans, domestic workers, and shop clerks) would gather together—in churches, factories, apartments, hospitals, and flophouses throughout the capital—to listen to clergy read the Bible and discuss a variety of popular themes, including Christ's life on earth, the ten commandments, the lives of the saints, and salvation. In contrast to the typical liturgy, meetings were conducted informally, beginning with prayers sung by a workers' choir, followed by the lecture (often with a lantern show), and then by further discussion of Scriptural readings. Eyewitness accounts suggest that emotional intensity at the meetings was often very high. "After a full day's work," missionaries reported, "the weary factory people ... listen to the *besedy* intently, as if afraid to miss even one word uttered by the preacher, and usually thank him at the end."[91] As one worker from the Vyborg district, a father of five, explained, "I go to the [spiritual] lectures just to relax. When I go home, [I am confronted by] great need [*nuzhda*], and by my wife's deep sighs of exhaustion [and] despair. I could listen to the Word of God forever; it gives me strength and patience."[92] During the singing, the mood

---

[87] RGIA, f. 1574, op. 2, d. 63, l. 1.

[88] Brooks, *When Russia Learned to Read*, 31.

[89] See, for example, A. Artamanov, *Ot derevni do katorgi: Vospominaniia* (Moscow, 1925), 12–15.

[90] On at least one occasion, a group of working women got down on their hands and knees to beg for admission to an overcrowded lecture. Runkevich, *Studenty-propovedniki*, 14.

[91] RGIA, f. 796, op. 442, d. 1632, l. 56.

[92] "Eparkhial′naia khronika," *Izvestiia po S.-Peterburgskoi eparkhii* 2 (1910): 21–22. Descriptions of Sunday prayer meetings offered by Ivan Churikov suggest a similar atmosphere, in which spiritual intensity was so high that those in attendance often shouted out and erupted into spontaneous song. A. S. Prugavin, *"Brattsy" i trezven-*

was "especially reverent" and "prayerlike," with many participants crying, sighing, or genuflecting.[93] Some workers compared the effect of the lectures to that of a "sunny day." When the series ended for the summer, they complained bitterly.[94]

The *beseda*, which also existed outside the city, evolved into a very popular form of Orthodox teaching in the urban environment, in part because of its flexibility in terms of scheduling and addressing the changing needs of a highly mobile population. In 1887–88 alone, approximately 50,000 workers flocked to 161 lectures from all parts of the capital, including the Petersburg and Vyborg districts. By 1904, two million persons attended 6,000 lectures at some eighty locations annually.[95] The impetus to establish lecture series often came from workers themselves, much in the same way that peasants petitioned for the founding of a chapel in the absence of a nearby parish. In 1894, for example, the residents of Peskov, many of whom were "poor working people," rented out a room for as much as sixty rubles a month in order to set up a program of religious lectures.[96] On opening night, almost 350 people attended, many of whom showed up in work clothes, having rushed from the factory to the lecture.

The enduring popularity of the *beseda* among workers in the pre-revolutionary period reflected its function as a forum in which to engage actively with scripture and learn more about the faith. Attendance was often very high, ranging typically from 200 to 1000 men and women. The relatively informal atmosphere relieved the sense of alienation that some workers felt in their own parishes, while fostering a closer relationship between workers and local clergy members.[97] The format of the *beseda*

---

niki: Iz oblasti religioznykh iskanii (Moscow, 1912), 17–18.

[93] TsGIA SPb, f. 2215, op. 1. d. 4, l. 164ob.

[94] Working-class parishioners from the Holy Trinity church in the Nevskii Gate region also requested religious lectures. "Eparkhial′naia Khronika," *Izvestiia po S.-Peterburgskoi eparkhii* 2 (1910): 21.

[95] *Otchet po deiatel′nosti Obshchestva*, 22.

[96] RGIA, f. 796, op. 442, d. 1632, l. 55–55ob. Another program was begun on Boldyrev pereulok at the request of factory workers in the Narva Gate region. Workers used their own funds to transform the rented meeting place into a richly decorated chapel with an abundance of icons. When workers at the Goldarbeiter factory petitioned the ORRP for spiritual lectures, the owner donated a small room for lectures, apparently sufficient for the 300 workers there. RGIA, f. 796, op. 442, d. 1632, l. 75.

[97] RGIA, f. 796, op. 442, d. 1632, l. 74ob. Attendance at the Vargunin lecture series, for example, typically ranged from 50 to 250, mostly men, some of whom came from the nearby Thornton textile factory. Some workers came from as far away as the Obukhov metalworks (12 versts from Vargunin), even in the dead of winter, Runkevich, *Studenty-propovedniki*, 25.; RGIA, f. 796, op. 205, d. 801, l. 2. Some local clergy became very popular. In 1905, workers were attracted by the thousands to the funeral procession for

encouraged a degree of lay participation in ways that traditional forms of liturgy did not (discussions, for example, were in Russian.) For the most part, though, the clergy continued to select the topics and lead the discussions. That some Orthodox workers wanted less clerical control is suggested by the increasing popularity of similar Bible and prayer meetings sponsored by Evangelical Christians, like the *pashkovtsy*, and by the lay preacher, Ivan Churikov, who actively advocated the rights of the laity to interpret scripture.[98]

In addition to whatever benefits it may have had as an intellectual and spiritual exercise, the *beseda* provided workers with a much needed avenue for relaxing and socializing within the context of a broader spiritual community.[99] It drew workers together, not only to study the Bible and to drink tea but to discuss their lives, to learn, and to enter into dialogue with one another. Especially for women, lectures offered an escape from the oppressive environment of factory barracks or overcrowded apartments. The singing of prayers and religious hymns was appreciated by many workers as an antidote to factory noise, just as pilgrimages served as a means to escape the filth and smoke of the city, if only temporarily.[100] As one of the few legal avenues for large groups of workers to gather in public until 1905, these rituals filled an important void in

---

Father Rozhdestvenskii, the adored head of the Aleksandr Nevskii Temperance Society and an active missionary on the lecture circuit, who had died of an illness contracted on a pilgrimage. N. Pal'mov, "Pamiati vydaiushchagosia pastyria—pobornika narodnoi trezvosti," *Otdykh Khristianina* 8 (August 1905): 19–26.

[98] RGIA, f.821, op. 133, d. 212, ll. 320–328ob. Among workers, a more critical attitude towards the Church and its control of virtually all aspects of religious life was very apparent after 1905. Noting the vast amount of material devoted to workers' efforts to secure more control on the factory floor, Dixon has suggested that "there is just as much to say about the consequences of [workers'] vain search for an established and dignified role in the affairs of their church." Dixon, "The Orthodox Church," 130–131.

[99] At times, however, workers involved in Church-sponsored activities demonstrated a very clear sense of the difference between spiritual and recreational pursuits. For example, in one of the many locations where religious lectures were held, local clergy suggested that a dance be held during crossworshiping week "in order to entice the narod away from the tavern." City officials approved the plan, but when workers found out that some would be dancing and having fun at the same time that others were worshipping the cross, they tore the posters down in protest. The dance was cancelled. RGIA, f. 796, op. 442, d. 1632, 1896, l. 58ob.

[100] M. Gorev, *Kak trezvenniki ezdili na Valaam* (St. Petersburg, 1909), 8. On a regular basis, Petersburg missionaries reported on the encouraging level of devotion exhibited by working-class pilgrims, parading through the streets of the capital to worship their favorite icons and shrines. See, for example, RGIA, f. 796, op. 442, d. 1577, ll. 73–74. *S.-Peterburgskii dukhovnyi vestnik* 35 (1895): 825–32.

working-class life. They enabled workers to come together as a community, as Orthodox believers, and as laborers. As Shapovalov explained, before there were legal political parties, trade unions, independently organized cooperatives, mutual aid societies, and a labor press, "the disunity (*raz"edinenie*) among workers was so great, the night so dark, that the [temperance] society ... seemed like a ray of light amidst the dismal darkness of the night."[101]

Icon Worship

Icons were very visible both in workers' homes and in the factory, serving as the focal point of both individual and community worship. The factory shop often acted as an urban substitute for the local village community in organizing icon-based rituals. In contrast to peasants, who were known to pray to a host of saints representing the various aspects of the agricultural cycle, workers tended to pray at most to a couple of images, one of which was usually St. Nicholas (the most popular saint in Russia). Still, the workday began in many factories with the singing of prayers before the shop icon, and saint's days were typically celebrated as a welcome holiday from work, and as an occasion for drinking, fun, and friendly competitions. In shops with a high percentage of recent migrants, workers habitually performed prayer services on the day of their village holiday as well.[102] Workers typically pooled their money to buy lamp oil and then elected a trusted elder to keep the icon clean and the flame alive.[103]

As these examples suggest, most rituals performed on the shop or factory floor were not undertaken as a necessary complement to the labor process (in the way, for example, that the priests' blessing of the cattle and the fields in the springtime was seen as vital to the economic livelihood of the village). More commonly, icon rituals in the urban workplace served as a means by which Orthodox workers celebrated shared notions of sacredness and expressed gratitude for good fortune. In 1893 workers at the Pal' factory asked the local priest to organize an icon procession to give thanks for being spared from the recent cholera epidemic.[104] Some-

---

[101] Shapovalov, *Po doroge*, 26.

[102] *Rabochii zavod "Serp i Molot,"* 61. Even after 1917, it was apparently still common practice for women weavers in Kharkov to cross themselves before beginning the machines. See A. Kostitsyn, *Trudiashchaiasia zhenshchina i religiia* (Moscow-Leningrad, 1929), 46.; RGIA, f. 796, op. 442, d. 1577, l. 68.

[103] See P. Timofeev, "What the Factory Worker Lives By," in *The Russian Worker: Life and Labor under the Tsarist Regime*, Victoria E. Bonnell, ed. (Berkeley, 1983), 97.

[104] TsGIA SPb, f. 19, op. 85, d. 16, l. 1. In 1902, a group of female work-

times workers from the same factory or shop also petitioned collectively for the purchase of an icon, which they then donated to their local parish. Sometimes, prayer services were used as a forum for celebrating political change as well: it was not uncommon for workers to gather together before the shop icon to commemorate the anniversary of the Emancipation, for example, or to give thanks for the issuing of the October Manifesto.[105] And on at least one occasion, workers at the Nevksii factory requested a prayer service (*moleben*) at the conclusion of a strike.[106]

As the labor movement gained momentum towards the end of the century, Orthodox rituals of community served quite naturally to organize the collective participation of workers not only as Orthodox believers but as laborers. Lacking legitimate channels through which to voice their grievances or offer support to one another, workers relied on various everyday religious practices for "secular," even radical ends. Collections for the lamp oil were used to generate sick funds; prayer meetings became forums for discussing and voting on strike issues; and icon and funeral processions were transformed into political marches.[107] While religious rituals provided workers with the behavioral texts for collective acts of protest, shared notions of sacredness helped to promote worker solidarity in opposition to the authorities, both within and without the factory.[108] For example, attempts by factory owners to limit the celebration of religious holidays evoked strong expressions of worker solidarity and collective protest, including strikes.[109]

Limited evidence suggests that individual workers turned to their icons most frequently to express gratitude for their blessings, to seek help from God to deal with the difficulties of everyday life, and to remember

---

ers from Moscow's Meshcherinovskii factory joined together to purchase a silver lamp to commemorate the anniversary of the opening of the relics at the Danilov monastery. "Prazdnovanie 250-letiia otkrytia moshchei sv. blagovernogo kniazia Danilla v Danilovom monastyre," *Moskovskie tserkovnye viedomost* 36 (8 September 1902): 418.

[105] *Moskovskie tserkovnye vedomosti* 9 (29 February 1904): 112.

[106] TsGIA SPb, f. 1229, op. 1, ed. kh. 253, l. 42ob.

[107] E. I. Nemchinov, "Vospominaniia starogo rabochego," in *Na zare rabochego dvizheniia v Moskve*, 160; *Staraia i Novaia Danilovka*, 11.

[108] Attempts to restrict workers' access to religious rites, as in the case of baptizing a child or burying a co-worker in a proper ceremony, form the basis of what E. P. Thompson labeled the "moral economy" of the crowd. E. P. Thompson, "The Moral Economy of the English Crowd in the Eighteenth Century," *Past and Present* 50 (February 1971): 76–136.

[109] Zelnik, "'To the Unaccustomed Eye,'" 297–326. See also RGIA, f. 20, op. 13a, d. 40, l. 22.

the dead.[110] The fervent prayers of a young worker hoping to be transferred to a better position in the drafting shop at the Izhorsk ironworks were probably typical of many workers (as well as peasants) seeking to bargain with God for a better livelihood.[111] Also common were the many prayers by working-class wives with alcoholic husbands, and those offered by widows, like Valentina Petrova, the daughter of a radical metalworker, whose husband's premature death left her and her infant impoverished. "There was not a day when I did not go to church," Petrova wrote, and in 1915 she followed the holy icons on a pilgrimage to Sergiev.[112]

Prayers for the sick were also common, since many workers (like peasants) believed in the miraculous power of icons and relics to heal the body. According to one Soviet source, workers flocked regularly to witness "healings" in front of the church at the Izhorsk ironworks, and the practice of kissing the "miraculous" icon there was so popular that it had an appreciable effect on the spread of disease among the urban population.[113] Recalling a healing he had witnessed at the Monastery of the Caves in Kiev, Kanatchikov's co-worker, described as a "dogmatist and churchgoer," defended his belief in miracles to an atheist in the factory with the argument that "seeing is believing":

> I saw with my own eyes how they tended to this very sick man—he couldn't use his legs at all, couldn't take a step—and how they brought the holy relics to his lips. Well no sooner had he kissed the relics and said his prayers than he was up on his feet. He just walked out of the monastery as if nothing had happened![114]

Many workers were drawn to religious figures like Ivan Churikov, with a reputation for "miraculous" healing powers and "magical" potions.[115] And in Shapovalov's case, the "miraculous" efforts of a priest to cure the young worker of a life-threatening hangover convinced him to renew his commitment to the faith and to join the temperance movement.[116]

---

[110] Most textile workers spent a large portion of their budget on icon oil, much of which was devoted to remembering the dead. Davidovich, 82.

[111] I. K. Mikhailov, *Chetvert' veka podpol'shchika na Izhorskom zavode v Kolpino* (Moscow-Leningrad, 1928), 8. Mikhailov's pragmatic and utilitarian attempts to bargain with God for a better job seem to coincide with traditional peasant practices. See Henri Troyat, *Daily Life in Russia Under the Last Tsar*, trans. Malcolm Barnes (Stanford, 1979), 209.

[112] *Rabochie Trekhgornoi manufaktury*, 191; Chaadaeva, *Rabotnitsa*, 45.

[113] Zavaialov, 61.

[114] Kanatchikov, *Autobiography*, 29.

[115] Prugavin, *"Brattsy" i trezvenniki*, 62.

[116] Shapovalov, *Po doroge*, 9.

In 1911, an article in the spiritual press suggested that belief in the miraculous healing powers of icons was waning among workers. While many peasants still clung to their icons out of a fear of doctors, it noted, workers were becoming accustomed to controlling their environment "at their benches," and tended to overestimate the power of medical science to heal.[117] Although medical care became more readily available and workers became comfortable about consulting doctors, the old ways did not die out quickly. Shortly after the turn of the century, the zemstvo physician Mariia Pokrovskaia went to treat the sick child of a young unskilled factory worker in Petersburg, whom she described as sober, hard-working, educated and interested in "politics." Despite the father's "urban" appearance, Pokrovskaia found that the family continued to regard one corner of their rundown, overcrowded apartment as a sacred space; there they had hung icons, beneath which they had lain their ill five year old.[118] While it is certainly possible that the young father was more of a traditional, pious patriarch than a budding radical typical of his generation, it may be that the icon had been hung by the child's mother, without his father's full approval. A different, but equally possible explanation is that the family's reliance on both icons and prayers (that is, "religion") as well as doctors ("medical science") was typical of many workers, who were trying to maximize their chances for survival in an environment rife with disease and uncertainty.

Until 1917, when artistic postcards begin to replace traditional religious scenes, the presence of icons in workers' living quarters remained so common that only their absence was considered remarkable. Given the various difficulties associated with parish life, it is possible that the act of praying before the icons, like the reading of scripture, assumed an even more important role relative to other rituals, since it was relatively easy to perform in the urban environment.[119] "Unlike the Eucharist, which only priests and bishops could administer," Vera Shevzov has written, "icons provided for a means of 'communion' of which anyone potentially could 'partake' without clerical mediation." She also points out that for

---

[117] "L.S-ii," "Iz nabliudenii nad sovremennoi religioznoi zhizn'iu," *Tserkovnyi vestnik* 26 (30 June 1911): cols. 797–99.

[118] M. I. Pokrovskaia, *Po podvalam, cherdakam, i uglovym kvartiram Peterburga* (St. Petersburg, 1903), 33–34.

[119] L. Kleinbort, "Khudozhestvennye zaprosy proletariata," *Vestnik Evropy* (September–December 1917): 357; In 1906, K. Mironov recalled the experience of two "conscious" workers whose landlady tried to hang her own icons on their wall. When they refused her, she reported them as "atheistic socialists" to the local authorities. K. Mironov, *Iz vospominaniia rabochego* (Moscow, 1906), 23; Buiko, *Put' rabochego*, 10.

many rural Orthodox believers, "prayer was prayer," even if performed in the absence of a priest.[120]

Given the lack of privacy so common in workers' living spaces, the potential for quiet prayer and veneration varied considerably, depending on the worker's living situation. At the massive Trekhgornaia textile factory in Moscow, for example, walking into the women's sleeping barracks was "like finding oneself in a monastery, with icons all around"; even on the men's side, there were usually three or four small icons on each floor.[121] The factory clergy routinely brought icons and prayers into the dormitories to reach exhausted workers, much in the same way that they made rounds in the village. But as many memoirists have recalled, the factory barracks were typically not a holy place: "We slept in one large room, crammed with 150 people," wrote one female textileworker,

> noise, drunkenness, and the swearing of obscenities gave us no peace—although I plugged my ears .... Usually the noise and arguing was started by old Natal'ia Sharapikha, who loved to indulge herself in vodka. There were many older women [tet'ki] like Natal'ia in the dorms. They get drunk and become rowdy: we young girls could not get away from all [their] noise, drunken songs, and obscenities. [T]here was no peace day or night.[122]

For Petersburg workers, who tended to live in overcrowded apartments, privacy and moments of peace and quiet were similarly lacking. And as the population of workers indifferent or hostile to Orthodoxy grew, it became increasingly common for the presence of icons to incite conflict between roommates. In M. Petrov's *artel'*, for example, a bitter argument erupted between members over the possession of the only icon in the apartment. When one worker tried to pray before it, another claimed it as his own and refused to allow others to pray to "his God"; the "owner" subsequently ripped the icon off the wall, put it under his pillow, and lay down on top of it. In response, the other members of the *artel'* decided to leave the icon corner empty after the incident, reasoning "if there are no icons, there's no point in praying [either]." So traumatized was Petrov by the course of events that he began to contemplate the meaning of faith.[123]

---

[120] Vera Shevzov, "Icons, Laity, and Authority in the Russian Orthodox Church," *Russian Review* 58 (1999): 26–48; Shevzov, "Popular Orthodoxy," 606.

[121] Lapitskaia, *Byt rabochikh*, 73.

[122] Krylova, *Zapiski tkachikhi*, 17–18.

[123] M. P. Petrov, "Moi vospominaniia," in *Na zare rabochego dvizheniia*, S. I. Mitskevich, ed. (Moscow, 1932), 183.

By the late nineteenth century, conflicts over the icons between believers and non-believers apparently became a regular feature of working-class life. Like Petrov, the worker A. Buiko had vivid memories of an iconoclastic blacksmith named Skliar who rented a corner of his apartment in the Narva District in 1902. Habitually drunk on Saturday nights, Skliar would threaten his pious landlady as she lit her icons: "There is no God! That's all stupidity. Bring me a thousand of your icons and gods, and I will smash them, and nothing will happen to me."[124]

Although his older roommates found nothing but nonsense in Skliar's ideas, Buiko admitted he was intrigued by them, particularly the concept of human evolution. Thus inspiring fear in some, fascination in others, conflicts over the holiness of icons and the debates that followed ultimately helped problematize the issue of faith among Orthodox workers.

Conclusions

In contrast to rural Orthodox believers, who were usually able to maintain a balance between sacred acts and labor practices within the context of a broader religious community, urban workers experienced a permanent tension between their needs as believers and the everyday realities of factory life. They often had to struggle to find a consistent, communal context in which to worship, celebrate, and acknowledge the sacred. When work and faith came into conflict, as they often did, the consequences varied. These ranged from a minor degree of inconvenience, as in the frequent headaches and dizziness workers had to endure while fasting on the job, to tragic loss, as in the case of the worker whose child died before being baptized. Even as workers commonly shared certain obstacles to the practice of the faith—exhaustion, lack of time, poverty, absence of privacy, loss of family and community structure—not all workers experienced these challenges to the same degree or in the same way. Aside from personal faith, factors such as age, sex, and the strength of ties to the village community influenced the way workers responded. Taken together, workers' religious behaviors reflect great fluidity in cultural norms, making it impossible to speak of any single model of "urban Orthodoxy."

Even as the demands of the urban factory challenged the worker's ability to maintain an active Orthodox way of life, they often increased the same worker's need for the consolation, sense of community, and aesthetic pleasure offered by religious practice. At the same time, pilgrimages, icon processions, singing groups, and prayer meetings brought workers together, not only as exercises of religious devotion, but as occasions for

---

[124] Buiko, *Put' rabochego*, 17.

socializing and relaxation. Prior to 1905, Orthodox rituals of community, particularly those related to icon veneration, also helped to organize early forms of labor protest. As Surh has argued, the popularity of the Gapon movement in 1904–5 emerged from this tradition of protest and reflected the extent to which Orthodoxy coexisted with, and actually facilitated and inspired workers' more "secular" goals and actions.[125]

As some aspects of traditional ritual life were undergoing change (as in the simplification of funeral practices) or even declining in importance (as in Sunday attendance at mass), other forms of religious behavior (like private prayer and the *beseda*) appear to have become more central to everyday religious practice. On the whole, workers demonstrated a stronger need for scripture and prayer than liturgy; although there is evidence that attendance at *besedy* actually increased the likelihood that a worker would perform his or her Orthodox duties (especially fasting, confessing, and communicating) more regularly and readily than before; for some, it may have served as a substitute for church-going.[126] Nonetheless, outside of church, workers spent a lot of their free time reading scripture and debating religious issues, both in organized settings like the *beseda* and the temperance tearoom, and more informally, in their homes and on the shop floor. Taken together, these various opportunities for religious "enlightenment" and debate enabled some workers to acquire a greater, and perhaps even more critical, understanding of Orthodoxy. Thus, with the gradual decline in certain aspects of traditional ritual life in the factory environment, a new, more conscious relationship to the faith was emerging. The experience of the 1905 revolution further deepened religious consciousness among some workers.[127]

---

[125] Gerald Surh, "Petersburg's First Mass Labor Organization: The Assembly of Russian Workers and Father Gapon," *Russian Review* 40 (October 1981): 440–41. See also chap. 5 of my unpublished doctoral thesis, "Class, Piety and Politics: Workers, Orthodoxy, and the Problem of Religious Identity in Russia, 1881–1914" (University of California, Berkeley, 1996); Zelnik, "'To the Unaccustomed Eye'"; Dave Pretty, "The Saints of Revolution: Political Activists in 1890s Ivanovo-Voznesensk and the Path of Most Resistance," *Slavic Review* 54 (Summer 1995): 276–304; and Steinberg, "Workers on the Cross," 213–239.

[126] TsGIA SPb, f. 2215, op. 1, d. 4, ll. 163–64.

[127] Some observers felt that, under the influence of the liberation movement, the Orthodox faithful appeared to be reaching a new level of religious consciousness. "The narod," a leading clerical journal in St. Petersburg pointed out, "not only wants to pray but to understand the meaning of that prayer, to live a religious life consciously, and to understand the meaning and sense of the religious service." "Letopis'tserkovnoi i obshchestvennoi zhizni," *Tserkovnyi vestnik* 24 (12 June 1908): col. 745.

Workers and the Orthodox Church in Early Twentieth-Century Russia

Sergei L. Firsov

Translated by Oksana Fedorova

The relationship between the Russian Orthodox Church and the working class in autocratic Russia during the reign of the last tsar has received insufficient attention. Although Russian historians have attempted to examine the spiritual demands of the Russian proletariat and the growth of atheistic views in its midst, rigid ideological stereotypes prevented an objective analysis of all such questions.[1] Although historians forced in the past to follow non-historical constructions are hardly to blame, the result is that many questions require investigation. This paper attempts to outline some important aspects of the Church-worker relationship, without claiming that any of the conclusions are complete or final.

First of all, it seems useful to note that the Russian Orthodox Church, the empire's predominant denomination, a formally powerful organization supported by the state, was neither free nor independent. It followed the directives of a secular official, the Procurator-General of the Holy Synod, and thus never had (and could not have had in principle) a social policy of its own, nor its own, independent views on the internal political problems of Russian society. The Church was simply the "department of orthodox creed," and the words of religious thinker P. Ivanov in reference to the second half of the nineteenth century seem fully justified. "The Church," Ivanov wrote, "had finally become a temple where separate individuals came to pray, who had nothing in common and even shunned each other, instead of being brothers and sisters in Christ. That which was referred

---

[1] See, for example, M. M. Persits, *Ateizm russkogo rabochego* (Moscow, 1965); I. S. Rozental', "Dukhovnye zaprosy rabochikh Rossii posle revoliutsii 1905–1907 gg.," in *Istoricheskie Zapiski* 107 (Moscow, 1962): 69–99.

to as Church, had lost any influence over society."[2] The fact that "faith had become scanty" was recognized by many priests (and the hierarchy), however, no constructive solutions were put forward.[3] It is in the light of these circumstances that the question of the influence of the Orthodox Church on the working class should be considered.

When discussing the religiosity of Russian workers, we need to take into account a number of issues, such as the differences in the perception of religious values by various categories of the proletariat and their general cultural level. It is necessary to distinguish between the religious conceptions of the so-called "conscious workers," and those of the recent immigrants from rural areas who came to the cities to earn their living and were witnessing, for the first time, "the seamy side of city life."

The active participation of the working class (and first and foremost, of its "conscious" section) in the 1905–07 revolutions, together with its general politicization and the rapid growth of its numbers, had contributed to the emergence of a clear crisis in the relationship between the workers and the official Church by the beginning of the twentieth century. V. V. Zen′kovskii, a philosopher and a public figure, wrote:

> The fact that in an Orthodox country, the sociopolitical movement is developing, for the most part, irrespective of Orthodoxy, and frequently in direct antagonism to it, clearly illustrates the detachment of our Orthodoxy from everyday life. This is especially disturbing in the context of the increasing political maturity of the Russian people, for if this process of political maturing develops in the same way as it did in the case of the intelligentsia, then Orthodoxy will find itself completely isolated from life, and Russian culture will not fulfill Orthodoxy's wonderful beginnings, but will share the west's sad destiny of fruitlessly searching for its soul.[4]

Although Zen′kovskii did not explain what he meant by the expression "political maturity," it is possible to assume that at issue here was, first and foremost, the proletariat, whose deficit of (or even lack of) religiosity had become the "talk of the town" in the first decade of the twentieth century.

In fact, the question of working class religiosity seriously worried many political, religious, and public figures of the time. Thus in 1907, in his

---

[2] P. Ivanov, "Taina Sviatykh," *Vvedenie v Apokalipsis* (Paris, 1949), ii, 567–68.
[3] See Aleksandr Vvedenskii, *Religioznye somneniia nashikh dnei* (Odessa, 1914), vol. 1. Vvedenskii became a leader of the religious 'rebirth' movement.
[4] V. Zen′kovskii, *Rossiia i Pravoslavie* (Kiev, 1916), 31.

brochure "Religion and the public," Professor I. Ozerov admitted that "workers need improved factory legislation, the right of assembly, freedom to organize labor unions, and so forth. Without these conditions, the worker will be unable to rise to religious creativity, and the Divine image will be erased from his mind."[5]

As we can see, Ozerov linked the question of workers' religiosity to economic and even political problems. Moreover, the official reports of the Procurator-General of the Holy Synod, when referring to Church affairs, stated:

> everywhere where large-scale industry has had time to develop, socialism captivates into obedience a multitude of laborers. Not limiting themselves to the class of factory workers, socialists also aspire to tear the peasantry away from the Church. The struggle against the eternal and the spiritual, in favour of the transitory and the material, is being conducted everywhere, systematically and with a concerted effort, and it has, to some extent, achieved its goal already. In a word, the Russian people's Orthodoxy has fallen under hostile and impudent attack.[6]

One could not state the matter more clearly than Fomenko:

> The Church unequivocally recognizes, as an accomplished fact, that the proletariat has already broken away from its influence; our current concern is to see that "socialists" do not pull the peasantry away from the Church. The way that the question is formulated is in itself rather indicative. The Orthodox Church is beginning to consider the question of peasants' religiosity *through the lack of faith* (emphasis in the original) of factory workers. Thus, the question of the proletariat's attitude to the Church begins to function as a kind of a litmus paper, which is used to try to determine some "average religiosity" of an orthodox person and, accordingly, to forecast the development of religious "moods" in the future. Moreover, frequent references to socialism as a godless doctrine should be understood in the context of the 1905–07 revolutionary events when the Church, for the first time, encountered an open advocacy of godlessness (for which it was unprepared), and which was perceived as an integral part of "socialism."[7]

---

[5] I. Ozerov, *Religiia i obshchestvennost'* (Moscow, 1907), 6.

[6] *Vsepoddanneishii Otchet Ober-Prokurora Sviateishego Pravitel'stvuiushchego Sinoda po Vedomstvu Pravoslavnogo Ispovedaniia za 1911–12 goda* (St Petersburg, 1913), 151–52.

[7] Many priests applied the well-known phrase "We will turn your temples into our

The task of "protecting" the peasants against the "noxious spirit of modern false doctrines" was thus directly related to a struggle against the penetration of urban influences into the masses. Annual reports on the situation in the dioceses noted with alarm that it was precisely the city that exercised a negative influence on rural religious moods. For example, the 1911 report on the situation in the capital states that one of the reasons for the "moral decline" amongst rural youth was their "departure from the native village to city factories in search of earnings." In cities, wrote the priests, "rural youth becomes influenced by bad examples of non-religious and immoral lifestyles and corrupted by the godless and anarchical propaganda."[8] It would be possible to cite many more examples, as almost every cleric in the official reports drew a dismal picture of the "impoverishment of faith" in the village as a logical consequence of "city life."[9]

Similar statements can be frequently encountered in the church press of the time. The priest Feodosii Pavlovskii wrote in 1913:

> When observing the modern village, one feels particularly saddened by peasant youths, who have grown up in the epoch of political ruin, worked as seasonal laborers in factory centers or in America and tasted the seamy side of city culture. The youths have no stable world outlook and often no religiosity; they are unruly and self-satisfied.[10]

As we can see from the above examples, by emphasizing the anti-social tendencies among non-religious youth, Orthodox priests were talking not

---

stables" to the period of the 1905 Revolution. In this article, the author Klavdii Fomenko (a senior priest) states hooliganism was the primary reason for such sayings, and also notes that "hooliganism is an embittered child of those counting themselves among the 'unemployed'. Hooliganism and the proletariat are related." K. Fomenko, "Khuliganstvo," *Kievskie Eparkhial'nye Vedomosti* 40 (1913): 1028.

[8] Rossiiskii gosudarstvennyi istoricheskii arkhiv (hereafter RGIA), f. 796, o. 442, f. 2473, ll. 285–6.

[9] For example, the Bishop Ioann of Riga and Mitava wrote: "Those who have visited cities and factories, are cold and even hostile towards religion." Also, the Novgorod Eparchy Report stated that "seasonal [factory] work disturbs the villages' spiritual life." Similar thoughts were expressed by the priest in the fifth *okrug* (subdistrict) of Kirillovskii *uezd* (district): "Under the influence of seasonal labour migration, an indifference towards religion can be observed in people, especially among the younger generation. Most of the young men and women from our area leave to work for the Northern Railway or in the city of Arkhangelsk. Once there, they abandon God's temple." See L. I. Emeliakh, *Krestiane i tserkov' nakanune Oktiabria*, (Leningrad, 1976), 48.

[10] F. Pavlovskii, "Po voprosu o narodnykh nravakh v sovremennoi derevne," *Kievskie Eparkhial'nye Vedomosti* 44 (1913): 1129.

so much about urban professional workers, as about those "proletarians" who used to come to the city for limited periods of time to earn money in the factories and plants. In relation to this, it seems useful to consider the question of whether the external manifestation of the workers' negative attitudes to religion and the Church resulted from conscious outlooks developed out of their own thinking processes or whether they were merely an indication of social protest and therefore had other causes.

The pre-revolutionary decade witnessed a serious "moral crisis" in society. Several years after the end of the Civil War, while describing the early twentieth century, General A. I. Denikin stated as a firm fact the deep and significant process of spiritual transformation that Russian people underwent at that time.[11] Many commentators made similar apocalyptic statements that forecast looming catastrophes.

Thus, the final 1910 edition of the extreme-right weekly journal, *Kronshtadtskii Maiak* (*The Kronstadt Beacon*) contained an editorial announcement informing the readers that during the next year the journal would contain "a whole range of articles concerning the evident proximity of the end of the world."[12] The existence of such moods in a society is symptomatic of advanced illness. Writing after the revolution, in 1918, N. A. Berdiaev also noted that "the illness of the Russian moral consciousness was ... prolonged and ... serious."[13] This crisis also had a material expression. According to S. S. Ostroumov, "the crime pages in the contemporary press offer a huge number of examples of mass suicides and dreadful crimes caused by the marasmus and the decay of bourgeois society during the last years of tsarism."[14]

Ostroumov perhaps exaggerated the alleged cause (the decay of bourgeois society) for increases in suicides and crimes; nevertheless his overall conclusions seem fair. Besides, when discussing the growth of crime in the pre-war years, we are reminded that "in those years, the intensification of crime in general, including crimes against property, went hand in hand with the growth of industry."[15] It is against this complex background that the question of workers' attitudes to religion should be investigated.

While admitting that the majority of workers were indifferent to the official Church, Orthodox clergy did not have any clear ideas about how

---

[11] A. I. Denikin, "Ocherki russkoi smuty," *Voprosy Istorii* 3 (1990): 122.

[12] *Kronshtadskii Maiak* 46 (1910): 5.

[13] N. A. Berdiaev, "Dukhi russkoi revoliutsii," *Literaturnaia ucheba* 2 (1990): 139.

[14] S. S. Ostroumov, *Prestupnost' i ee prichiny v sovremennoi Rossii* (Moscow, 1980), 71.

[15] Ibid., 69.

to return them to the "bosom of the Church" or even about what initial steps might be taken. Attempts to attribute industrial workers' lack of religiosity to their mastery of tools and machines, a phenomenon that supposedly induces them to perceive themselves as "masters of the world," do not stand up to criticism, as we shall see below.

According to Professor Ozerov, "today's workers leave religion simply because the modern Church is nothing more than a known capitalist organization which sanctifies a lie and sides with capital and the powers that be."[16] Of course, this explanation cannot fully satisfy us either. A proper examination of the relationship between the Church and the Russian working class in the pre-revolutionary epoch needs to take into account the whole complexity of social, psychological and other factors, without giving undue priority to any particular aspect of Russian reality.

Before the revolution, Archpriest S. N. Bulgakov wrote that "Russia experienced [simultaneously] a spontaneous and rapid economic growth and spiritual decay." Precisely because of this, we can't really list specific reasons for this "impoverishment of faith" among the working class; the process was actually "normal" for those conditions.[17] Additional questions are: exactly what did the concepts of "religion" and "atheism" mean to the workers; and exactly how did they understand religious issues and how did they relate to the Orthodox Church, in light of their cultural and socio-political development?

Of course, the working class was not homogeneous: its ranks included both the qualified skilled workers, grappling with the pressing issues of the day; and the unskilled manual labourers newly-arrived from the village. In addition to these "conscious" and "unconscious" proletarians, there was also a very large category of workers who did not fall under these definitions. Therefore, any one-sided assessment of the spread of atheistic sentiment in the workers' milieu would be unhelpful. Regardless, it seems necessary to point out that a feeling of gloom seems to permeate contemporary writing about this issue.[18]

As regards workers' religious indifference, the increased influence of socialist ideology on the proletarian environment clearly played a role.

---

[16] N. Ozerov, op. cit., 11.

[17] S. N. Bulgakov, *Avtobiograficheskie zapiski* (Paris, 1946), 81.

[18] For example, the priest, M. Galkin, wrote that "in the workers' milieu, we are encountering an explicit mockery of [church] rituals and especially of our Orthodox clergy." See M. Galkin, "Dumy o pastorstve," *Prikhodskii Sviashchennik* 11 (1912): 3; See also L. S-ii, "Iz nabliudenii nad sovremennoi religioznoi zhizn'iu," *Tserkovnyi Vestnik* 26 (1911): 799.

An indirect indication of this phenomenon is the two-volume "On the peaceful Struggle against Socialism" (1911) by V. K. Sabler, the Deputy Procurator-General of the Holy Synod under K. P. Pobedonostsev. The author insisted that it was necessary to struggle against the spread of "anti-state socialist doctrines," primarily by means of reforming the factories and improving the workers' living conditions, which, in his opinion, European capitalists had already undertaken.[19]

Many similar works appeared that recommended "pulling" workers away from socialism. Well known at the time was the uncompromising opponent of "socialist ideals," a Moscow missionary and member of the Black Hundreds, Archpriest I. I. Vostorgov. Two volumes of his writings contain articles in which the Archpriest attempted to examine "socialism in the light of Christianity," some of them addressing those workers who were "intellectually advanced through courses and reading."[20] Although admitting that there was a grain of truth in socialism, especially in its elaboration of questions related to the workers' hardship and insufficient wages, Vostorgov emphasized that before any economic and political innovations "it is necessary to achieve people's moral development and re-education."[21] The Moscow missionary's writings were not limited to a critique but offered a program of refutation of "the doctrine of socialism" which, in his opinion, was "in an irreconcilable conflict with the Christian worldview."

The increased influence of socialist doctrine in cities also led in 1910 to the Holy Synod's adoption of the document "On the Introduction of Teaching the Denunciation of the Foundations of Socialism in Theological Seminaries." In his review of the document, the theologian Professor V. Ekzempliarskii noted that "the denunciation of socialism has undoubtedly been introduced into seminary teaching because of the increasing influence of socialist views among the workers and sections of the intelligentsia; and, on the other hand, because of modern socialism's clearly hostile attitude towards religion in general and Christianity in particular." The "Denunciation of the Foundations of Socialism" course was also part of a broader course of "moral theology."[22] At the same that the Holy Synod was in the process of developing and approving its "Denunciation

---

[19] Vladimir K. Sabler, *O mirnoi bor'be s sotsializmom: Putevye vospominaniia Vladimira Sablera*, 2 vols. (Sergiev Posad, 1911).

[20] I. I. Vostorgov, "Beregis' obmannykh rechei" [against the socialists of all parties] in *Polnoe sobranie sochinenii*, 5 vols. (Moscow, 1913), 3: 38. The article was originally written in 1905.

[21] Ibid., 12.

[22] RGIA, f. 802, op. 10, f. 186, l. 63; ibid., f. 796, op. 209, f. 2430, l. 111.

of the Foundations of Socialism" course, V. I. Lenin published his work on religion (1909), in which he emphasized that the proletarian party "must become the ideological leader in the struggle against all manifestations of the 'Middle Ages,' including the old formal religion and all attempts to improve or revive it."[23]

For Orthodox religion, the situation was further complicated by the fact that the crisis of faith coincided with a crisis in the Church itself. This, naturally, led to an even greater increase in the number of workers breaking away from the Church.

To understand this "cooling of faith" and to find its causes was a persistent concern in official publications and current affairs articles. For example, one of the church figures of that epoch noted that the psychology of workers was determined by the fact that they attributed all their achievements to "efforts of personal will" and emphasized that it was precisely this "group that had the most negative attitudes to the Church and its principles."[24]

This and other similar documents contain more questions than answers. While stating unpleasant and painful facts for the Russian Orthodox Church, the writers mainly focused on working class deficiencies in moral education, as well as the underdevelopment (or absence) among the working class, even among its "conscious" elements, of a "moral gauge" for evaluating religious or other doctrines, including socialism.

An eloquent illustration of this position is provided by E. Grekulov's study which used a rather unusual "proof" of the proletariat's atheistic mood. When discussing the workers' lack of faith, the author cites the memoirs of an old Bolshevik F. N. Samoilov, who wrote:

> During the time of the 1905 general strike in Ivanovo-Voznesensk, representatives of the Soviet of Working Deputies came to see the governor for negotiations. During the conversation, there was thunder and lightning. The governor and others began to cross themselves, while none of us batted an eyelid or even thought of crossing ourselves. We stood there calmly, looking on as they were crossing themselves. "Don't you really believe in God?" exclaimed the Governor, who was surprised by our behavior. "To us, a thunderstorm is nothing to fear, but we are a bit scared of famine," we answered.[25]

---

[23] See V. I. Lenin, "Ob otnoshenii rabochei partii k religii," *Polnoe sobranie sochinenii*, 55 vols. (Moscow, 1961), 17:425.
[24] L. S-ii, "Iz nabliudenii nad sovremennoi religioznoi zhizn'iu," 799.
[25] See Y. F. Grekulov, *Tserkov', Samoderzhavie, Narod (Vtoraia Polovina XIX -*

E. F. Grekulov also cites a verse expressing, in his opinion, the workers' atheism:

> So let us rise up bravely, brothers!
> And we shall have land once again!
> And on bitter aspens, we shall hang
> The priests, and the noblemen, and the tsar![26]

This kind of "proof" presents a serious problem in an exaggerated way and can not be usefully employed when considering the complex processes taking place in Russia. (Sentiments similar to those in the above verse, by the way, were expressed frequently at the time and, as a rule, were associated with displays of hooliganism.)[27]

Lack of education, difficult living conditions, long working hours—all these factors gave rise to feelings of protest, the first step of which was, naturally, hatred toward the oppressors or simply those who were better off.[28] The task was to direct this hatred into certain channels: for some, this meant a revolution and a fundamental reorganization of society, while others searched for peaceful solutions to the problem and sought to "guide" hatred into "legitimate channels." Discord in the Church itself in many respects encouraged the process of workers' withdrawal from religion.[29]

There was, however, a segment of proletarians who, despite their withdrawal from the Orthodox Church, did not wish to abandon earlier traditions and attempted to reconcile the concept of social justice with belief in God. This trend was especially notable in St. Petersburg, where workers (some of whom, probably, had earlier belonged to Gapon's organization) severed their links with the official Church after the infamous events of 1905. Their desire to remain "Christians with a church" led some of

---

Nachalo XX v.) (Moscow, 1969), 147–48.

[26] Ibid., 146.

[27] See, for example, Fomenko, "Khuliganstvo," 1028.

[28] For example, Duke S. G. Leikhtenbergskii said to the Russian Army and Navy Archpresbyter that "I used to change my clothes and visit St. Petersburg factories and plants, getting right into the crowd and talking to workers; I know their mood. This is where all this hate is disseminated. You'll remember my words, the time is approaching when all that rabble [i.e., the Grand Dukes, etc.] will be swept away so fast that many won't even have a chance to run from Russia." See G. Shavelskii, *Vospominaniia poslednego protopresvitera russkoi armii i flota* (New York, 1954), 26.

[29] For example, during the years of the 1905 Russian Revolution, even the Church hierarchy admitted that "our Church, insofar as it is a human community, has, in fact, stagnated." See Bishop Evdokim, *Na zare novoi tserkovnoi zhizni (Dumy i chuvstva)* (Sergiev Posad, 1905), 12.

them to form a rather remarkable sectarian religious organization, known as *Golgofskie Khristiane* (Golgotha's Christians). The Golgothans' theoretical basis reflected the writings of an Old Believer bishop Mikhail Semenov, previously Orthodox Archimandrite and professor in the capital's Ecclesiastical Academy. Bishop Mikhail Semenov was summarily forced to sever his ties with the Orthodox religion during the years of the 1905 revolution. Mikhail's fair-minded position attracted the Golgothans, who followed his example and collectively applied to withdraw from the Church.[30] Trying to keep to the "pure Gospel" and therefore not paying much attention to rituals, the Golgothans nevertheless wanted to be headed by a bishop.

The main feature of the Golgothan movement was their readiness to suffer, to prepare themselves to accept Golgotha. Naively aspiring to follow their rejection of "human untruth" to the end, the followers of the movement expressed their creed in the following words: "The Golgothan movement has grown among those workers who stayed believers. They participated in revolution, while believing in God. They would find it difficult to discard this belief. But Mikhail is a bishop, and a learned clergyman. We badly need him at the moment."[31] Bishop Mikhail did, in fact, participate in the Golgothans' assemblies at some point, but he was not prepared to head this kind of Christian workers' movement. Not only official church authorities viewed the Golgothans as "religious dissidents"; they were also perceived in this way by the Old Believer hierarchy, which was disturbed by Bishop Mikhail's activities. Eventually, about 1912, the Golgothan movement broke up, and Bishop Mikhail was obliged to criticize its "careless form," the "excessive harshness of its theses," and so forth; he also noted, however, that he did not consider them to be "in particular contradiction to the spirit of the Church." He declared, moreover: "I do not wish to be responsible for that which is not mine to the last word and idea, and I think it is unfair to present me with such accusations."[32]

The movement created by idealist workers had thus completely failed. Neither Bishop Mikhail nor the writer D. S. Merezhkovskii, whom the workers also called to join the movement, were prepared to connect their names with this initiative. In our opinion, this was understandable: by

---

[30] Marietta Shaginian, *Chelovek i vremia: Istoriia chelovecheskogo stanovleniia* (Moscow, 1980), 410. M. Shaginian attended the Golgothans' meetings for some period of time.
[31] Ibid., 415.
[32] Ibid., 445.

that time, the Golgothans had become, by and large, a rudiment of the past, or using M. S. Shaginian's apt words, "a splinter from the positive part of the Russian national phenomenon of 'narodnichestvo' (populism)," and for this reason alone were doomed to fail.

Another example of a workers' religious community in pre-revolutionary Russia is even more interesting and surprising. I am talking about the under-researched mystical sect the "Shchetinintsi," which existed in the capital approximately between 1908 and 1914. The members of this sect (or, more precisely, community), called "Nachalo Veka" (The Beginning of the Century), were the St. Petersburg workers, former followers of G. A. Gapon, who led the demonstration on 9 January 1905. These workers recovered from the defeat of the revolution and the profound disappointment that followed by finding themselves a "teacher-mystic," a "wise man," A. G. Shchetinin, who was also a completely immoral person, a drunkard, and a sadist. M. M. Prishvin, who became interested in the Shchetinin phenomenon, wrote about him:

> His outward lifestyle, however, does not prevent them from believing in the God living in him; physical nature is that of the angel who, when incarnated, said "farewell" to Our Lady. The teacher told them: life needs to be arranged according to the principle of "you is more than I." The disciples enter into a kind of a mystical contract with their leader, which amounts to the following: they give themselves into slavery to the master, they die for him; he kills them, takes this sin on himself, but then revives them to inherit God's kingdom.[33]

Of course, the "murder" was meant in a figurative, mystical sense and its point was cleansing from sins. For this reason, the workers forgave Shchetinin's behavior and depravity, submitting to all his demands without complaint. According to Prishvin, "this 'teacher', the drunkard and the debauchee, undoubtedly had some mysterious power about him."[34] For the moment, the Shchetinin phenomenon escapes analysis since the people involved need to be considered in a broader Russian socio-psychological context. (That Shchetinin was well acquainted with G. E. Rasputin was probably no accident.)

Eventually, however, the workers began to demand from their teacher the same moral lifestyle as the one they were following themselves. Al-

---

[33] M. M. Prishvin, "Religioznyi ekstaz. (Po povodu dissertatsii D. G. Konovalova)," *Russkaia Mysl'* 2 (1909): 51.
[34] Ibid., 52.

though he did not agree to this and left St. Petersburg to join his other followers in the Caucasus, the group survived and continued to live by the evangelical principle of "loving one's neighbor as oneself." However, their brand of Christianity was rather specific and it was not just Prishvin who noted their socialist and revolutionary background (which must have played a major role in their "revolt" against Shchetinin). Z. N. Gippius, who was in touch with the group before their break with Shchetinin, noticed this straight away:

> [I] cannot remember now all of their undoubtedly Marxist formulas which were poured on me, dressed up in old religious words, or sometimes openly stated. Christian terminology utterly obscured their anti-Christianity, their anti-religiosity, itself a religious force. The Bazarovs and the Lunacharskiis, had they met this "teacher" today, would not have understood that all of them are leaders of one and the same movement. Their disciples will understand tomorrow, when the disciples of their disciples will join together. They will develop a common language too.[35]

What seems remarkable here is that religious workers of the pre-1917 decade (primarily those in the capital who had participated in the 1905 events) began to view religion and the official Church through the prism of the idea of social justice clearly wrapped in a socialist "package."

In any case, both those workers who were indifferent to religion and the Church and those who remained believers were situated, in the main, in opposition to the existing regime and were therefore perceived by official church authorities as a potential threat to the country's "faith and piousness."

We must not generalize too much: among the workers were "traditional" believers genuinely devoted to the Church. The fact remains that Church authorities viewed factory workers as the least religious members of Russian society. Exactly how the situation might be changed, the authorities did not know. Some Church leaders such as Bishop Veniamin Kazanskii, who later became Metropolitan of Petrograd, were influential, popular, and respected by the working class. This was, however, the exception rather than the rule.

---

[35] L. Pushchin, "Literaturnyi dnevnik," *Prishvin*, 173–74.

The Collective Psychology of Russian Workers and Workplace Self-Organization in the Early Twentieth Century

Nikolai V. Mikhailov

Translated by Gerald D. Surh.

The economic and political movement of Russia's workers during the First Russian Revolution—compared with the preceding period—reached not only an unanticipated scope, but also an unprecedented degree of organization, which even official Soviet historiography did not attribute to Bolshevik leadership alone. This occurrence has been explained by Lenin's thesis on "the creativity of the masses," a concept that has remained abstract and unsubstantiated by concrete historical research. The tendency to contrast workers with the Russian peasantry, to which Communist Party ideology gave clear expression, forced Soviet historians to stress precisely those features of the proletariat that distinguished it from the peasantry, leaving in the shadows the immense influence that the village exercised on the psychology of workers. The individual attempts to escape the limits of the official framework, successful though they have been in the work of, for instance, Iu. I. Kir'ianov and V. F. Shishkin,[1] have been unable to change the overall situation in the historiography.

This paper will attempt to gauge the influence of the peasant commune tradition on the psychology and organizational creativity of Russian workers. Without denying the important influence of the intelligentsia on workers, we have consciously accentuated the divergences in their positions, insofar and in those cases where workers' own original ideas have appeared.

---

[1] Iu. I. Kir'ianov, "Ob oblike rabochego klassa Rossii," in *Rossiiskii proletariat: Oblik, bor'ba, gegemoniia* (Moscow, 1970), 100–40; V. F. Shishkin, *Tak skladyvalas' revoliutsionnaia moral'* (*Istoricheskii ocherk*) (Moscow, 1967).

Peasants, who regularly filled the ranks of factory workers, possessed the experience of many centuries of communal self-organization. The Russian commune was not simply a territorial association of rural residents, but an entire social organism with its system of self-government (*samoupravlenie*), labor organization, social protections, moral values, and established norms of behavior. The peasant commune was a stable psychological community, and it was conscious of itself as an integral and self-sufficient institution possessing an elevated authority. Custom was the main factor in any important decision the commune took, and a collective, clannish consciousness dominated the individual and the personal.

The basic cell in the commune's system of social relations was the peasant family, whose function was not only the perpetuation of the clan. It was also the primary production unit (*kollektiv*). Therefore, the village commune was at once both a union of families and an association of farm holdings. On a peasant farm, the joining of the producer with the means of production was realized by the most natural, organic means: the peasant acted simultaneously as both owner and laborer, the roles of supervision and execution being unified in a single laboring individual, which in industrial society take the form of opposing social forces. In conditions of combined property and labor, the peasant family—the primary laboring collective—could not but be a collective subject of the property, and the subject of the peasant farm could not but be a collective personality.[2]

Leaving the village for the city, the peasant lost the social relations he was used to and experienced a psychological uneasiness in the strange, new conditions, and he tried to find a place for himself in this unfamiliar setting. Village migrants, though no longer performing peasant labor, tried to reproduce a communal style of life in the city and, where they lived on city territory in a sufficently concentrated mass, they sometimes succeeded. However, examples of this at the end of the nineteenth century were rather exceptions than the rule.[3]

The unfamiliar urban setting, so distinct from the village, where solid family and neighborly relations existed, forced the village migrants to

---

[2] S. V. Lur'e, "Kak pogibla russkaia obshchina," in *Krest'ianstvo i industrial'naia tsivilizatsiia* (Moscow, 1993), 137; A. V. Gordon, "Tip khoziaistvovaniia—obraz zhizni—lichnost' ," ibid., 116–19; and M. M. Gromyko, "Sem'ia i obshchina v traditsionnoi dukhovnoi kul'ture russkikh krest'ian XVIII–XIX vv.," in *Russkie: Semeinyi i obshchestvennyi byt* (Moscow, 1989), 7–20.

[3] Lur'e, "Kak pogibla," 159–60.

cling to one another, to seek the support of *zemliaki* (persons from the same locality). They often moved in together, renting an apartment as an *artel'* (a small group of workers from the same locality who jointly sought employment). P. Timofeev, who observed such *zemliachestva* (associations of persons from the same locality) at the beginning of the twentieth century, noted:

> ...This *artel'* lived together in surprising harmony. Quarrels and fights almost never happened . . . The *zemliachestvo* drew them into a single family, and several members of the *artel'* sacrificed a great deal for its sake. Thus, one of them had to get up at three o'clock in the morning and walk from Narva Gate to beyond the Nevskii Gate, which made for a roundtrip of about ten–twelve *versts* [about eleven–thirteen km] per day. Another one worked on the Vyborg Side [a workers' district in St. Petersburg] and made a similar trip every day.

The *zemliachestvo* was the basic channel through which migrants from the villages filled the ranks of [urban] workers. Heading to the city, a peasant already knew that a *zemliak* would find him work and would support him for a while. Some workers of peasant origins, having become bosses, turned into great patriots and accepted into their shops only those who approached them as *zemliaki*. "In Petersburg, there is a factory," wrote P. Timofeev, who had in mind the Baltic Shipyards, "in one of whose sections worked migrants from only two districts of Tver Province—Staritskii and Novotorzhskii—from which two of the 'bosses' stemmed."[4] The *zemliachestvo* helped peasants adapt to the new milieu, although they were no longer able to reproduce in the city the style of life to which they were accustomed.

A much stabler community than the *zemliachestvo* also arose in the person of certain collectives in industrial establishments. That is precisely where elements of the experience of communal organization began to show themselves quite early. In 1800 the Senate granted the request of the workmen (*masterovye*) of the Frianovskaia Possessional Factory in Bogorodskii district (Moscow province) that "to keep order in the factory and to look after the payment of their money, six persons elected by them from their ranks were to be in charge." The female owner of the Krasnosel'skaia Paper Factory near Petersburg complained to the Minister of Internal Affairs that "the workmen have fallen into disobedience, have formed a society among themselves which governs them while rejecting

---

[4]P. Timofeev, *Chem zhivet zavodskoi rabochii* (St. Petersburg, 1906), 11, 15–16.

any authority over itself."[5] In the period 1870–80, a demand for the introduction of elected worker delegates in enterprises set off the very largest strikes such as those at the New Spinnery in Petersburg (1878) and at the Nikol'sk Manufactory of the Morozov Company (1885). At the end of the nineteenth century, several Petersburg factory administrations, on their own initiative and untroubled by the absence of legislation, met the desires of workers and "arranged a special means of dealing with workers by the mediation of deputies or 'elders,' sometimes elected by the workers from their ranks, sometimes designated by the factory management from the same ranks." Thus, elected deputies existed at the Izhorsk Works from the middle of the 1890s, and at the Siemens and Halske plants, from the founding of the firm (1854).[6]

The vigorous growth of Russian industry in the 1890s sharply increased the flow of migrants from the village to the old industrial centers. Thus, in Petersburg the proportion of migrant workers and domestics—according to the 1897 census—was the highest in Russia, constituting 80.3 percent of the total for that category in the capital. The vast majority of peasants entering factories and mills had left their families at home (*na rodine*). Only eight percent of Petersburg textile workers in 1897 lived with their families and among metalworkers, ten percent.[7] The absence of the usual family surroundings further increased the severity of the psychological unease that afflicted village migrants, binding them even more to the factory collectives. However, the nature of the interrelationships among participants in the production process in industrial enterprises, having its roots in the serf factory, was fundamentally distinct from that which was practiced in the peasant family labor collective.

The underground revolutionary activist P. G. Smidovich, a participant in the group Rabochaia Mysl' (Workers' Idea) who worked at the Nevskii Machine Works in the 1890s, observed how the behavior of young village migrant workers literally changed before one's eyes under the influence of the factory order. Van'ka, a boy of fourteen or fifteen from a remote little village in Tver' Province, was sent by his father to Peters-

---

[5] A. M. Pankratova, *Fabzavkomy Rossii v bor'be za sotsialisticheskuiu fabriku* (Moscow, 1923), 35–36.

[6] Ibid., 253–253 ob., "Kopiia predstavleniia nachal'nika Admiral'teiskikh Izhorskikh zavodov ot 26 iiunia 1905 g."; *1905 v Peterburge*, 2nd series: *Sovet rabochikh deputatov. Sbornik materialov* (Leningrad, 1925), 180 ("Pokazaniia A. N. Rastorgueva 12–18 fevral'ia 1906 g.").

[7] E. E. Kruze, *Polozhenie rabochego klassa Rossii v 1900–1914 gg.* (Leningrad, 1976), 142–43.

burg to earn money. Here is how Smidovich described his appearance and manner when he began work at the plant:

> He arrived a quite young little peasant man [*sovsem malen'kii muzhichok*] with an original voice and original manners. In the beginning he worked in my group: 'Van'ka, bring us such-and-such...'—'Ah, what's the hurry' (Van'ka replies). Or: 'Van'ka, run quickly and tell them to bring...Hurry up...We're all waiting...'Van'ka barely begins to move and, falling over himself in his father's gigantic felt boots, heads toward the door. 'Van'ka, what's wrong with you?!'—'Ah, what's the hurry, no need to run...things can wait...why the shouting...'

The obvious crudeness and unhurried manner mirroring the behavior of a stolid, self-assured, adult peasant provoked mirth among the workers and ill will among the foremen.

The crudeness and mockery of the foremen, the threat of a fine, fear of the possibility of losing pay—all this literally chained Van'ka to his broom, which he wielded incessantly throughout the workday, and even in sleep, when his roommates, wanting some fun, shouted, "Van'ka! Where's your broom?!"—he gave a muffled groan and began to move his arms as though sweeping. "A month later," Smidovich recalled, "I meet him again, and I had to chew him out. Van'ka remained silent. This was so unexpected that I stop and ask him what's the reason he doesn't answer. 'Foreman sir, don't think I don't know how to behave...I couldn't be rude to you...'" Before me stood no longer the little jackdaw with his mouth open, but the 'beginnings of a human being' who was able to address you politely and perhaps, eventually, critically."[8]

It is noteworthy that Smidovich saw in this sharp change in Van'ka's mode of behavior not a breakdown of personality, not the meekness of a young worker, but only an outward reaction to rudeness, the reenactment now not of peasant habits, but of the manners of workers with seniority, who were also able in a polite answer to express their rejection of treatment that management forced upon them. The contrast between the relations occurring in peasant family collectives and those that village migrants met with in the factory was so great and so obvious that only a complete lack of rights compelled them to bear the rudeness and humiliation. In those cases when workers decided upon open conflict, they

---

[8] P. G. Smidovich, "Rabochie massy v 1890-kh gg. Ch. IV. Peterburg," in *Avangard: Vospominaniia i dokumenty piterskikh rabochikh 1890-kh gg.* (Leningrad, 1990), 369–70.

put forward, along with purely economic demands, other demands that showed their attempt to change their relations with the employer. As early as the 1890s there were widespread demands for polite treatment, dismissal of management representatives who engaged in rudeness and mockery, and rehiring of comrades who, in the collective's opinion, had been unjustly dismissed.[9]

The police official, S. V. Zubatov, sought to take advantage of the workers' striving for self-organization. On his initiative informal factory committees of elected workers were created under the supervision of the Okhrana in Moscow, Minsk, and Odessa that acted as intermediaries between the collectives and enterprise managements on problems of pay and the internal factory order. The creation of conditions for the semi-legal activity of elected factory representation gave such a push to the development of an organized labor movement in 1902–03 that the government was forced to hurriedly abolish the famous Zubatovist experiment. Thanks to the factory committees, the maturity and organizational firmness of the protest movement against arrangements prevailing in the enterprises defeated the police's hopes of taking the labor movement under its control.[10]

A Ministry of Finance conference on measures to ensure tranquility at factories and mills, after studying the causes of disorders at Petersburg enterprises during the 1901 strikes, found it helpful to propose that workers choose *starosty* (elders) from their own ranks in order to conduct negotiations with management or the Factory Inspectorate. The same opinion was held in the Ministry of Internal Affairs as well, its representatives noting however that the already existing practice of introducing factory *starosty* would be in conflict with the law.[11] Yet the norms of the subsequent 10 June 1903 Law on Starosty were aimed not so much at legalizing factory committees as at limiting the functions of the workers' delegates in transmitting complaints and conducting discussions in cases of conflict. Aside from its rather high age qualification for *starosta* candidates (twenty-five years) and the complete dependence of the delegates on management, the law did not permit *starosty* to act as a collegial representative organ of the factory. The factory collective was not permitted to gather in general meetings, but only in groups, and gatherings of the *starosty* were allowed only with the permission and under the supervision

---

[9] *Rabochee dvizhenie v Rossii. 1895–fevral' 1917 g. Khronika.* 1st series, *1895 god.* (Moscow, 1992), passim; and ibid., 2nd series, *1896 god.* (Moscow, 1993), passim.

[10] Pankratova, *Fabzavkomy,* 69–73.

[11] "Materialy po voprosu ob uchrezhdenii starost," l. 7ob.

of management. Furthermore, the Law on Starosty pertained only to private enterprises subordinated to the Factory Inspectorate.[12]

In any case, the Law on Starosty did not achieve wide application. Thirty-six Petersburg industrialists, including the president of the Petersburg Society of Factory and Mill Owners, S. P. Glezmer, resolutely opposed the establishment of the institution of *starosty*.[13] During the first year after the adoption of the law, only five Petersburg enterprises introduced it.[14] Nor did the workers manifest any interest in the legislative innovation. In their struggle for elected representation, they relied not on the law, but on tradition, and they acted by "seizing the moment," winning recognition of their deputies' rights from management by stubborn persistence.

On 5 January 1905, workers of the Putilov Plant presented management with the demand, among others, to form a permanent commission of [worker] delegates with guarantees of their inviolability.[15] In the course of the January general strike in Petersburg the enterprise collectives demonstrated their ability to organize themselves very rapidly. "For organizational purposes," recalled Ekateringof Factory worker V. A. Lemeshov, who was a member of the Petersburg Assembly of Russian Factory Workers, "Gapon [priest and worker leader] proposed that the shops in every mill and factory elect deputies who would be obligated to clarify the workers' demands and to present them to management. Those demands which management could not satisfy were to be written into a petition, which Gapon would take to the Tsar."[16] As a result of that proposal the Gapon Assembly began to grow rapidly; from 6 to 8 January entire factories of workers came to its locals to sign up, and the elected delegates signed the petition in the name of their collectives.[17]

T. A. Rubinchik, an active participant in the trade union movement of printers, observed that workers' efforts to make deputies a permanently

---

[12] "Ob uchrezhdenii starost v promyshlennykh predpriiatiiakh. Vysochaishe utverzhdennoe mnenie Obshchego sobraniia Gosudarstvennogo soveta. 10 iiunia 1903 g.," in *Sobranie uzakonenii i rasporiazhennii pravitel'stva, izdavaemoe pri Pravitel'stvuiushchem Senate. 1903 god. Otd. 1. Vtoroe polugodie.* (St. Petersburg, 1903), 1559–1560.

[13] *Krizis samoderzhaviia v Rossii, 1895–1917 gg.* (Leningrad, 1984), 89–90.

[14] Tsentral'nyi gosudarstvennyi istoricheskii arkhiv goroda S.-Peterburga (hereafter TsGIA SPb), f. 1229, op. 1., d. 368, ll. 13–13ob. ("Donesenie starshego fabrichnogo inspektora Peterburgskoi gubernii v Otdel promyshlennosti Ministerstva finansov ot 25 fevralia 1904 g.").

[15] U. A. Shuster, *Peterburgskie rabochie v 1905–1907 gg.* (Leningrad, 1976), 72.

[16] Tsentral'nyi gosudarstvennyi arkhiv goroda S.-Peterburga (hereafter TsGA SPb), f. 9618, op. 1, d. 26, l. 70 ("Vospominaniia V. A. Lemeshova. 25 fevralia 1935 g.").

[17] Shuster, *Peterburgskie rabochie*, 78–79.

recognized institution at enterprises were nothing new as they had fought for this continuously in 1903–04.

But the great novelty of 1905 was the joint actions of delegates from different factories and different trades uniting among themselves. This began systematically when the struggle broke out in favor of the four workers dismissed from the Putilov Plant and when neighboring factories, under the general sponsorship of the so-called "Russian Assembly" supported them.[18]

When in spring 1905 the election of deputies or *starosty* began to be conducted everywhere in Petersburg's mills and factories, the process reflected not the workers' recognition of the 1903 law, but a completely different phenomenon. In the conditions of a rising revolutionary tide, workers swept aside the original framework of the Law on Starosty and, by extra-legal means, created organs of factory collective representation— soviets of *starosty*, deputies' commissions, or factory committees. Their appearance was spurred by the elections of worker representatives to the Commission of Senator N. V. Shidlovskii in February 1905, which strengthened further the confidence among workers in their right to have permanent elected factory representation.

In response to the labor movement's growing politicization and organization, the government attempted to broaden the application of the Law on Starosty by extending it to state factories. The specially reworked statute was by and large based on the 1903 law, although there were substantial differences, dictated by the desire to diminish worker dissatisfaction with the earlier limited coverage. Thus, the "Regulations on Starosty in Ports and at Factories of the Naval Department," which were sent out to the department's plants in May 1905, foresaw the payment of an additional twenty-five percent of basic earnings to *starosty*.[19] However, the attempt to revitalize the 1903 law met with the opposition of workers at the large machine plants, where the committees made up of former Shidlovskii Commission electors were the most active.

Workers of the Aleksandrovsk Machine Works in Petersburg simply refused to choose *starosty*. At the Nevskii Ship and Machine Works elections were conducted without being inhibited by the Law on Starosty.[20]

---

[18]TsGA SPb, f. 9618, op.1, d. 32, l. 101 (T. A. Rubinchik, "Peterburgskii Sovet rabochikh deputatov 1905 g.").

[19]TsGIA SPb, f. 1304, op. 1, d. 2387, l. 133 ("Pravila o starostakh v portakh i na zavodakh morskogo vedomstva. Aprel' 1905 g.").

[20]*Materialy ob ekonomicheskom polozhenii i professional'noi organizatsii peterburgskikh rabochikh po metallu* (St. Petersburg, 1909), 24.

Workmen at the Izhorsk Plant declared through their delegates that they did not want the "Regulations on Starosty" introduced at the enterprise. Their dissatisfaction was provoked by the amount of supplemental pay for *starosty*, the high age qualification, and the right of management not to approve the elected candidates which, "in the workmen's opinion, deprived them of their right to choose." The workers regarded the obligatory presence of management representatives at their meetings as "extremely inhibiting," and they expressed the apprehension that "persons speaking against management would subsequently be persecuted." The introduction of *starosty* at the Izhorsk Plant had to be postponed till a better time, leaving in place the institution of "unpaid delegates," which had already existed at the enterprise for more than ten years.[21]

The election of *starosty* at the Baltic Shipyards that took place 19 and 21 July 1905 also ended without result: in the Copper Boiler Shop they "did not take place due to the unwillingness of the skilled and unskilled workers [*masterovye i rabochie*],"[22] and candidates elected in other shops refused to carry out the obligations of *starosty*. At a general meeting of *starosta* candidates on 17 August, thirty-three of them explained their refusal by a reluctance to take on themselves the responsibility of this post at such a troubled time for workers, while the rest expressed their dissatisfaction "with the twenty-five percent of shop pay defined by the rules."[23] No doubt, the motives indicated by the workers did not include all of the reasons for their decisions. In analyzing the causes of the failed elections, Baltic Shipyard Director K. Ratnik saw as the chief one the fact that "the newly-introduced rules on *starosty* proved to be obsolete and satisfied no one." No less important was another observation of the director: the workers expressed dissatisfaction not so much with the amount of supplemental pay for *starosty*, as one might think, but rather with supplemental pay in principle, because it would make them dependent on management.

> But the big question is, from whom should the *starosta* receive the pay for his position [Ratnik noted in a letter of 11 September 1905]? In order not to be in an artificial position between workers and management and to be for management's sake an independent representative of his groups, he must receive his financial support

---

[21] "Kopiia predstavleniia," l. 253 ob.

[22] TsGIA SPb, f. 1304, op. 1, d. 2387, l. 202 ("Soobshchenie o vyborakh starost na Baltiiskom zavode. 19 iiulia 1905 g.").

[23] Ibid., f. 1304, op. 1, d. 2387, ll. 263–263ob. ("Prikaz nachal'nika Baltiiskogo zavoda ot 25 avgusta 1905 g.").

from the workers themselves and not from management, and also not be replaceable by it.[24]

Elections of *starosty* at the Baltic Shipyards designated for 18 and 19 May 1906, also failed to be held "in view of the opposition to these elections that exists among the workmen."[25] The unyielding opposition of workers to the introduction of the institution of *starosty* did not at all mean that they did not want elected factory representation. The institution of elected worker deputies existed at the Baltic Shipyards before the adoption of the "Regulations on Starosty" and it was preserved after unsuccessful attempts to apply them. Thus, according to the shipyard's "Chronicle Book," a "reelection of deputies and deputy alternates" took place at the enterprise on 16 February 1905, and "the election of delegates and their alternates" was conducted 25 October 1905.[26] The date of the first "reelection" coincided with elections to the Shidlovskii Commission, and in October 1905 elections to the Soviet of Workers' Deputies were held in Petersburg factories. On 18 July 1906, the "reelection of shop deputies and their alternates" again took place. Only in the last case did the management succeed in conducting elections according to the "Regulations on Starosty," the supplemental pay for fulfilling delegates' duties having been increased by fifty percent of the basic wage (*oklad*).[27]

The concerted boycott with which the workers of Petersburg's state factories greeted the 1903 Law on Starosty—completely independent of and without any kind of appeal from the revolutionary parties—bears convincing witness to their preference for traditionally elected factory groups representing the workmen before management over the institution of *starosty*, with which the traditional groups contrasted. It is evident that the already established, traditional standard of relations between workers and factory managements, though not formulated in law, made possible worker representation more independent and less subordinated to management than the 1903 law permitted. The boundaries of this independence, unwritten and set only by custom, were quite mobile, being dependent on the ability of a given collective to stand up for the rights

---

[24] Ibid., f. 1304, op. 1, d. 2387, ll. 266–267 ("Chernovik pis'ma nachal'nika Baltiiskogo zavoda v Schetnyi otdel Glavnogo upravleniia korablestroeniia i snabzheniia ot 11 sentiabria 1905 g.").

[25] Ibid., f. 1304, op. 1, d. 2387, l. 283 ("Donesenie nachal'nika Baltiiskogo zavoda morskomu ministru ot 19 maia 1906 g.").

[26] Ibid., f. 1304, op. 1, d. 678, ll. 107, 110ob., 115 ("Kniga-khronika Baltiiskogo zavoda").

[27] Ibid., f. 1304, op. 1, d. 678, ll. 48ob.–50, 53 ("Prikazy nachal'nika Baltiiskogo zavoda ot 11 i 18 iiulia 1906 g.").

of those it elected as well as on the policy of a given management, on its acceptance or rejection of the worker deputies.

When in 1905 a universal excitement took hold of Russian workers, enterprise collectives not only reproduced a form of communal organization with ease, adapting it to purely proletarian ends, they also utilized the institution of elected deputies to coordinate their actions on a city-wide scale. Thus arose the soviets of workers' deputies, for which the organized laboring collectives, led by the factory committees, served as the mass base and support. It has been thought that with the onset of reaction at the beginning of 1906 elected worker representation at the enterprise level ceased to exist. However, this did not happen; the factory committees turned out to be the soundest link of the soviet structure, outlasting the soviets themselves. Thus, for instance, after the destruction of the Petersburg Soviet of Workers' Deputies by the police, the factory committees served in January–February 1906 as the foundation of the Commission on Unemployment, which rendered aid to locked-out workers, and in March–April the committees sent their delegates to the Petersburg Soviet of the Unemployed.[28] This is not to say that the factory committees were preserved or revived at all enterprises in spring 1906, but evidence shows clearly that factory representation remained a very widespread phenomenon.

In the "Days of Liberty" the factory managements did not dare to dismiss all the worker deputies, but with the onset of reaction and mass firings, they got rid of the more radically inclined representatives. As regards the institution of elected deputies itself, they restricted themselves to try to establish stricter control of it. Thus, at the Sestroretsk Armaments Works the worker leaders, who had been elected to the Shidlovskii Commission and the Soviet of Workers' Deputies, were arrested on the eve of the *starosta* elections of 23 December 1905, so that the new slate of delegates could not help but be more moderate. Despite the Law of 10 June 1903, however, the *starosty* acted as an all-factory, corporate body, while, at the initiative of the Main Artillery Administration, the position of permanent president of the factory's *starosta* assembly was introduced on 15 January 1906. Judging by the surviving minutes, management representatives were not present at the assembly's sessions.[29] At the Nevskii

---

[28] V. S. Voitinskii, *Peterburgskii Sovet bezrabotnykh: 1906–1907 gg.* (New York, 1969), 2–17.

[29] TsGIA SPb, f. 1290, op. 1, d. 659, ll. 95–95 ob. ("Kopiia prikaza nachal′nika Sestroretskogo oruzheinogo zavoda ot 28 dekabria 1905 g,"); d. 672, ll. 1 ob.–3 ("Prikaz nachal′nika Sestroretskogo oruzheinogo zavoda ot 4 ianvaria 1906 g.") and

Ship and Machine Works in Petersburg in 1906, even the composition of the *starosta* council was little changed—thanks to manager I. I. Gippius's liberalism—and as before, radically-inclined workers predominated. According to S. V. Matveev's memoirs, seventeen Social Democrats (SDs) and five Socialist Revolutionaries (SRs) entered the factory committee at the beginning of 1906, and after new elections in June of that year, out of a thirty- to thirty-five person committee, by P. A. Garvi's calculation, seventeen or eighteen were SDs, eleven were SRs, and six were non-party.[30]

Those party activists closest to the proletarian masses were compelled in their everyday work to turn to the non-party factory committees because without their participation not a single event in the life of the collective could be managed, be it a strike or even a meeting.[31] The revolutionary parties' committees plainly underestimated the universal character of the soviet form of organization in 1905–07 and the factory representation it encompassed, which were equally suited to coordinate economic and political struggle. They saw in the soviets only an organ for preparing and conducting an armed uprising, and they turned to the non-party factory committees with the aim of mobilizing workers for political action. That is what happened in Petersburg in June and July 1906, when the SD and SR committees attempted for the first time to make use of the factory committees to create a citywide political organization. But the lack of coordination in the actions and summonses of the party committees brought to the workers chaos and confusion instead of consolidation. At one enterprise deputy elections were carried out several times, and the workers, used to acting as an entire collective, no longer understood where and with what aim their representatives were moving.[32]

The attitude of workers toward attempts of the SD and liberal intelligentsia to transfer onto Russian soil the experience of the West European trade union movement was highly instructive. Workers readily agreed to an industrial and not a narrowly trade-oriented structure of unions. Individual membership, however, proved to be unfamiliar to them, a fact revealed by the irregular payment of membership dues and

---

d. 48 ("Kopiia protokolov sobranii starost Sestroretskogo oruzheinogo zavoda, nos. 1–11 za 1906 g.").

[30]Tsentral'nyi gosudarstvennyi arkhiv istoriko-politicheskikh dokumentov S.-Peterburga (TsGAIPD SPb), f. 4000, op. 5, d. 857, ll. 26–27 ("Vospominaniia S. V. Matveeva"); P. A. Garvi, *Vospominaniia: Peterburg—1906 g.* (New York, 1961), 49.

[31]V. I. Nevskii, *Sovety i vooruzhennye vosstaniia v 1905 g.* (Moscow, 1932), 12.

[32]Voitinskii, *Peterburgskii sovet*, 87.

the relatively small membership of the unions that rigidly held to this principle. Thus, the Petersburg Union of Metalworkers (*Soiuz rabochikh po metallu*), founded in spring 1906, brought into its ranks no more than one-sixth of the city's metalworkers. The union's leaders, creating citywide and district centers, did not even try to take the factory representative organizations under their control or to spread their influence in them.

F. Bulkin, a participant in the trade union movement of Petersburg metalworkers, described the mutual relations of the union and the nonparty factory committees in this way:

> They (the factory commissions) consisted of the delegates of the separate shops and were the intermediaries between the workers and management. But their functions were broader. They entered into all the details of everyday factory life, saw to management's observation of contracts, resolved ripening conflicts through negotiations, traced orders the factory received and the distribution of the work, organized aid to those unemployed, exiled and arrested; and finally, led strikes if factory conflicts were unsolvable by peaceful means. This role of the factory commissions in the economic struggle, further reinforced by the fact that they sometimes took on political functions as well, naturally moved the union into second place. At large factories the commissions enjoyed great influence and possessed a rich treasury; during conflicts one turned only to them for aid.... The commissions almost completely ignored the union and did not take it into consideration. The factory commissions did not invite the union to participate in the resolution of conflicts and even bypassed it in entering into relations with other factories.[33]

In contrast to the metalworkers' union, the Petersburg Union of Printing Workers (*Soiuz rabochikh pechatnogo dela*)—the most influential trade union in the country in 1905—was able to combine formal, individual membership with the actual collectives. Out of 18,000 Petersburg printing workers, approximately 11,000 registered with the union by summer 1906, but only 3,000 to 4,000 formal members of the trade association paid dues regularly. However, delegates to the Council of Deputies (*Sovet upolnomochennykh*), which had replaced general meetings, were elected not from members of the union, but from the printing establishments and represented the interests of the collectives. This allowed the enterprise

---

[33] Bulkin, *Materialy po ekonomicheskomu polozheniiu*, 54.

organization's governing board to act in the name of the whole profession, and all printers, irrespective of their relation to the union, felt themselves to be its members. The collectives of the printing institutions went farther than other trades in strengthening elected representation, and in spring 1906, with the union's support, they began to introduce worker self-government into the printing establishments, which they called "autonomy."[34] The Union of Printing Workers knew how to make use of the traditional attraction of workers to collectivism. It was an organization like the soviets, though confined by the boundaries of a single trade, and this permitted it to achieve significant concrete results in improving the economic condition of the profession's workers.

In 1905–07 the worker collectives put forth such demands, along with purely economic ones, as inviolability of elected delegates and acceptance of their rights in establishing factory regulations, in working out wage rates, and in resolving questions of hiring and firing. The collectives delegated administrative rights to the factory committees and strove to apply them not only in relations among individual workers, but also to management representatives, whom the deputies attempted to fine, and even to factory managers and directors, who were [sometimes] required to dismiss themselves "voluntarily," under threat of removal in a sack. A good many cases are known when collectives succeeded in introducing worker self-government and self-management *kontrol'* beyond the actions of printshop administations. This kind of arrangement the workers called a "worker constitution" or (among printers) "autonomy."

"Autonomy" was recognized by the majority of Petersburg's large printing houses in the course of 1906. In many of them the autonomy commissions consisted in the beginning of worker and management representatives but they quickly became purely worker. The internal regulations of the Energiia printers were developed by a mixed commission and sanctioned by a general meeting of the collective. They enabled the delegates to receive compensation for the performance of their duties only from the workers, not from the proprietor. The owner could be present at general meetings only with the permission of the workers. All questions of hiring, firing, and punishment for violations were to be resolved by a joint commission.[35]

A characteristic feature of the self-rule of the printers' collectives was their effort not only to defend their members' interests before the own-

---

[34] *Istoriia Leningradskogo soiuza rabochikh poligraficheskogo proizvodstva. Kniga 1: 1904–1907 gg.* (Leningrad, 1925), 146, 172–73, 225–26, 255, 282–83, 420.

[35] Ibid., 273–75.

ers, but to regulate relations among the workers. Petersburg's autonomy commissions fought against such widespread occurrences among workers as drunkenness, absenteeism, foul language, and "uncomradely treatment of women workers," applying fines and dismissals broadly and frequently punishing violations more strictly than management. The Union of Printing Workers Council of Deputies established a court of honor for the examination of conflicts among workers, and its authority quickly became so great that even management representatives, wanting to justify themselves in the eyes of the workers, had resort to it.[36]

A. M. Pankratova contended that printers, in their effort to win as many rights as possible from the entrepreneurs, went beyond the boundaries of "genuine worker self-rule" in taking over management functions, and their autonomy commissions "served as a catalyst of disintegration and demoralization among workers." To the worker representation of the printers, Pankratova contrasted the factory committees of the metalworkers which, in her opinion, did their work "in a revolutionary manner," combining economic struggle with political.[37] In our view, this comparison is not correct. Not only printers, but metalworkers and generally all Russian workers without distinction of trade manifested a tendency to intervene in the regulation of the work process.

Both the authorities and the enterpreneurs clearly acknowledged this feature of worker psychology. Thus, in November 1905 the Orlov province governor saw in the demands of the Diat'kovskaia Crystal Factory (Briansk district) collective "the deceptive hope that workers could take over the factory and its administration and run things independently."[38] Baltic Shipyard Director K. Ratnik voiced the warning that the further broadening of the rights of the factory deputies "without proper labor organizations" would make "the owners of industrial establishments into the humble servants of their workers and their *starosty*" and would lead "to the closing of these establishments due to the impossibility of two bosses of one and the same enterprise."[39] Aware of the danger of disorganizing production by the interference of workers in the process of production, entrepreneurs actively opposed attempts to introduce worker self-management and gave way only under strong pressure. As a result,

---

[36] Ibid., 279–82.

[37] Pankratova, *Fabzavkomy*, 114, 115, 118.

[38] A. S. Kasimov, *Khronika rabochego dvizheniia v tsentral'no-chernozemnom raione (1895–fevral' 1917 g.)* (Penza, 1993), 78.

[39] TsGIA SPb, f. 1304, op. 1, d. 2387, ll. 266–267ob. ("Chernovik pis'ma nachal'nika.")

few collectives achieved a significant extension of the rights of elected representatives.

The misgivings of the industrial owners were not in vain. In a number of cases, collectives that had won self-governance proved incapable of maintaining a basic procedural order, which led to a halt in production. Thus, Petersburg ship stevedores (*katali*) succeeded in eliminating contractors and taking affairs into their own hands as the result of a victorious strike in summer 1906. The result was complete disorganization. Drunkenness, hiring independently of the needs of the work, extortion, violence toward the representatives of entrepreneurs–all this paralyzed the unloading of ships. It is noteworthy that even in this situation the owners saw a solution not in stronger repression but in an arrangement "whereby the vessel owners would have to deal not with individual workers, but with an organized entity in the form of a trade association established by them."[40] Of course, the capacity of workers for self-organization and self-discipline did not best show itself in this temporarily and accidentally formed collective of low-skilled workers. It was a very different matter in the longstanding collectives of highly skilled factory workers.

So for instance, the self-governing collectives of Petersburg printers proved their ability to maintain discipline. They also had enough insight to confine their designs on participation in management to limits that would permit entrepreneurs to conduct business. In this case we can agree with A. M. Pankratova's statement that the autonomous commissions of printers objectively worked "to the benefit of the capitalists" by strengthening and not disorganizing production.[41] A similar scene occurred in the public works for Petersburg's unemployed in 1906–07, which a labor organization—the Unemployed Council (*Sovet bezrabotnykh*)—helped to open and to lead. Worker self-management was made a basic principle, and the administration performed only technical supervision. And if the intervention of the Unemployed Council in small and unstable collectives was often required, and if the work performed departed from the norm, then in the shops on Gagarinskii Wharf, where working conditions differed but little from a factory's, the committee of elected deputies dealt with the task independently.[42]

---

[40] Rossiiskii gosudarstvennyi istoricheskii arkhiv (hereafter RGIA), f. 150, op. 1, d. 656, ll. 7–8ob. ("Kopiia dokladnoi zapiski peterburgskikh sudovladel'tsev. Ranee 2 aprelia 1907 g."); ibid., f. 150, op. 1, d. 656, ll. 9–11ob. ("Kopiia prosheniia sudovladel'tsev gorodskomu golove N. A. Reztsovu. Ranee 2 aprelia 1907 g.").

[41] Pankratova, *Fabzavkomy*, 118.

[42] Voitinskii, *Peterburgskii sovet*, 181–85.

At the beginning of the twentieth century the traditions of communal self-government, surmounting the opposition of the authorities and the entrepreneurs and frequently encountering lack of comprehension from revolutionaries and the liberal intelligentsia, manifested itself in the striving of workers for self-organization within the bounds of laboring collectives which, in 1905–07, took the form of a struggle for worker self-management. The laboring collective did not simply advance from its ranks leader-deputies who defended their members' interests before management and represented them in citywide proletarian organizations; it turned itself into a new, stable community, which the workers' consciousness invested with the same rights as the commune had in the thinking of peasants: with the highest authority in addressing any question in the life of the collective, with the right to judge its members and to act in their name, [yet] not allowing or expelling from their midst those displeasing to the majority. Collective responsibility [*krugovaia poruka*] recognized the right of each person to his or her job and guaranteed the material and moral support of those dismissed or arrested in a "social cause."

The worker, like the peasant, remained a collective personality, felt himself part of a "worker family," and preferred collective forms of participation in citywide organizations to individual ones. The laboring collective did not include management representatives in its make-up, stood against them as a single whole, and saw in them the basic obstacle to the realization of its rights. The nature of management's relations with workers called forth in the "worker family" not only protest, but also a continuing effort to recover a lost human dignity which, among peasants, was directly linked with the right to take part in managing the labor process, the carrying out of not only fulfillment but also oversight functions. Worker intervention in the management of production objectively encompassed two tendencies—a destructive one (as with the stevedores) and a constructive one (as with the printers). By and large, the negative attitude of Russian entrepreneurs toward worker self-management embittered workers and sometimes encouraged in the labor movement the first, destructive tendency.

The processes of industrialization and urbanization at the end of the nineteenth century in Russia proceeded with great dynamism, and workers taking jobs on the eve of the new century preserved in their consciousness traditional, communal values. In the course of adapting to the new life circumstances, these values were not displaced by others and were not lost, but were transformed within the framework of a new community—the laboring collective—and very quickly showed themselves in that sharply expressed anti-entrepreneurial, anti-bourgeois trend that the labor movement demonstrated during the First Russian Revolution.

The Liquidationist Controversy: Russian Social Democracy and the Quest for Unity

Alice K. Pate

In 1908 the St. Petersburg workers and activists read articles in the pages of the Social Democratic press with titles such as "What is liquidationism?" "Liquidationism and anti-liquidationism," and "Around the liquidators." This rhetoric emerged from the rise of a workers' movement that required radically different party organizations than had previously existed. When Petr Stolypin, Minister of the Interior, ended the "days of freedom," the revolutionary fervor of 1905–07 subsided and the underground party organization, under constant attack from the police, all but disappeared. "Legal" organizations and party activists operated primarily in accordance with the Law of 4 March 1906, which allowed properly registered "societies" to exist. From these legal workers' associations there arose a new group of party activists known as *praktiki* who had their own ideas about building revolution, and who resisted the control of the émigré leaders (prominent individuals such as Lenin, Martov, Plekhanov, and Trotskii living outside Russia). Efforts to resuscitate the weakened underground and connect its dwindling committees with the expanding workers' associations brought about a tactical and organizational debate within the Social Democratic (SD) movement between the *praktiki* and the émigrés. These debates sparked the famous "Liquidationist Controversy." At SD plenums, conferences, and in the press over the next four years, émigrés attempted to define and control the newly emerging *praktiki*. The activists' revolt signaled the appearance of a separate revolutionary culture, involving a new cadre of party workers, trained in unions, workers' clubs, and cooperatives, and indifferent to the early ideological disputes upon which the émigrés had focused their attention.[1]

---

[1] Although this study focuses on Social Democracy, analogous developments oc-

Historians of Social Democracy have interpreted the Liquidationist controversy as further evidence of Menshevik reformism, which, in this view, placed the Menshevik wing of the Russian Social Democratic Workers' Party outside an increasingly radicalized workers' movement, especially by 1912–14. The accepted interpretation, outlined by Leopold Haimson in two influential *Slavic Review* articles, argues that younger, more radicalized workers, drawn to the Bolshevik wing of the party beginning in 1912, voted for Bolshevik candidates for the governing boards of workers societies and associations.[2] By 1914, this generational conflict supposedly produced "Bolshevik hegemony" within St. Petersburg workers' associations. Formally accurate in some of its parts, this analytical tendency overlooks much of significance in the era's workers' and SD movements.

This paper reexamines aspects of the "Haimson thesis" through analysis of contested discourses rather than high politics. Language, rather than ideology, dictated the course of the Liquidationist controversy. From 1906 to 1914, the changing revolutionary culture produced new perceptions of social and political realities among the *praktiki*. However, earlier ideological conflicts among the émigrés had produced a limited discursive territory, which had little application to the new culture. Inside Russia, the *praktiki* and worker activists became prisoners of the language they chose. They refused to break free of old narratives and allowed the Leninists to seize legitimizing labels. Further examination of the differentiation within the revolutionary discourse derived from émigré, *praktiki*, and worker "realities" will shed light on the collective identity of the *praktiki* and Russian workers.

Before the 1905–07 Revolution, SDs utilized a variety of competing voices—revolutionary and reforming, spontaneous and conscious, passive and active. Before the Liquidationist controversy emerged, émigré theorists assigned value to each of these voices, forcing the marginalization of some of them, who became, in essence, the "other." When the revolutionary culture changed, as it did after 1905, Russian Social Democracy was not receptive to the reassertion of the defeated voices. Émigrés continued to demand one voice, preferring to ignore the plurality of voices that better represented new Russian realities. A set of terms and their associated values set the parameters of the debate. These must be traced in order

---

curred within the Socialist Revolutionary (SR) Party.

[2]Leopold Haimson, "The Problem of Social Stability in Urban Russia, 1905–1917," *Slavic Review* 23 (December 1964): 619–42, and 24 (March 1965): 1–22.

to comprehend the failure of Liquidationism and, more significantly, the related movement to reform the party [3]

In earlier polemical battles, Plekhanov, Lenin, and other Marxist émigrés saw two alternatives in their approaches to workers: propaganda and agitation. As is well known in Social Democratic historiography, theorists argued that propaganda advanced revolutionary goals, while agitation temporarily postponed those goals by focusing workers' attention on reform. For example, during the Economist struggle, language excluded the young Marxists—the so-called "Economists"—who had sought approval for their activities from the émigrés before the Second Congress in 1903. The older theorists subordinated economics to politics and spontaneity to consciousness, arguing that trade unions and a broad movement would produce an unorganized, indeed chaotic, movement rather than a core of professional revolutionaries armed with Marxist theory.

After the Second Congress in 1903, Iulii Martov and the Mensheviks rejected Lenin's famously restrictive definition of "party member." Lenin used the term "member" in the manner inherited from the Economist controversy for the purposes of exclusion. According to Lenin, spontaneity was chaotic, anarchistic, and weak. Socialism would be successful in Russia only through the actions of party members who, armed with correct theory, would bring consciousness to the workers' movement.[4]

This conflict, so apparent at the Second Congress, was not reflected in practice, that is, in the actual workers' movement. Inside Russia, during the 1905–07 Revolution, revolutionaries were drawn into a broad workers' movement. Local activities thrived in unions, cooperatives, libraries,

---

[3]Such analysis is drawn from Dominick LaCapra, *Rethinking Intellectual History Texts, Contexts, Language* (Ithaca, NY, 1983), 36–60; The concept of revolutionary voices was the subject of a AAASS panel held at Boca Raton in September 1998 and Michael Melancon, "A Chorus of Voices: A Bakhtinian Approach to the History of the Russian Labor and Revolutionary Movements," unpublished manuscript. See also Cathy A. Frierson, *Peasant Icons: Representations of Rural People in Late Nineteenth-Century Russia* (New York, 1993).

[4]For thorough treatment of the early history of Social Democracy see Abraham Ascher, *Pavel Aksel'rod and the Development of Menshevism* (Cambridge, MA, 1972); Samuel H. Baron, *Plekhanov: The Father of Russian Marxism* (Stanford, 1963); Jonathan Frankel, *Vladimir Akimov and the Dilemmas of Russian Marxism, 1895–1903* (Cambridge, MA, 1969); Israel Getzler, *Martov: A Political Biography of a Russian Social Democrat* (Cambridge, MA, 1967); Leopold H. Haimson, *Russian Marxists and the Origins of Bolshevism* (Cambridge, MA, 1955); John L. H. Keep, *Rise of Social Democracy in Russia* (Oxford, UK, 1963); Leonard Schapiro, *Communist Party of the Soviet Union* (London, 1960); Allan K. Wildman, *Making of a Workers' Revolution: Russian Social Democracy, 1891–1903* (Chicago, 1967).

and campaigns for better working conditions and the eight-hour day. One might say that the underground organizations' loss was the open workers' movement's gain. The activities of Bolshevik and Menshevik factions and those of other revolutionaries were collaborative, especially at May Day and on the anniversaries of Bloody Sunday. Party activists frequently ignored polemical conflict, produced joint leaflets, organized mass meetings and cooperated in strike activities. Within Social Democracy, Bolshevism and Menshevism were labels that applied primarily to theory, not practice. Workers often looked to revolutionaries for leadership on governing boards of organizations. Drawing on long-term relationships and encouraged by calls for unity from all sides within the workers' and revolutionary movements, party activists and workers often ignored party and factional allegiances to came together in a unified dynamic movement or, in this study's terminolgy as adopted from that era, "unity." At the local level, the concept (and practice) of unity came to predominate in the workers' movement, a fact not clearly delineated in existing histories.[5] The revolution of 1905–07 forced new definitions, and in 1906 the Russian Social Democratic Workers' Party (RSDRP)[6] reached a formal compromise at the Fourth "Unification" Party Congress, which formally ended the separate Bolshevik and Menshevik factions.

Nevertheless, among émigrés "unity" was neither fully recognized, nor realized. After 1907, as reaction reasserted itself, the old party concepts and languages reemerged. What resulted was an ongoing discursive conflict among upper-level party members—a divisive battle of redefinition, exclusion and inclusion that was not mirrored at the local level. The émigrés sought to interject their theoretical battle onto Russian soil. Local activists envisioned a different sort of party, a different reality and a different set of meanings. A struggle involving Leninist émigrés, Menshevik émigrés, and local activists emerged. Although this social, political, and discursive battle was not finally settled until 1918, the revolutionaries' perception of party, movement, and class, defined during 1908–12, set the agenda for SD actions in 1917.

Worker activists and party *praktiki* fought against the inclination back toward old party forms in favor of new forms or, simply, for party reforms.

---

[5]For studies of 1905 and early labor history which do not always share this study's analytical tendencies, see Victoria E. Bonnell, *Roots of Rebellion: Workers' Politics and Organizations in St. Petersburg and Moscow, 1900–14* (Berkeley, 1983); Laura Engelstein, *Moscow 1905: Working Class Organization and Political Conflict* (Stanford, 1982); Gerald D. Surh, *1905 in St. Petersburg: Labor, Society and Revolution* (Stanford, 1989).

[6]The transliterated Russian name is abbreviated RSDRP.

The Menshevik A. N. Potresov and others rejected the conspiratorial underground party, seeking instead an active existence for the party in legal workers' organizations. It was this movement that Lenin labeled "liquidationism" for its alleged desire to do away entirely with underground or illegal work. The existing party, which as of the 1906 unification congress officially proclaimed unification, had no choice but to reply. In response to Bolshevik demands for close ties—indeed virtual identification—between the party and workers' organizations, Martov wrote that the unity of class forces in trade unions depended upon political non-affiliation.[7] His perceptions, formed from his place in Russian society, experience in student circles, and active participation in agitation among workers, provided broad definitions for a new type of "party." For Martov and the Mensheviks, "party" stood apart from the revolutionary "movement" which had enveloped the old party. In this equation, Martov denoted "unity" as a combination of internalized general socialist theory and unionized workers that produced the "movement." In the final analysis, class and action held hegemony over party and theory. It should be noted that, although many of the early reformists rejected the predominance of an illegal party organization, especially one led by émigrés on the Leninist model, few, if any, rejected the concept of illegal work under tsarist conditions, as long as this did not define the movement. In any case, reformists' approaches, for instance, those of Potresov and Martov, were not identical and certainly could not all be fit to the Leninist Procrustean bed of "liquidationism."

Between the revolutions, theory not practice remained the environment for Lenin's views. In the emigration, social experience separated Lenin and the other émigré theorists from the more dynamic *praktiki*, the practical revolutionary activists. Not only old forms but also old discourse dictated his and their responses. In direct contact only with a few central leaders, Lenin was unable to experience revolutionary activity in Russia. Thus isolated, by 1908, Lenin's well-known disagreements with Bolsheviks on the left and Mensheviks on the right reflected a power struggle between the émigrés and the activists inside Russia.[8] In language designed to redefine the movement, Lenin called for a "struggle on two fronts" against "liquidationism" on the left and the right. On the left, Lenin had in mind Bolshevik "recallists" who rejected SD participation

---

[7] "Sotsial-demokratiia v professional'nom dvizhenii," *Golos sotsial-demokrata* 4/5 (April 1908): 13–16.

[8] For analysis of Lenin's polemics with almost everyone in those years, see Robert C. Williams, *The Other Bolsheviks: Lenin and His Critics* (Bloomington, IN, 1986).

in the State Duma (which Lenin favored) and therefore demanded the recall of party Duma deputies. Although Lenin successfully arranged the expulsion of the recallists, his polemical attack on the Menshevik "liquidators" (that is, those who merely wanted to dethrone illegal work) won few recruits among Bolsheviks inside Russia, most of whom sought reconciliation with the Mensheviks. These Bolshevik "conciliators" included trade unionists such as I. P. Gol'denberg, S. I. Kanatchikov, and N. I. Lebedev of the Textile workers', and Roman Malinovskii of the Metalworkers' Union, all of whom struggled to establish politically independent trade unions.[9] The multi-faceted Bolshevik split weakened Lenin's leadership and opened the door to the ascension of legal activists, that is, those who focused primarily on legal or trade unionist activities inside Russia. Tied to theory, Lenin's only recourse was high-level organizational struggle and polemics.

At the time, Leninists dominated the Petersburg Committee (PK) which had the duty of coordinating RSDRP actions in the capital.[10]. The PK argued for a return to the underground and rejected close ties with legal organizations. Leninists also argued that Mensheviks comprehended "cultural" but not "revolutionary work." Such criticism drew on old debates over the value of agitation and propaganda. Cultural work such as Sunday schools, combatting literacy, developing libraries, and organizing lectures or excursions, did not immediately produce "conscious" revolutionary workers; hence, in the Leninist view, it was inferior.

Menshevik publicists or *literatory*, many of whom had much closer ties to the workers' organizations than the Leninist PK, defended the *praktiki* and rejected PK hegemony within the RSDRP in the capital. A letter by "I.," published in *Golos sotsial-demokrata* (*Voice of the Social Democrat*), blamed the organizational crisis in the capital on the Bolshevik-dominated committee's hostility to the Duma faction and trade union work. These Mensheviks (or so-called "liquidators") viewed the party as

---

[9] On liquidators, see also Ronald Grigor Suny, "Labor and Liquidators: Revolutionaries and the 'Reaction' in Baku," *Slavic Review* 34 (1975): 319–46. N. I. Lebedov was president of the Textile Workers' Union and was active on the Central Bureau of Unions. He also played an active role in the insurance campaign after 1913. I. P. Gol'denburg served on the party's Russian Bureau in 1907, edited a number of trade union and party newspapers, joined the Mensheviks in 1917 and the Communist Party in 1920. S. I. Kanatchikov was an active trade unionist, editor and organizer. The provocateur, Malinovskii, was secretary of the Metalworkers' Union from 1906–09 and was elected to the Fourth Duma.

[10] For a complete history of the PK see M. Moskalev, *Biuro tsentral'nogo komiteta RSDRP v Rossii (avgust 1903–mart 1917)* (Moscow, 1964)(hereafter *Biuro*)

a section of a broad movement and saw future dynamism and growth primarily in the legal organizations. Conversely, illegal work, especially in its old forms, represented a step backwards, into a static arena of inactivity and propaganda, a postponement and rejection of revolutionary possibilities. The author, probably B. I. Gorev, summoned the *praktiki* to work toward unity within the movement.[11] In Gorev's view, PK methods forced an unwelcome change of course that drove a wedge between legal activists and the underground. Unity was not a theory; it was a practice undertaken by members of a broad labor movement. Incorporating the spontaneity of the masses, Gorev's vision of the movement was fully democratic, decentralized, and nonexclusive.

The émigré Feodor Dan, who, unlike Lenin, remained close to the *praktiki* inside Russia, wrote in the Menshevik paper *Golos sotsial-demokrata* that propaganda, agitation, and organization were all necessary for the proper development of a working class political party. Dan explained that current police repression hindered propaganda. At present, the party could only direct agitation through the Duma faction, the trade unions, and other related organizations and, only after utilizing these methods, connect these actions to more significant political issues. Dan further explained that refurbishing the party required a change in personnel. As the Party reorganized, Dan warned its members to avoid the preservation of "fossils" which would create "barriers" to a unified party. He argued that party cells obstructed unification since they excluded legal activists. The entire discussion revealed that despite the formal acceptance of unity by the 1906 party congress, a new split, along old lines, was emerging. To avoid this Dan argued for a new definition of party membership that would unite legal and illegal activists. Dan stood solidly on the side of reform and advocated the "liquidation of the old party." At this point, Dan both adopted and broadened Lenin's epithet "liquidator" since, in Dan's view, the new party encompassed both legal and illegal activists.[12]

In July 1908, the Menshevik attack on the old party structure reached a peak with the circulated letter of two Menshevik members of the SD Central Committee, Martynov and Gorev. The authors protested plans for a party conference to be held abroad since such a meeting would by

---

[11] Letter signed "I.," *Golos sotsial-demokrata* 4/5 (March 1908): 28. Although the leftist Menshevik Boris Nikolaevskii also used the pseudonym "I.", the tactical line of this "I." clearly represented the views of V. I. Gorev (Goldman), who served on the SD Central Committee and on the editorial board of many papers. The Russian name for Central Committee in transliteration is TsK.

[12] F. Dan, "Posle buri," *Golos sotsial-demokrata* 1/2 (February 1908) and "Na sovremennuiu temu" *Golos sotsial-demokrata* 8/9 (July/September 1908).

definition exclude "vital and active elements of Social Democracy." To increase the authority of the *praktiki*, they suggested that the Central Committee, a defunct "simple fiction," be replaced by an "Information Bureau." In this approach, the party's vital elements were activists inside Russia, not émigrés. Martynov and Gorev, like Dan, attempted in a variety of ways to redefine the party as activist-oriented and active, rather than furtive and passive. By refraining from involvement in the open labor movement, the party would have remained isolated and weak. The emerging struggle consisted of a battle on the part of the reformers to prevent the marginalization of activists in the open workers' movement (also known as "legalists"). Characterizing future participation in the Central Committee as "useless and giving rise to harmful organizational illusions," Gorev and Martynov threatened to resign from the party if their suggestions were ignored.[13] Reflecting their perception of the changing Russian revolutionary culture, the authors intended to challenge émigré control of the movement. Just as utopians tried to bring about revolution without material foundation, the Central Committee, they claimed, had no link to the mass of workers. Gorev and Martynov believed that their resignation from the party would throw the underground into a kind of alienated isolation from the new movement's vital segments.

The circulated letter tied the "movement" to class and revolution in a host of new codes and conventions. As a category, "movement," since it included legal and illegal party activists and workers, was superior to "party." The Party envisioned by Lenin that brought consciousness to the workers and therefore was necessary for the success of the revolution should, in this vision, be only one part of a broader movement. Information needed only to be disseminated by the party; organization was not essential. *Praktiki* and worker resistance to both employer and state expanded the definition of class to include revolutionary activity rather than a simple relation to production. Gorev's and Martynov's perception of unity collapsed the difference between political and economic struggle. The underground party (understood as the party defined and led by the underground), they argued, disrupted this relationship by attempting to eject the *praktiki* and impose on workers and activists a different sort of movement: centralized, organized, and restrictive. Such an organization

---

[13]The letter was later published in *Sotsial-demokrat* 13 (26[9] May 1911): 9, as "Perly likvidatorstva"; Schapiro, *Communist Party*, 113. The letter was signed by I. Dniprovskii and according to *Sotsial-demokrat* involved at least one editor of *Golos sotsial-demokrata*. The Soviet historian Moskalev credits Gorev and Martynov as co-authors; Moskalev, *Biuro*, 130–31.

would dissolve unity. For Gorev and Martynov, only a reorganized party could reflect the newly evolved movement.

Unfortunately for the reformists, the SD Plenum, which met during August 1908 in Geneva (and which therefore could not be a real party plenum), condemned the Menshevik resolution "On the Reorganization of the Central Committee." The resolution had proposed a set of reforms sponsored by Menshevik *praktiki* and *literatory* aimed at strengthening legal activity. Instead of favoring reform, the Plenum, dominated by the émigrés, voted to strengthen the underground and revive the Russian Bureau as representative inside Russia of the Central Committee. By an odd twist, the émigré-dominated Plenum then selected a five-member Russian Bureau of the Central Committee that in effect gave authority to the very legalists who wished to dismantle the old organizational apparatus. The concession was not deliberate: at the time, legalist-oriented party activists were a majority of party leaders inside Russia. There was no way to create an authoritative Russian Bureau other than by utilizing legal activists such as the Bolshevik I. P. Gol′denberg, former member of the Russian Bureau and the Trade Union Commission, the Menshevik M. I. Broido, a cooperative and trade union *praktik*, and the Bundist (member of the Bund or Jewish branch of the SD movement) I. L. Iudin, who worked in the Petersburg Metalworkers' Union and was close to the "liquidators."[14] The Polish and Latvian Social Democrats, sometimes unpredictable in allegiance, were also represented. The legal activists in the Russian Bureau, whose specific task was to represent the émigré-dominated Central Committee, were instinctively suspicious of party institutions governed from abroad. The whole matter, which in one sense was quickly rendered moot by the arrests of the bureau's entire membership by the year's end, demonstrates the acute differences between party activists located inside Russia and those abroad.

The reformists' suspicions about the nature of a party conference held abroad (like the misnamed Plenum) received confirmation when the Fifth Party Conference in Paris, 21–27 December 1908, rejected the Mensheviks' resolutions. Gorev and Martynov had correctly predicted the limited *praktiki* attendance. The minority Menshevik delegates hoped to integrate the reemerging illegal components with the legalists.[15] In a se-

---

[14] As mentioned, legal activists had difficulty attending the Plenum, which consisted of five Bolsheviks, three Mensheviks, one Polish Social Democrat, two Bundists and one Latvian Social Democrat. See Ascher, 163; Moskalev, *Biuro*, 131–32; "Iz deiatel′nosti Ts.K.," *Sotsial-demokrat* 2 (28[10] February 1909).

[15] Gosudarstvennyi arkhiv Rossiiskoi federatsii (hereafter GARF), f. 111, op. 5, d.

ries of proposals, the Caucasus delegation, SD and Menshevik stalwarts such as Dan, M. Ramishvili, and P. Aksel′rod, all staunch reformers, suggested defining party members quite broadly, as "conscious elements actively working in the name of revolutionary socialism in any section of the workers' movement." Since active work could only be realized inside Russian legal organizations, this definition reaffirmed the Menshevik concept of party membership. To strengthen the authority of the legal activists, the Mensheviks even proposed that émigrés be prohibited from serving on the Russian Bureau. The activists also planned a joint conference of legal and illegal party groups.

The conference struggle over the term "illegal" ultimately demonstrated the superiority of Lenin's discursive grasp. Instead of rejecting the Leninist hegemonic use of the word "illegal," the Mensheviks attempted to adopt an illegal identity, in effect, joining their own opposition. Conventional party wisdom, reflecting past struggles and now attacked by the reformists, had defined activities in the legal realm as anarchistic, unguided, and disorderly since such activities escaped strict control by the guardians of theoretical purity. In reply to accusations of a "cult of legality" and the "negation of the illegal organization," the Caucasus delegation reminded their critics that they were "delegates of an illegal party organization to an illegal conference." Further, they argued, their own proposal that legal elements merge with the underground had illegal status in Russia. In this debate, the Mensheviks aimed to prevent their marginalization by stating they were the truly illegal faction.[16] They accepted the term "illegal" as a legitimizing label; hence its very proponents in the struggle for control of the party dismissed the "legal" status. Party was linked discursively to the illegal underground, not to the unified legal and illegal party group which existed inside Russia. Unwittingly, the Caucasus delegation, struggling against the conference's émigré majority, legitimized Lenin's definition of party.

Appealing to the principle of democracy, Menshevik delegates challenged the voting status of Bolsheviks from St. Petersburg. The Caucasus delegation reported that a Menshevik conference of delegates from seven of the city's districts representing 300 organized workers opposed the Petersburg Committee's right to represent the city since it constantly put up obstacles to unity.[17] Conspiracy in underground cells isolated

---

263, l. 98; Moskalev, *Biuro*, 138.

[16] *Otchet kavkazskoi delegatsii ob obshchepartiinoi konferentsii* (hereafter *Otchet*) (Paris, 1909), 30–31, 33; Moskalev, *Biuro*, 141–42.

[17] *Otchet*, 10.

the party from the movement, the Caucasus delegation argued. In the absence of reform, the party's "liquidation... becomes inevitable" as the "Social Democratic movement will pass it by."[18] Movement—vital and dynamic—would in the end dissolve the party, the reformers believed.

Lenin naturally joined the fray against the Menshevik delegates for identification as the representative of the legitimate party. Using language similar to that used to isolate the "Economists" years earlier, Lenin labeled as "liquidators" anyone who challenged the party center as defined by the conference. The Leninist resolutions compelled the "minority to submit to party discipline [and] work loyally within the limits of a single establishment and its executive organs" and resolved that "rejection of this work signifies boycott of the party."[19] In one resolution, Lenin summoned "all true party workers without regard to faction and tendencies" to struggle against those who wanted "to liquidate the existing RSDRP and to substitute shapeless associations within the bounds of legality." Reaffirming the necessity of forming party cells in every factory, the conference delegates carried through Lenin's proposals. On the work of the Central Committee, the conference endorsed the existence of its Foreign Bureau, despite the opposition of the reformist "Caucasus delegation," and advocated stronger control and connections to local, regional, and national party organizations.[20]

Hence, the Leninist resolutions imposed accepted conventions onto the movement. Party discipline would dominate the broader movement. Who would disagree that only those who worked within the party/movement should be admitted into the party? The real question, as years earlier, was the definition of the party. Also striking was the Leninist definition of the minority, an old definition, reminiscent of the Second Party Congress, which privileged an accidental group at a conference over an entire movement. The opposition to these resolutions, as at the Second Congress, were a minority only at the conference not within the movement as a whole.

The context of the debate to this point was a simple power struggle; however it revealed a deeper crisis within Russian Social Democracy. While denouncing "factions" and "tendencies," Lenin was in fact creating them by appropriating "unity" as a term for those who opposed the "liq-

---

[18] Again, the significance for the reformers of the "movement" in relation to the "party" must be noted. *Otchet*, 5, 9, 32–33.

[19] *Partiia bol'shevikov v period reaktsii (1907–1910 gg.) Dokumenty i materialy* (hereafter *Partiia bol'shevikov*) (Moscow, 1961), 209–12.

[20] Ibid., 217.

uidators." In fact, the current life experiences of the *praktiki* and worker activists were poorly reflected in the old party structure. Abroad, the party center refused to recognize the new conditions and reverted to familiar organizational forms which seemed to offer security in the years of reaction.

The defeat of the *praktiki* at the party conference shifted the struggle to Russia where the authors of the reform movement had aided in critically weakening the old organizational structure. Since the central party structures refused to acknowledge the growing authority of those who worked in trade unions, clubs, and cooperatives, the SD movement's only recourse, according to the reformists, was to reject the existing party. The *praktik*, F. A. Cherevanin (F. A. Lipkin) had already urged Petersburg Mensheviks to leave existing party organizations and form a non-party club-cooperative organization. Shaped by experiences in the workers' movement, the *praktiki*, already submerged in this new revolutionary environment, sought new organizational forms.

A central question arose for the reformers and, in a different sense, for historians: could new organizational styles develop in a repressive society? It would seem that they could. The very context of the *praktiki*'s struggle for reform was the revolutionary culture which had evolved since 1907, under the extremes of the Stolypin reaction. Fluid and dynamic, the movement involved party members and non-party activists who cooperated with each other within the entire spectrum of revolutionary socialism. Workers, drawn to socialism through years of contact with party personnel, did not necessarily commit to party. In fact, party members often switched affiliation depending on location or other factors. For example, where Mensheviks were highly organized, socialist-oriented workers cooperated with and often joined the Mensheviks. Likewise, in factories where Bolsheviks were a major force, many joined the Bolsheviks and the same applied to the Socialist Revolutionaries (SRs). Regardless of party influence, the revolutionary culture was socialist, oppositional, and generally non-affiliated after 1905–07. Lenin and other Marxist theorists, including some Mensheviks, in emigration, alienated from and unfamiliar with this new revolutionary culture, sought to reaffirm party as the central feature of the movement—in the process marginalizing the legal activists who had contributed to its evolution. The émigrés defended old organizational methods against the threatening new culture, while the *praktiki* fought to reform the party by downplaying party affiliation.

Examples of this sort of activist tendency abound. Throughout 1909, *praktiki* and worker activists in Petersburg and other areas cooperated with the SD Duma faction in the by-election campaign of 1909.[21] In trade unions and workers' clubs throughout Petersburg, both Bolshevik and Menshevik activists distributed leaflets and held six public meetings to support the SD candidate N. D. Sokolov's bid for a vacant Duma seat. In September, encouraged by their collaboration, party activists and trade unionists met to discuss the creation of a nonparty party.[22] Present at the meeting were Bolshevik conciliators, Kanatchikov, Lebedov, and Malinovskii, all of whom voted to concentrate activity on the legal arena so that the SDs would "become a solid mass, and not act separately but according to a definite plan." They also voted for the creation of an illegal organization of the most experienced workers who could lead political activity.[23] At the rank and file level, the majority favored a merger of legal and illegal work. These proposals epitomize "liquidationism" in practice. The party's rejection of resolutions defended by the Caucasus delegation at the Fifth Party Conference left the *praktiki* no alternative but to support the continued existence of an independent SD party inside Russia. Even so, by 1909 most factions leaned toward SD unity and hoped to blot out the dividing lines between Bolshevik and Menshevik, between legalists and the underground.

To coordinate the merger of legal and illegal groups, another assembly of thirty-five to forty party workers endorsed the formation of initiative groups throughout the city.[24] Trade unionists advanced collaboration of illegal and legal forces into one illegal SD Party to prevent the continued estrangement of SDs from each other. In the discussion that followed, the PK representative announced that any cooperation with legal activists was "already condemned at the party conference" and that the meeting's participants were "liquidators!" M. B., probably the Menshevik Broido, recorded the meeting's proceedings and claimed that after November the activists in the capital were united with the exception of

---

[21] For a thorough treatment of *praktiki* activities in legal congresses and other venues, see Alice K. Pate, "Liquidationism and Failure of Unity: Russian Social Democracy and the St. Petersburg Metalworkers' Union, 1906–14," unpublished Ph.D. dissertation (Ohio State University, 1995), chapter 3.

[22] See Michael S. Melancon, "'Marching Together!' Left Bloc Activities in the Russian Revolutionary Movement, 1900–February 1917," *Slavic Review* 49 (Summer 1990): 239–53 and "'Stormy Petrels': the SRs in Russia's Labor Organizations, 1905–14," *Carl Beck Papers* (Pittsburgh, 1988).

[23] Bulkin, "Soiuz metallistov i department politsii," *Krasnaia letopis'* 8 (1923): 225. See the Bolshevik account in *Proletarii* 50 (1909).

[24] The most significant of these groups, the Petersburg Initiative Group, organized in 1911 at the Congress of Handicrafts' Trades, would be closely identified with the Metalworkers' Union.

the now alienated "recallist" PK.[25] The legal activists never accepted the label of "liquidators," but nonetheless lost the battle to reject openly old party forms. Language delineated the conflict.

Reform not liquidation of the party in fact defined the actions of the Menshevik *praktiki*. In an "Open Letter" published in *Golos sotsialdemokrata* in 1910, sixteen Menshevik *praktiki* identified party reform as a developing process within Russian Social Democracy.[26] More than any other platform, the "Open Letter" defines the reformist movement known to this day as Liquidationism. Mentioned only in passing in most studies, this document occupies a central place in SD discourse of the interrevolutionary years and is essential to an understanding of the dilemmas of Russian revolutionaries in general. The activists acknowledged that "circles abroad"—opponents of "Menshevik Orthodoxy"—were trying to split the Menshevik wing of the party. Taking aim at Plekhanov and the Party Mensheviks (those who wished to retain old forms of party organization), they compared their rebellion to 1903 when the Mensheviks "raised the banner of revolt against bureaucratic centralism." The *praktiki* charged that the party membership was alienated and demoralized, leaving the party in a state of impending collapse. In order "not to break, but on the contrary to pick up the thread of the development of Menshevik thought," they encouraged SD activists to relocate the party center to the workers' movement. True unity, they insisted, could only be achieved at the cost of the destruction of the old party. Workers' organizations would serve as the "fulcrum" for the formation of the "independent political movement." Attempting to turn the tables on their accusers, the *praktiki* argued the true "liquidators" were those "holding onto obsolete forms, preventing the free development of the party." Now the party was developing along predetermined lines in keeping with Menshevik and Russian Marxist ideology; the "liquidators" simply proposed an acceptance of reality.

Clearly, the authors of the "Open Letter" hoped to include a plurality of voices in the reorganized party. Members were revolutionary, active, and, at the same time, spontaneous. The *praktiki* envisioned new organizational forms which did not require discipline and theory. The future brought into being through party activities would be thoroughly

---

[25] At the time, the PK was dominated by those who wanted to recall SD deputies from the Duma, a position opposed by Lenin. "Iz rabochei zhizni: S.-Petersburg," *Sotsial-demokrat* 15/16 (12/30 September 1910): 13–14.

[26] "Otkrytoe pis′mo," *Golos sotsial-demokrata* 19/20 (January–February 1910): 23–24.

revolutionary in its political and social context. Workers voting for governing boards of labor associations and at meetings and conferences in the months following publication of this letter supported this vision.

Privately and in the press, émigrés and the *praktiki* addressed the issues presented in the "Open Letter." Dan accepted the emphasis on legal work, summoning unified SDs to a "Struggle for Equality." As the "Social Democratic vanguard," the *praktiki* should work to acquire full, legal rights for the workers' movement.[27] On 7 January 1910, Aksel'rod, whose ideas closely resembled those of the "Open Letter," praised the "tact and dignity" of the document in a letter to A. N. Potresov, whose approach also closely resembled that of the "Open Letter." A founder of the Petersburg Union of Struggle and the famous newspaper *Iskra*, Potresov had criticized Lenin's centralization of the party at the Second Congress. In a letter to the German Social Democrat Karl Kautsky, Potresov now admitted that SD activists should have joined workers' organizations as early as 1901. Potresov was ready to correct earlier errors. One of a very small group of SD intellectuals in St. Petersburg during 1910, Potresov undertook to defend Menshevik *praktiki* who worked in the open labor movement. His article "Critical Sketches" asserted that the Party's "old organizational forms" were powerless under current conditions. He characterized "the first cadres of [working class] *intelligenty*" just then taking shape as the real inheritors of socialist ideology. According to Potresov, the new working class revolutionary culture would replace the old party structured around the intelligentsia.[28]

Inside Russia, all reformers recognized unity as the fundamental principle proposed by the "Open Letter." Movement gained precedence over party and encompassed revolutionary activists and workers who worked in legal and illegal organizations, attended meetings and lectures, and joined cooperatives and educational societies. As noted, this approach attained very wide acceptance. To defeat this dangerous concept, Lenin would have to reclaim and redefine the unity movement as socialist, conscious, and disciplined, in other words in such a way that "unity" would apply solely to a Leninist party. As usual, Lenin proved equal to this daunting task.

First and foremost, Lenin used both the "Open Letter" and Potresov's defense of it as kindling for his fiery attack on the "liquidators" and on the Mensheviks, just as years earlier he had used the Economist "Credo,"

---

[27] F. Dan, "Bor'ba za legal'nost'," *Golos sotsial-demokrata* 19/20 (January/February 1910): 2–3.

[28] Potresov, "Kriticheskie nabroski," *Nasha zaria* 2 (1910): 59, 61–62.

to discredit the supporters of the new revolutionary culture. Most of the signatories, such as F. A. Cherevanin and E. A. Maevskii, remained on the right wing of the party their whole lives.[29] Since they frequently contributed to the Menshevik journals *Nasha zaria* and *Luch*, Lenin's vituperative attacks characterized those publications as "liquidationist" as well, just as earlier on he had identified and excoriated *Rabochee delo* as "Economist." Any Menshevik who favored the cause of a focus on legal activities, Lenin painted with the wide brush of "*likvidarstvo*," embellished with various insults and belittlements. How and why the Leninist tactics once again worked is of great interest for the history of the period.

Processes already at work in the movement allowed the discussants to further adapt the texts of the debate to the power struggle. With the simultaneous publication in the Bolshevik *Proletarii* and the Menshevik *Golos sotsial-demokrata* of the "Letter to Social Democratic Comrades Working in the Trade Unions, Educational Societies, Schools, Cooperatives and other Legal Organizations" from the Vyborg district SDs (St. Petersburg), both sides of the debate claimed victory.[30] To the delight of the Bolsheviks, the Vyborg party activists admitted that their decision to work in legal workers' associations in defiance of central party decrees had created a party organization plagued by "parochial politics" and "narrow local egoism." The "lack of discipline," they continued, had alienated the Duma faction from the workers. Although their criticism appeared to be directed at the legalists, the authors of the letter adopted a slogan that both Menshevik *praktiki* and Bolsheviks interpreted as a vindication of their positions: "Unity of the working class, unity in the ranks of the illegal RSDRP, do not abandon your legal work!" From the Bolshevik side, *Proletarii* asserted that the Vyborg letter proved that liquidationism and its problems were not Bolshevik inventions. *Proletarii* then called for broadening the base of legal work and improving its quality and, implausibly, described this approach as "Bolshevik." The editors denied they had ever opposed legal work, as accused by "liberal scribblers" and some

---

[29] The complete list of the signatories of the "Open Letter" is as follows: K. Avgustovskii (S. O. Ezhov), Anton (M. S. Panin-Makodziub), Vadim (V. K. Ikov-Mirov), V. Petrov (L. N. Radchenko), Georgii (Kotelevtnets?), Georg (V. O. Levitskii), Evg. Ga-aza (V. A. Gutovskii-Maevskii), Kramol′chikov (G. I. Prigornii), D. Kol′tsov (B. A. Ginzburg), Nad. Mikhailova (E. M. Aleksandrova), Solomonov (St. Ivanovich-Portugeis), Cherevanin (F. A. Lipkin), Iurii (P. A. Bronshtein-Garvi), and Ia. P-ogo (Piletskii). Ezhov (S. O. Tsederbaum) was Martov's brother, editor of many journals labeled liquidationist by Lenin, and later a worker insurance activist.

[30] "Iz partii," *Golos sotsial-demokrata* 14 (May 1909): 15–16 and "Pokhmel′e legalistov," *Proletarii* 45 (13 [26] May 1909): 2.

"Menshevik writers." Yet, the Leninist position had indubitably scorned legal work in public organizations. This linguistic legerdemain constituted the opening shots in the renewed struggle for control of discourse and, it would follow, the movement and party inside Russia.

Simultaneously, the Menshevik editors of *Golos sotsial-demokrata* extolled the Vyborg comrades for "invit[ing] Social Democrats to implement tasks" already presented in the newspaper's pages and in the resolutions of the Caucasus delegation at the all-party conference. Unity of illegal and legal work, they argued with some accuracy, had always been a Menshevik tactic. They alleged that *Proletarii*'s editors only "pretended to detect" movement toward Bolshevik positions in the Vyborg letter.[31] They felt that its publication clearly placed unity and legal work on the agenda for everyone within the movement. In summary, both sides had scored points: the Vyborg SDs seemed to question the revolutionary and socialist nature of legal work and at the same time promoted legal work and inclusive party unity. Questions remained about how best to utilize the evident stand-off.

At first, things seemed to go well for the reformists, for instance at the January 1910 Plenum of the Central Committee in Paris, attended by fourteen central committee members, including Lenin, Martov, and Trotskii. Aided by the predominance of Menshevik and Bolshevik conciliators, the delegates attempted to sort out the factional disputes of the last two years. The recallists expelled from the Bolshevik faction in 1909 were readmitted in their reformulation as the Vpered (Forward) group. The Bolshevik paper *Proletarii*, and the Menshevik *Golos sotsial-demokrata* were to be discontinued and replaced by a revised, non-factional newspaper, *Sotsial-demokrat*. The formerly Bolshevik editorial board now included Martov, Dan, and the Polish Social Democrat, A. Varskii. Trotskii's *Pravda (Truth)*, which pursued a policy of SD unity, was also given financial backing. At the Plenum, a majority rejected Lenin's intransigent positions on many of these issues and voted that any "Social Democratic groups in the legal sphere, which were prepared to affiliate with the party," as well as "individual activists," could be represented at the Sixth Party Conference to be convened in six months. More ominously for the Menshevik reformers, the Plenum passed a Leninist-sounding resolution that defined "liquidators" as Social Democrats who rejected "revolutionary goals" and who would "at any cost adjust themselves" to conditions in Russia.[32]

---

[31] See Martov's editorial, *Golos sotsial-demokrata* 13 (1909).

[32] Moskalev, *Biuro*, 162; *Sotsial-demokrat* 11 (13 February/31 January 1910): 10–

Elated at the improving prospects for party unity, the Menshevik editors of *Golos sotsial-demokrata*, including Dan and Martov, praised the Plenum's decisions, which, they asserted somewhat prematurely, had "liquidated" the Bolshevik-Menshevik party split. The Menshevik émigré leaders chose to interprete the delegates' condemnation of liquidationism as aimed at elements—that is, a complete rejection of illegal revolutionary work—that did not exist within their own faction. The *Golos sotsial-demokrata* editors felt that if they attacked this resolution, they would disrupt the Plenum's desireable process of unification. Unwilling to force a split, they emphasized the conciliatory gestures made by the Bolsheviks at the Plenum and remained silent on the misinterpretation of liquidationism, thus creating the possibility of future conflict. Although the Leninists had yielded considerable ground on substantive issues, they had retained control of crucial linguistic ground by having the Plenum define liquidationism in a way that divided Social Democrats into good ones and bad ones.

Regardless, at this point an array of party forces—Menshevik *praktiki*, Bolshevik conciliators, and worker activists—all stood together in opposition to Lenin. If a real unified all-party conference had been held, the reformers would have won a clear majority. Still, Menshevik and Bolshevik leaders obviously could not resolve their differences on reform and "liquidationism" without intense political infighting. Lenin remained adamant in his rejection of reform: in the absence of democracy, the party, with the correct theory guiding it, had to be distinguished from the class whose interests and aims it promoted. Mere "conciliationism" could not bridge over such differences. Aksel′rod warned the reformers that nonfactionalism under present conditions "means behaving like an ostrich, means deceiving oneself and others," since only by factional organization could party members achieve reform "or, to be more exact, a revolution in the party."[33] In a letter to Potresov, Martov admitted that the final defeat of Leninism required a complete wrecking of the old party. Martov and the other émigrés refused to be responsible for such a schism.[34]

The editors of *Golos sotsial-demokrata*, at least, openly welcomed Trotskii's call for unity within the Russian SD movement. As planning

---

11; G. Swain, *Russian Social Democracy and the Legal Labor Movement, 1906–1914* (London, 1983), 94, citing Nikolaevskii, *Materialy* 2, item 32, notes by V. L. Shantser; Schapiro, *Communist Party*, 116–17. Schapiro does not mention the agreements concerning plans for the Sixth Conference, but instead focuses on Lenin's determination to resist implementation of the decisions of the Plenum.

[33] *Nevskii golos* 6 (1912) and *Nasha zaria* 6 (1912).

[34] Schapiro, *Communist Party*, 118, citing Martov to Potresov, 23 February 1910.

began for the all-party conference foreseen by the Plenum, Trotskii's connection to the *praktiki* inside Russia was sealed by their mutual agreement to give authority to legal activists. Bolshevik conciliators V. Nogin and I. Gol'denberg promptly began instituting the conciliationist party directives in St. Petersburg. The Russian Bureau, with two seats each for Bolsheviks and Mensheviks, and one position for each of the three major nationality factions (Poles, Jews, and Lithuanians), had the responsibility for planning the Sixth Conference. Gol'denberg began work on a project to revive the newspaper of the SD Duma faction newspaper *Novyi Den'* (*New Day*) with the assistance of Potresov and other Petersburg Mensheviks. Meanwhile Nogin attempted to recruit two Mensheviks to the Russian Bureau. Despite Nogin's efforts, the important SD legal activists P. Garvi, I. Isuf, and K. Ermolaev, who had refused when asked to join the work of the Russian Bureau in 1909, once again refused to be associated in any way with the Central Committee.[35] The cause of reform was in part hampered by leading reformists! Eventually Sverchkov, a Menshevik close to Trotskii, accepted the responsibility of entering the Russian Bureau. In May 1910, Russian Bureau delegates arrived in Moscow for their first meeting. Before the meeting began, Sverchkov met with representatives of the local Moscow journal, *Vozrozhdenie* (*Resurrection*), known to be sympathetic toward the right-wing Mensheviks, possibly to convince another Menshevik to join the Russian Bureau. However, with negotiations incomplete, arrests ended the meetings and further damaged possibilities for unity and conciliation.[36] Thus for varying reasons the 1910 plans for organizational unification were stillborn.

This failure was soon enough coupled with the revival of factional newspapers. Lenin's polemical article "K edinstvu" ("Toward unity") in *Sotsial-demokrat* led to the resignation of Martov and Dan from the editorial board, as was likely his intention. Consequently, the Menshevik émigrés continued to publish *Golos sotsial-demokrata* as a rival to *Sotsial-demokrat*. In St. Petersburg, Potresov introduced the legal journal *Nasha*

---

[35] "Razrushennaia legenda," *Golos sotsial-demokrata* 24 (Prilozhenie) (February 1911); Garvi, *Revoliutsionnye siluety* (New York, 1962), Introduction, 9; Moskalev, *Biuro*, 165. Martov, Martynov, Gorev and Ramishvili sent a letter to the Foreign Bureau approving the withdrawal of the Mensheviks from the Russian Bureau 27 April 1910, Moskalev, *Biuro*, 167 citing RGASPI, f. 18, op. 39, ed. khr. 36036. However, Martov blamed Garvi, Isuv and Ermolaev for the failure of implementation of the Plenum directives. Schapiro, *Communist Party*, citing Martov to Potresov, 17 April 1910.

[36] L. Germanov, (Frumkin) "Iz partiinoi zhizni v 1910," *Proletarskaia revoliutsiia* 5 (1922): 232; "Razrushennaia legenda," *Golos sotsial-demokrata* 24 (February 1911); Garvi, *Revoliutsionnye silueti*, introduction and p. 9.

zaria with Garvi, Levitskii, and Ermanskii included among the editors. Strongly aligned with Party reformers, *Nasha zaria* was labeled purely liquidationist by Lenin, although Ermanskii was on the left wing of the Mensheviks.[37]

Along with the rapid resplintering of the SD press, there occurred a total collapse through arrests and other mishaps of all the central party bodies in 1910. This opened an unexpected window of opportunity for reform. Liquidationism in practice, that is, the unity of the revived underground and the legal workers' movement (rather than the Leninist exclusionary caricature of liquidationism), could have arisen, had someone acted. Party émigrés hostile to reform, totally lacking a party base, were politically impotent. Unfortunately, Menshevik émigrés underestimated the extent of Lenin's isolation and ignored evidence of the strength of the reform movement inside Russia. In a situation in which the old party organization had perished, those who favored a new reformed party waited for guidance but failed to find it among the intelligentsia, both Menshevik and Bolshevik, who remained locked into old organizational patterns. The only means for the success of the Menshevik reformers was a complete break with Lenin and the old bureaucratic party. For all their polemics, the Menshevik leaders proved unwilling to practice what they preached. A new party lay in wait; no one ushered it into being.

The Sixth Party Conference, conceived to end the party schism, never took place as expected; moreover, the whole affair rendered the party split absolute. Conference planning fell to the Foreign Bureau of the Central Committee, whose ranks were augmented by the Menshevik B. I. Gorev and the Bundist F. M. Iunov, bringing its make-up closer to the reformers. On 16 March 1911, the Foreign Bureau denounced conflicts and released a letter from the émigré Mensheviks addressed "To all our comrades from abroad" that espoused an end to the party split.[38] Regardless, for various reasons the Foreign Bureau itself temporized in its task of summoning a party conference. Not least at fault were Menshevik leaders who inexplicably failed to utilize pro-unity and pro-reform sentiment back in Russia to bring about a unified conference and achieve reform. As time passed without the summoning of the unified Sixth Party Conference, Lenin and Trotskii formed rival organizing committees that resulted in not one but two separate party conferences, at Prague and Vienna, during 1912.

---

[37] For examples of Lenin's condemnation of "liquidationism" see "Golos likvidatorov protiv partii," "Otvet 'Golos sotsial-demokrata'" and "Za chto borot'sia?" *Sotsial-demokrat* (23 March 1910); *Partiia bol'shevikov*, 117–123; Moskalev, *Biuro*, 165.

[38] Ibid., 168.

The Bolshevik-oriented Prague Conference achieved Lenin's unfulfilled objectives from the January 1910 Plenum. Repeating previous indictments, the conference dismissed as "liquidationism" (in the Leninist variant) all attempts to increase the status of legal activism. The delegates also resolved that "by its conduct the [reformist] group [around] *Nasha zaria...* has finally placed itself outside the party." The Prague delegates also banned all cooperation with liquidators in the upcoming elections to the Fourth State Duma. To reinforce tactical and programmatic unity, the conference delegates required that all communications with Russian organizations pass through the Central Committee.[39] Needless to say, these planks all represented Lenin's long-term thinking about the party.

The rival "Conference of RSDRP Organizations" assembled at the People's House in Vienna on 12 August 1912. Despite the disruptive efforts of tsarist police agents, conciliatory resolutions prevailed. A resolution "On the Organizational Forms of Party Building" suggested that "the existing and newly beginning illegal party organizations should be adapted to the new forms and methods of the open workers' movement." To broaden contact with the proletariat, the delegates agreed to increase participation in all forms of legal and illegal political institutions linked through the party to non-political workers' organizations. Only unity candidates arrived at through negotiation with all local Social Democrats were to be supported in the upcoming elections to the Fourth State Duma. Finally, delegates elected a seven-member Organizing Committee which would operate inside Russia, rather than a Central Committee located abroad. Based upon these resolutions, groups loyal to Vienna—the Mensheviks, Bundists, and non-factional Social Democrats—identified themselves as the "August Bloc."[40] After 1912, the reformers pursued a struggle against the Leninists, anticipating that a wave of conciliation would obliterate the remnants of the old party. In a sense, the Vienna Conference fulfilled Aksel'rod's injunction that only through factional work could the old party organization be destroyed and real unity be achieved.

As the rival party hierarchies attempted to carry out the mutually contradictory resolutions of Prague and Vienna, St. Petersburg *praktiki*

---

[39] *Vserossiiskaia Konferentsiia Ros. Sots.-Dem. Rab. Partii 1912 goda*, ed. R. Carter Elwood (New York, 1982), 28, 31; Schapiro, *Communist Party*, 133.

[40] P. A. Garvi, *Vospominaniia: Petersburg, 1906 g.; Petersburg-Odessa-Vena, 1912 g.* (New York, 1961), 10–12, 25; *Pis'ma P. B. Aksel'roda i Yu. O. Martova, 1901–1916* (Berlin, 1924), 227.; *Izveshchenie o Konferentsii Organizatsii RSDRP*, ed. R. Carter Elwood, (New York, 1982), 15, 28–29; Schapiro, *Communist Party*, 127–28.

and worker activists had the clear opportunity to found an independent unified working class political party. If questioned, both Lenin and Aksel′rod would have agreed that the Russian activists' success depended on the current level of the workers' political consciousness. In the actual event, as it turned out, the question of the day, namely, would the proletariat have the capability to engineer a party revolution?, would be answered during a period of revived revolutionary fervor in the prewar years. During the 1912–14 years, using time-honored political tactics, Lenin simplified the ideological battle by labeling all opponents "liquidators" and by continuing his assault on the reform movement, which, of course, he vilified as "liquidationist" according to his definition, which, unfortunately for the Mensheviks, had been accepted as the official one. Convinced that only the party with the correct theory could realize revolution, Lenin tirelessly battled Menshevik émigrés for control of a party that did not yet exist. Isolated, acting in a disintegrating apparatus, Lenin now seized the legitimizing label —unity—and used it to create loyal Bolshevik cadres who would serve as the nucleus of a pro-Leninist party, a reprise of his tactics at the Second Congress in 1903. Although at the local level Leninists would have to develop new tactics in association with the Prague outlook on unity, their task had been lightened by Lenin's victory in maligning all reformers as "liquidators."

As such, liquidationism, pushed outside the party by resolutions at Vienna, never reasserted itself. Rather, its proponents, discursively defeated, now rejected the label and instead endorsed the unity platform. From 1912 to 1914, during the elections for the Fourth State Duma and the campaigns for freedom of coalition and for social insurance, workers consistently voted for unity. Workers, socialists, and nonparty activists collaborated in strikes and in efforts to establish a workers' newspaper in St. Petersburg. Unfortunately for those who really wanted unity, the Menshevik émigrés and the Leninists ignored this cooperation and continued to pursue factionalism, thus ensuring that the battles would be fought on Lenin's preferred terrain. In this way, even the seemingly triumphant unity campaign ultimately failed.

Inside Russia, the election campaign for the Fourth State Duma was already underway. During October, Stalin, one of the Bolshevik leaders in St. Petersburg, actually deployed unity slogans so as to exclude Mensheviks from receiving Duma mandates, even accusing the Mensheviks of "playing at unity" in order to "smuggle their candidate through somehow."[41] One might note first the significant fact that inside Rus-

---

[41] I. V. Stalin, *Works* (Moscow, 1953), 2: 265–66.

sia the Bolsheviks had already commenced their appropriation of the unity slogan and second that Stalin was already proving himself a good pupil of Lenin. Regardless, seven Mensheviks and six Bolsheviks made up the Fourth Duma SD faction, most of whom were elected on unity platforms.[42] N. Chkeidze, as a leading spokesperson for the faction, encouraged conciliation and cooperation, and on 15 December four Bolshevik deputies approved a proposal to merge the Bolshevik and Menshevik newspapers and become collaborating editors.[43] On the one hand, this showed the continuing power of the real unity movement and, on the other, alarmed Lenin, who now became determined to split the Duma faction in disregard of activists' hopes for unity in the capital.

Increasingly factionalism, aggravated by the émigrés' haggling and intervention, damaged the possibilities for harmony among the deputies. Although unity platforms were the basis for their election, tension quickly arose between the deputies loyal to Lenin's Central Committee and those connected to the Menshevik Organizational Committee.[44] At a succession of party meetings, Lenin pushed for an end to compromise between the Menshevik and Bolshevik deputies.[45] At Poronin on 27 July 1913, the Central Committee heard conflicting reports on the prospects for unity.[46] In September 1913, the Central Committee rejected the Bolshevik Duma deputy A. Badaev's resolution "Unity in the Duma is Possible and Necessary." When the SD deputies met jointly on 16 October 1912, the Bolsheviks accused the Menshevik majority of hindering their access to committee assignments and not letting them speak for the faction. By 15 November, the Bolshevik deputies formed the SD Labor Group, effectively ending any possibility that the Social Democratic Duma faction would serve as unifier of the party in Russia.[47]

---

[42] For discussion of the lists, see *Luch* 10 (September 1912): 4; *Novaia rabochaia gazeta* 50 (2 July 1914): 2; *Luch* 29 (19 October 1912): 2; *Pravda* 153 (20 October 1912): 2; *Sotsial-demokrat* 30 (25[12] January 1913).

[43] Malinovsky and Muranov opposed this. *Luch* 78 (18 December 1912): 1.

[44] Robert McKean, *St. Petersburg between the Revolutions: Workers and Revolutionaries, June 1907–February 1917* (hereafter *St. Petersburg*) (New Haven, CT, 1990), 140–41; G. I. Zaichkov, *Bor'ba rabochikh deputatov gosudarstvennoi dumy protiv tsarizma v 1907–1914gg.* (Moscow, 1981); A. E. Badaev, *Bolsheviks in the Tsarist Duma* (New York, 1973), 43–44; M. L. Lur'e, *Bol'shevistskaia fraktsiia v gosudarstvennoi dume: Sbornik materialov i dokumentov* (Leningrad, 1938), 104–09.

[45] After a Bolshevik meeting at Cracow, four Bolsheviks in the Duma faction agreed to end collaboration with *Luch* while still rejecting allegiance to the Prague resolutions.

[46] V. I. Lenin *Collected Works* (Moscow, 1960–70), 18: 460–61; *Pravda* 167 (13 November 1912): 2, and 47/251 (26 February 1913): 1; "Lenin i *Pravda*," *Krasnaia letopis'* 1 (1924): 77; Badaev, *Bolsheviks*, 107–15.

[47] Badaev, *Bolsheviks*, 114–15, 116–22; *Novaia rabochaia gazeta* 61 (19 October 1913): 1.

The schism in the Duma faction did not, however, obliterate cooperative action between rank and file worker activists. Early in 1912, two different groups attempted to organize Marxist newspapers. The Bolshevik conciliators N. Baturin (the pseudonym of N. Zamiatin), an editor of *Zvezda*, and Frumkin (M. I. Germanov) created a fund for worker contributions to this venture.[48] At the same time, the left-wing Menshevik Initiative Group announced a project for a nonfactional newspaper edited by workers.[49] Hoping to unite the two efforts, the Initiative Group called a meeting in March to propose that the two groups merge. The Leninist Central Committee decided to hinder this venture by using money under Lenin's personal control to discourage cooperation and pursue instead the establishment of a separate Bolshevik newspaper, *Pravda*. At a meeting on 15 April 1912 set up by St Petersburg Metalworkers and attended by 500–600 activists, only forty supported the Bolshevik resolution that condemned the new workers' newspaper *Rabochaia gazeta* as "liquidationist." The majority voted for workers' control of the projected newspaper and selected a board of eight to start publication on 22 April, the very same date announced for the launch of *Pravda*. Arrest of the entire group on 18 April 1912 ended the possibility for workers' control of a worker-oriented newspaper.[50]

Instead of a workers' newspaper, both factions of the RSDRP now introduced their own newspapers. With financial support from Lenin, the Bolsheviks began the publication of *Pravda* on 22 April 1912. The Leninist M. Kalinin stated that the paper would be a "nonfactional" party paper that included all Marxists on the editorial board. Indeed, the paper's very first editorial, written by Stalin, stated that *"Pravda* will call above all else and in the main for unity in the class struggle of the working class."[51] In point of fact, Lenin was unable to use the newspaper for polemics against the "liquidator-Mensheviks" until February 1914,

---

[48] *Zvezda* 28 (5 November 1911): 1; 33 (10 December 1911): 2; 1/37 (6 January 1912): 1.

[49] See Nicolaevsky Collection, Hoover Institution, Stanford University, Series 16, Box 42, ff 7 for correspondence between Aksel'rod and Garvi on this issue. Lidiia Dan attended one of these meetings and Trotskii was interested in the project. *Zhivoe delo* 2 (27 January 1912): 2.

[50] F. Moravskii (S.P-skii) "Rabochaia gazeta," *Zhivoe delo* 2 (27 January 1912); "O rabochei gazete," *Metallist* 10 (11 February 1912); R. Gorin, "K voprosu o rabochei gazete," *Zhivoe delo* 10 (24 March 1911); Bulkin, *Na zare*, 237.

[51] In *Sotsial-demokrat* Stalin even called for cooperation with *Rabochaia gazeta*. See *Metallist* 13 (7 April 1912); "Rabochee izdatel'stvo," *Metallist* 15 (1 June 1912); Iurenev, "Mezhraionka," 112; Stalin, "Our aims" in *Works* (Moscow, 1953), 2: 255–56; R. G. Suny, "Labor and Liquidators," 338.

when Kalinin became editor.[52] After the arrests of the editorial board chosen to begin publication of *Rabochaia gazeta*, the Initiative Group lacked personnel and funds for continuing the project. Instead the more conservative Menshevik Organizational Committee, as rival to Lenin's Central Committee, launched a Menshevik journal, *Luch*.[53]

In spite of the appearance of factional newspapers, local activists cooperated in numerous strikes and demonstrations during the prewar years. From 1912–14, demonstrations and strikes, with the wide participation of workers and activists, either had general political goals or reflected particular economic or political policies at individual factories. These protests and associated work stoppages mostly occurred without control or coordination from above. The workers' demands and motivations suggest they collectively opposed authority in all its forms and sought a united movement against those who attempted to hold political, economic, or ideological power.

Local socialist groups cooperated in demonstrations summoned on May Day and the Bloody Sunday anniversaries of 9 January. Huge political demonstrations occurred after the news of the massacre of miners at the Lena Gold Fields on 4 April 1912 reached the capital. Encouraged by the Menshevik deputy G. S. Kuznetsov, local SDs and students called for a demonstration on Nevskii Prospect on Sunday, 15 April. Workers participated in a wave of spontaneous strikes from 14–22 April involving around 140,000 participants.[54] As May Day approached, the Central Bureau of 1 May Committees with joint participation of many SD and SR groups distributed leaflets calling for a strike, a democratic republic, Constituent Assembly, eight-hour day, and land confiscation.[55] In response to such widespread agitation, 150,000 laborers joined May Day strikes in 1912. Although activists made efforts to coordinate strike action after May Day, inviting formation of strike committees at district meetings, arrests curbed their success.[56] On their own initiative, the Bolshevik Pe-

---

[52] See R. Carter Elwood, "Lenin and *Pravda*," *Slavic Review* 31 (June 1972): 355–80.

[53] Martov to Garvi, 23 April 1912 and 27 July 1912; B. I. Nikolaevskii, L. Tsederbaum-Dan, eds., *Pis'ma P. B. Aksel'roda i Yu. O. Martova 1901–16* (Berlin, 1924), 222–23, 243; P. A. Garvi, *Zapiski Sotsial-demokrata* (Newtonville, 1982), 218–19.

[54] Rossiiskii gosudarstvennyi arkhiv sotsial'no-politicheskoi istorii (RGASPI), f. 6860, op. 1, d.173, l. 4; *Zvezda* 31/67 (17 April 1912); *Pravda* (Vienna) 25 (6 May–23 April 1912): 3.

[55] I. Iakovlev, "Aprel'sko-maiskie dni 1912 goda v Peterburge," *Krasnaia letopis'* 3 (1925): 230–37; Robert McKean, *St. Peterburg*, 90, citing GARF, f. 1405, op. 530, d. 824, ll. 82, 88; f. 102 (DPOO 1912), d. 341, l. 108.

[56] *Pravda* nos. 8 and 9 (May 1912); Iakovlev, 232, 234–35; McKean, *Petersburg*, 91, citing GARF, f. 102 (DPOO 1912), d. 341, ll. 136–37, 161, 181; d. 101, ll. 81, 225–26.

tersburg Committee decided to oppose strikes for 9 January 1913 (Bloody Sunday); regardless, 71,000 walked off the job with the support of other socialist organizations. Unilateralism was neither popular nor successful among this era's workers and activists.[57] For May Day 1913, the OK, PK, and Central Committee printed leaflets, and the PK formed a strike committee with local SRs.[58] In fact, collaboration continued into 1914, when, for instance, the Menshevik Initiative Group, the Bolsheviks, the Mezhraionka (a radical SD group aimed at party unity), and the SRs all coordinated strike plans for 9 January.[59] Workers' groups and activists coordinated demonstrations on 4 April, May Day, and in other stoppages even when various party institutions had been weakened by police harassment and arrests.

Workers and socialists openly embraced the unity campaign in all these activities. It became clear to Lenin that this campaign was central to workers' views of the movement. In 1913, invoking decisions made at Prague, the Leninist Central Committee resolved that:

> Social Democrats must attract into all workers' societies the broadest possible circles of workers, inviting into membership all workers without distinction according to party views. But the Social Democrats within these societies must organize party groups [cells] and through long, systematic work within all these societies establish the very closest relations between them and the SD Party.[60]

During elections to governing boards of clubs and societies and in Duma elections, Leninists successfully appropriated the unity campaign for their slates of "Marxist" candidates. The governing board of the St. Petersburg Metalworkers' Union, which had been dominated by Mensheviks, Bolshevik conciliators, and SRs since its formation in 1906, was altered through these election tactics. On 21 April 1913, 700–800 members of the reorganized union met to elect an interim board. *Pravda* passed out copies of a list of suitable candidates which it called the "Marxist" slate. The rival Menshevik journal *Luch* objected to factional lists: traditionally candidates had been chosen from district meetings based on personality

---

[57] *Listovki Peterburgskhikh bol'shevikov, 1902–17 gg. Tom vtoroi, 1904–1917*, 74–75, "Lenin i *Pravda*," *Krasnaia letopis'* 1 (1924): 71; E. E. Kruze discusses the PK leaflet in *Istoriia rabochikh Leningrada. Tom pervyi. 1703–fevral' 1917* (Leningrad, 1972), 431.

[58] *Listovki*, 82–84, *Pravda* 10/304 (3 May 1913): 3; *Luch* 100/86 (3 May 1913): 2.

[59] *Listovki*, 88–90, 102–03; *Novaia rabochaia gazeta* 8/26 (11 January 1914).

[60] Thomas Taylor Hammond, *Lenin on Trade Unions and Revolution, 1893–1917* (New York, 1957), 72.

and local loyalties. The assembly elected a temporary governing board which included thirteen Bolsheviks, five Mensheviks, one SR, and one non-party candidate. The conciliatory Bolshevik A. S. Kiselev became president, and the Mensheviks V. M. Abrosimov and N. K. Morozov were named secretary and treasurer respectively. Two Bolsheviks, A. S. Kiselev and A. A. Mitrevich, and two Mensheviks, G. O. Baturskii and S. M. Shvarts, were placed on the editorial board of the trade union's journal, *Metallist*.[61] At the election of the permanent board on 25 August, *Luch* and *Pravda* both presented lists that claimed the unity slogan and both of which included Kisilev and Mitrevich. Once again, members elected the *Pravda* list, which included three Mensheviks among the thirty-one full and candidate members.[62] When in 1912 the State Duma passed the "Law on Sickness Insurance," elections were held to choose worker administrators of factory benefit funds for ill workers. The socialist slates that won in the elections to insurance boards at the provincial and city level, whether Bolshevik or Menshevik (the law disallowed SR candidates because that party had declined Duma participation), encouraged responsibility to the "representative body of sickness funds" subordinated to "Marxist" leadership.[63] As was intended, workers interpreted these slogans as nonfactional, democratic, and pro-unity.

The Liquidationist controversy rested on old theory and discursive tactics. As in the earlier Economist debate, Leninism consisted of a tactic for excluding opponents through labeling. By successfully redefining themselves as "united" and "Marxist," Leninists won seats on governing boards of workers' organizations. Under no circumstances should one conclude that Leninist rhetoric duped an unsuspecting passive working class. The Leninist victory was hollow. Many of those elected to the "Marxist" slates were Bolshevik conciliators and long term activists with a record of service in legal organizations. Workers voted and marched for unity platforms, not specifically for Bolsheviks or Leninist programs. They demanded socialist organizers, not Bolsheviks. In reality, during 1912–14

---

[61] *Luch* 92/178 (23 April 1913): 2; Bulkin, *Na zare*, 261–62, 270–72; *Pravda* 83/287 (10 April 1913): 4; 92/296 (23 April 1913): 4,7; 93/297 (24 April 1913): 4; B. I. Gorev, "Demagogiia ili marksizm?" *Nasha zaria* 6 (1914): 80; For discussion of slates by *praktiki* see Gvozdev, *Novaia rabochaia gazeta* 65 (25 October 1913): 1.

[62] "Kogo vybirat'," *Novaia rabochaia gazeta* 14 (24 August 1913) and "Ob''iavlenie," *Novaia rabochaia gazeta* 15 (25 August 1913). Articles on the meeting from *Nash put'* can be found in GARF, f. 6860, op 1, d.1748; "Iz zhizni soiuza," *Metallist* 7 (24 August 1913); 8 (18 September 1913).

[63] *Voprosy strakhovaniia* 16/26 (19 April 1914): 3; "Iz zhizni soiuza," *Metallist* 4 (1 April 1914); Sher, "Vybory v strakhovie uchrezhdeniia v Peterburge i zadachi edinstva," *Bor'ba* 6 (1914): 22–23.

the overwhelming majority of workers adopted a "liquidationist" identity that promoted collaboration between legal and illegal activity inside Russia.

After 1908, Lenin's discursive superiority and the Menshevik émigrés' feckless defense of reform intensified higher level factionalism. This in turn, by accident, generated conditions suitable for reform because of the organizational disruption at the top. Locally, illegal party committees joined legal activists to demand a unified party. Inside Russia, SD identity paralleled that of the workers: collectively socialists embraced unity, non-factionalism, and socialist democracy, very broadly defined. The movement included those who opposed the state and the employers in and through legal and illegal organizations. Lenin's rigid categories of propaganda over agitation, consciousness over spontaneity, and party over movement had no basis in Russian realities. The Russian revolutionary movement rejected the hard discipline and enforced factionalism of the émigrés: its voice was not exclusionary. Movement both spontaneous and conscious, compassionate and reflective, dynamic and educational mirrored the new Russian revolutionary culture.

Social Democracy was unable to align itself to a unified workers' movement before 1914. If Menshevik leaders hoped to play a role in the reconstituted party, Lenin had to be removed from the party center. Unresponsive to that reality, the Menshevik leadership abroad failed to comprehend the utter devastation of traditional organizational forms. Thus bounded by the discourse of the Liquidationist controversy, they could not act. The so-called "liquidators," in reality revolutionary *praktiki*, by acquiescing in Lenin's labeling tactics, accepted their own marginalization. The fate Gorev had predicted for the Leninists became that of the liquidators creating a gap between the movement and the party. New forms were proposed but not established. Unity was accepted but not enacted. One can only surmise the revolutionary possibilities. Haimson has indicated that revolution was possible before the First World War. This paper suggests, that even if this were the case, the revolutionary possibilities did not rest on "Bolshevik" hegemony. Revolutionary action founded upon unity and opposed to capitalism, the tsarist autocracy, and monologic political infighting reflected worker practice in their quest for a socialist society in Russia.

Proletarian Knowledges of Self: Worker-Poets in Fin-de-Siècle Russia

Mark D. Steinberg

Plebeian Russian authors—writers with little or no formal education who began writing poetry, prose, and essays while employed in various wage-earning jobs—were preoccupied with questions of selfhood in the critical years of crisis, reform, and consequence between Russia's two revolutions, 1905 and 1917. Self-reflection obsessed them and was connected strongly to reflections on the nature, social place, and moral significance of the individual. Keywords like *lichnost'* (self, person, personality, individual) and *chelovek* (the human person, man) saturate their writings, typically as grounding for moral or political appeals. As one contemporary observer of prerevolutionary working-class attitudes put it, an elaborate "cult of the self" (*kul't lichnosti*) and "cult of man" (*kul't cheloveka*) pervaded the discourse of activist and outspoken workers in Russia.[1]

Conceptions of self, of course, are not universal. Indeed, the variability in their form and in their dialogues with morality, identity, and ideas of truth are precisely what makes their examination so revealing. As much recent study has shown, notions of the self, and appeals to it as a value or a principle, are remarkably contingent. Shaped on the indeterminate terrain where the natural actions of the mind grapple with external worlds of experience and meaning (ranging from material life and political structures to cultural landscapes of language, imagery, and symbol), the self has been variously recognized, imagined, presented, and

---

[1] L. M. Kleinbort, "Ocherki rabochei demokratii," *Sovremennyi mir* 1 (March 1913): 32–44; and 5 (November 1913): 178–85 (for use of term, see 182, 185). This term was earlier used by Emile Durkheim, whose work was known in Russia. See Durkheim's "L'Individualisme et les intellectuels" (1898), trans. Steven Lukes, *Political Studies* 17, no. 1 (March 1969): 19–30. Although Kleinbort employs "*kul't cheloveka*" in quotation marks, he mentions no source.

M. Melancon, A. Pate, *New Labor History*, Bloomington, IN: Slavica, 2002

used. In these cognitive journeys of the mind in the social and cultural world, varied conceptions of self have taken form, together with varied existential and moral ideas that tend to be intertwined with ideas of self. One particular notion, the mainly Western idea of an interior and autonomous self, by nature endowed with a universal humanity and dignity, is only one of a range of self concepts, but it is one that has had a powerful historical effect in shaping moral thinking, and social and political reasoning, in much of the modern world. It has nurtured the very consequential view that every person possesses certain natural rights, not because of any particular status, situation, or role, but simply by virtue of being human. At the same time, we should not impute more cohesion or orderly progress to this particular history of self and morality than it has had. Some recent work has described a more fractured, ambiguous, and darker history of the self and self-awareness: one in which selfhoods and ideas of self are shaped also by feelings of angst, guilt, melancholy, alienation, and fear, and by the self's own leanings toward narcissism, deceptive presentations of the self, and irrational desire.[2]

The Proletarian "Cult of Man"

The modern ideal of the self as the inward source of human identity, dignity, and rights shared by all human beings occupied a central place in the discourse of activist workers in Russia in the late nineteenth and

---

[2] Influential studies in a variety of disciplines have explored varied self-concepts and especially the interrelations among the self, ideas about the self, and moral reasoning. Among the works I have found most useful are (in order of publication, not value) Stephen D. Cox, *"The Stranger Within Thee": Concepts of the Self in Late Eighteenth-Century Literature* (Pittsburgh, 1980); Lawrence Kohlberg, *Essays on Moral Development*, 2 vols. (San Francisco, 1981 and 1983); Clifford Geertz, "'From the Native's Point of View': On the Nature of Anthropological Understanding," in *Local Knowledge* (New York, 1983), 55–70; Michael Carrithers, Steven Collins, and Steven Lukes, eds., *The Category of the Person: Anthropology, Philosophy, History* (Cambridge, UK, 1985); Roy F. Baumeister, *Identity: Cultural Change and the Struggle for Self* (New York and Oxford, 1986); Charles Taylor, *Sources of the Self: The Making of Modern Identity* (Cambridge, MA, 1989); Richard Eldridge, *On Moral Personhood: Philosophy, Literature, Criticism, and Self-Understanding* (Chicago, 1989); Richard A. Shweder, *Thinking Through Cultures: Expeditions in Cultural Psychology* (Cambridge, MA, 1991), 113–85; Jerome Levin, *Theories of the Self* (Washington. D.C., 1992); Gil Noam and Thomas Wren, eds., *The Moral Self* (Cambridge, MA, 1993); *Rewriting the Self: Histories from the Renaissance to the Present*, ed. Roy Porter (London, 1997). Michel Foucault's work on the history of sexuality was focused strongly on the constitution of the self and the historical importance of ideas about the self in the genealogy of ethics. See the introduction to his *History of Sexuality* (New York, 1978), and his interview in Hubert L. Dreyfus and Paul Rabinow, *Michel Foucault: Beyond Structuralism and Hermeneutics*, 2nd ed. (Chicago, 1983), 229–52.

early twentieth centuries. Historians of Russian labor, of course, have often noted workers' demands for "polite address" and, more generally, for treatment befitting their worth as "human beings."[3] These challenges to "humiliation and insult" (*unizhenie i oskorblenie*), however, were very often much more than mere items on a list of demands. They were at the heart of an ethical vision with which many workers judged the entirety of social and political life. At the core of this ethics, though often stated indirectly, was the belief in the inward self as the source of universal human identity, hence natural and equal worth, and hence the moral rights of the individual person as a human being. The natural dignity of the person, not the particularistic interests of a class, became a foundation for social judgment and for imagining a just society.

Variations on these themes pervaded workers' critical writings in the years from 1905 to the revolution. When, writing on the eve of the First World War, Lev Kleinbort surveyed the Russian labor press of recent years, he found a fundamental, even obsessive, preoccupation with questions of "honor and conscience" (*chest' i sovest'*) and of insult and humiliation, and pervasive demands to be recognized as "human beings," not slaves, machines, or animals. Indeed, this language and argumentation was inescapable in the labor press. Hundreds of articles, essays, and letters by workers (encouraged and echoed by these papers' non-proletarian activists) repeatedly voiced moral outrage at the treatment of workers as "beasts of burden" (or "camels," "cattle," "machines"), at conditions that forced workers to sell not only their labor power but also their human dignity, at society's blindness to workers' "human personality" (*lichnost' chelovecheskaia* or *lichnost' cheloveka*), and at the refusal of upper classes to recognize the "freedom" and "autonomy of the human person" or the simple fact that "a man is a man."[4] An essayist in the journal of the

---

[3] V. F. Shishkin, *Tak skladyvalas' revolutsionnaia moral': istoricheskii ocherk* (Moscow, 1967); Reginald E. Zelnik, "Russian Bebels," *The Russian Review* 35 (July 1976): 265, 272–277; Victoria E. Bonnell, *Roots of Rebellion: Workers' Politics and Organizations in St. Petersburg and Moscow, 1900–1914* (Berkeley, 1983), 43–72, 90, 102, 170–71, 183–84, 191, 264, 449, 452; Tim McDaniel, *Autocracy, Capitalism, and Revolution in Russia* (Berkeley, 1988), 161, 169–74, 194–95; Leopold H. Haimson, "The Problem of Social Identities in Early Twentieth-Century Russia," *Slavic Review* 1 (Spring 1988): 1–20, esp. 2–8; Diane P. Koenker and William G. Rosenberg, *Strikes and Revolution in Russia, 1917* (Princeton, 1989); Mark D. Steinberg, *Moral Communities: The Culture of Class Relations in the Russian Printing Industry, 1867–1907* (Berkeley, 1992), 235–36, 242–45.

[4] Kleinbort, "Ocherki rabochei demokratii," *Sovremennyi mir* 1 (March 1913): 26–29; *Pechatnyi vestnik* 3 (23 June 1905): 21–23; 9 (28 August 1905): 8; 11 (11 September 1905): 3, 7; *Vestnik pechatnikov* 3 (9 May 1906): 4; 5 (20 May 1906): 3, 5; 6 (28 May

St. Petersburg Metalworkers' Union argued typically that ethics must be grounded above all in "honor, feelings of dignity, and consciousness of the rights of the human personality." The leaders of the Moscow Tavern Workers' Union emphasized these same points by naming their union paper *Man* (*Chelovek*), ironically appropriating the customer's conventional term of address for waiters. The point was to remind others (and workers themselves) that the tavern worker is not simply a "'man' in quotation marks" but a "living human personality" (*zhivaia chelovecheskaia lichnost'*) whose "all-human dignity" (*obshchechelovecheskoe dostoinstvo*) must be respected.[5]

In fiction and especially poetry, worker-writers articulated these same themes. Kleinbort, in a survey he also made of workers' literary writing, found the same obsession with human dignity, humiliation, and rights that he found in workers' journalism. The language of these "voices from the soul"—as the provincial glassworker Egor Nechaev titled a 1906 poem about the insulted dignity of workers[6]—was filled with the key words and images of this discourse: the "pain," "insult," and "depersonalization" (*obezlichenie cheloveka*) of workers due to their lack of freedom to act according to their own will;[7] the "spiteful" disdain of workers' "honor";[8] the degradation of workers into "literal automatons";[9] and the need for the world to see that "we are people, not animals, not cattle,"[10] and that "the soul of the worker is no different from that of the educated rulers of the world."[11] A telling elaboration on these themes was described by the

---

1906): 2–3; *Pechatnik* 3 (14 May 1906): 12–13; 8 (23 July 1906): 6–7; *Bulochnik* 1 (19 February 1906): 8; 3 (12 March 1906): 39–40; *Pechatnoe delo* 24 (11 September 1910): 4; *Metallist* 8 (13 January 1912): 8.

[5] *Nash put'* 10 (3 December 1910): 6; *Chelovek* 1 (13 February 1911): 1.

[6] Kleinbort, "Ocherki rabochei demokratii," *Sovremennyi mir* 5 (19 November 1913): 178–79; 6 (December 1913): 167–68; Egor Nechaev, "Golos dushi," *Zhurnal dlia vsekh* (1906). This poem, reprinted in *U istokov russkoi proletarskoi poezii* (Moscow and Leningrad, 1965), 87–88, was first published in *Zhurnal dlia vsekh* in 1906 and later in the 1914 collection of his poems, *Vecherniia pesni: stikhotvoreniia* (Moscow, 1914).

[7] *Ofitsiant* (waiter S. P.), "Sovremennye kuplety," *Rodnye vesti* 4 (Easter issue, 1912): 7.

[8] Quoted by Kleinbort, "Ocherki rabochei demokratii," *Sovremennyi mir* 5 (November 1913): 178.

[9] Chechenets (a metalworker), "Nevol'niki truda," *Nash put'* 17 (23 May 1911), reprinted in *Proletarskie poety*, 3 vols. (Leningrad, 1935-39) 2 (1936): 11. Also poem by the waiter S. P., "Sovremennye kuplety."

[10] Nechaev, "Golos dushi."

[11] Letter accompanying verses submitted to *Pravda* by the miner Aleksei Chizhikov (4 March 1914); Rossiiskii gosudarstvennyi arkhiv sotsial'no-politicheskoi istorii (hereafter RGASPI), f. 364, op. 1, d. 315, ll. 1–3 (quote from original p. 4).

metalworker Aleksei Bibik in his 1912 novel *K shirokoi doroge* (*Toward the Open Road*), the first Russian novel written by a worker. In the midst of a passionate discussion with a comrade from his factory about questions of pride, envy, dignity, art, morality, doubt, and death, Ignat Pasterniak, the young worker who is the semi-autobiographical hero of the novel, offers this moral fantasy:

> Imagine a huge hall. Before a crowd of thousands of self-important and conceited people, someone is playing piano. Or violin. It doesn't matter. His playing is so inspired, that everyone is spellbound by his music. They don't even move. Then there is some whispering: who is this, who is he? So he stands up and throws off some sort of cloak he has been wearing and stands there in a simple, dirty blue shirt. He's a worker!... Imagine the picture.... Everyone would be amazed and he would say to them, "So, you thought that under this dirty blue shirt was emptiness? An animal? What gave you the right to think that? To think that we don't feel or understand beauty? What made you think that only you are the salt of the earth. You are pitiful! I can't bear to remain any longer with you!"[12]

The seemingly simple identification of the worker as a human being—in fact, a very particular construction of all human beings as subjects possessing natural dignity and intrinsic rights—was in Russia, as elsewhere in the modern world, a potentially inspiring and explosive idea. It helped make sense of social structures and relationships—subordination and unequal exchange, in particular. Most essential in shaping these meanings were the perceived effects these relationships had on workers' inward selves (on their *lichnost'*). It mattered less that these were unequal relationships than that they "trampled in the dirt" workers' "feelings of human dignity."[13] It was a source of great interpretive and discursive power to be able to see and speak of capitalist social relationships not simply as subordination and unequal exchange, but, as the worker-critic Ivan Kubikov did, as "moral oppression."[14]

The moral poetics of suffering preoccupied Russian worker-writers, for it was strongly intertwined with these ways of experiencing and valuing the self and of deploying these notions critically. Suffering, it is worth

---

[12] Andrei Bibik, *K shirokoi doroge (Ignat iz Novoselovki)* (St. Petersburg, 1914), 80. The novel was first published in 1912 in the leftist journal *Sovremennyi mir*.

[13] *Golos portnogo* 1–2 (10 May 1910): 10.

[14] Kvadrat (Ivan Kubikov), "Vpechatleniia zhizni," *Pechatnoe delo* 24 (11 September 1910): 2.

emphasizing, is interpretation. Physical injury, disease, loss, and death are mainly material facts, but suffering is mainly a category through which people perceive, value, and represent such facts (and less tangible experiences—and already partly interpreted ones—such as oppression, insult, betrayal, and unfulfilled desire). As interpretation and rhetoric, the meanings of suffering are necessarily unstable and variable. Certainly, the naming and explaining of suffering has been shown to differ between cultures and over time.[15] Literature, art, and song in different places and times—from sacred liturgies, to the songs of slaves and workers, to modern philosophies—are filled with examples of various ways of naming, explaining, and valuing suffering, and of individuals and groups using discourses of suffering to argue about (often against) the world. There is one constant. Ideas of suffering are almost always tied up with notions of self and with the moral and spiritual meanings attached to varied self-concepts. It matters, for example, whether physical suffering—illness for example—is viewed as "immanent justice" punishing a sufferer for sin,[16] or is blamed on social conditions, thus externalizing the moral fault. More subtly, it matters how suffering is treated emotionally, aesthetically, and spiritually: as proof of a warrior's manhood, for instance, or of a saint's humility, or of an oppressed people's nobility (diasporic Africans or Jews, for example); as a devalued state of body and mind to be avoided, ignored, or cured (reflecting a definition of the good life, at least in part, as the absence of suffering), or as an edifying good and even source of great soulfulness, beauty, and inspiring power, to be contemplated and retold, often with various moral lessons attached. These meanings are not mutually exclusive. Sorrow and suffering, like tears, can express contradictory and ambiguous meanings. But ideas about the self—however variant the category—seem persistently to occupy the center.

In Russia, suffering had tangible social form and history (a "sociopolitical causal ontology," in the rich but inelegant language of social science.[17]) The everyday lives of the urban poor in Russia were harsh: crowded and unsanitary living conditions, wide social and political inequalities, low wages and debilitating working conditions, limited social protections, and restricted civil rights.[18] However, the organization of

---

[15]This is a major theme in Richard A. Shweder's collection of essays, *Thinking Through Cultures: Expeditions in Cultural Psychology* (Cambridge, MA, 1991), 313–31.

[16]Shweder, *Thinking Through Cultures*, 160–61.

[17]Ibid., 313.

[18]Scholarly study of the social history of Russian labor in the late nineteenth and early twentieth centuries is now very rich. See, especially, the studies by Victoria Bonnell, Joseph Bradley, Barbara Engel, Rose Glickman, Heather Hogan, Iurii Kirianov,

these raw facts into a narrative of suffering introduced layers of meaning and intent that were not intrinsic. When lower-class Russian authors did so, they necessarily drew upon what was culturally and intellectually available to them. Frequent use of literary form gave them more scope to articulate and employ possible meanings of suffering and more space to adapt and invent.

In emphasizing cultural context, one must be cautious in generalizing about the meaning of discourses of suffering in Russian culture. Recent efforts to demonstrate a persistent and deeply-seated Russian cultural inclination toward self-injury, self-humiliation, and self-sacrifice—what one author has called, borrowing a Freudian concept, "moral masochism"— tend toward cliché and stereotype, over-generalize from scattered evidence, and reduce the rhetorics of contemporary cultural criticism to objective views from inside the culture.[19] To the extent that there was a "cult of suffering" in Russian culture, it was diverse, changing, and contradictory (and not even strictly "Russian"). Most important, it also contained the opposite of "moral masochism": a self-elevating rejection of degrading and destructive humiliation. Orthodox Christianity certainly placed theological and liturgical weight on the inevitability, and sanctity, of suffering—as the fate of sinful humanity, but also as elevating practice of the virtues of humility, emulation of Christ's passion, and a way to transcendence and salvation.[20] Russian literature, especially from the mid-nineteenth century, also devoted a great deal of energy to exploring the complex psychic and moral meanings of suffering. Even a summary of common descriptions of the major writers in the Russian literary canon by the early 1900s conveys a clear enough idea of the centrality, and hence availability, of a complex poetics of suffering:[21] Mikhail

---

Diane Koenker, Robert Johnson, Tim McDaniel, Charters Wynn, and Reginald Zelnik.

[19] Anna Feldman Leibovich, *The Russian Concept of Work: Suffering, Drama, and Tradition in Pre- and Post-Revolutionary Russia* (Westport, CT, 1995); Daniel Rancour-Laferriere, *The Slave Soul of Russia: Moral Masochism and the Cult of Suffering* (New York, 1995).

[20] The classic accounts of Russian kenotic Christianity are Nadejda Gorodetzky, *The Humiliated Christ in Modern Russian Thought* (New York, 1938); and G. P. Fedotov, *The Russian Religious Mind* (Cambridge, MA, 1946), chap. 4. See also Mark D. Steinberg, "Workers on the Cross: Religious Imagination in the Writings of Russian Workers," *Russian Review* 53, no. 2 (April 1994): 213–39.

[21] Useful contemporary and later scholarly summaries of thematic trends in Russian literature can be found in *Istoriia russkoi literatury XIX v.*, ed. D. N. Ovsianiko-Kulikovskii, 5 vols. (Moscow, 1908–11); Renato Poggioli, *The Poets of Russia, 1890-1930* (Cambridge, MA, 1960); *Istoriia russkoi literatury*, 4 vols. (Leningrad, 1980–83); *Handbook of Russian Literature*, ed. Victor Terras (New Haven, 1985); Evelyn Bristol,

Lermontov's introspective and melancholy poetry, with its dominant motifs of sorrow, grief, and estrangement from the petty and sinful human world; Ivan Nikitin's "songs of sorrow, sadness, and bitterness;"[22] Nikolai Nekrasov's pathos-suffused portraits of peasant misery, grief, and death, written in a "sorrowing tone" that was still striking to mid-century contemporaries but would, critics noted, become familiar to readers of the many poets who followed Nekrasov;[23] Fedor Dostoevsky's psychological and metaphysical explorations of humiliation, guilt, cruelty, madness, and death; the melancholy and pessimistic visions of evil and death in the writings of many fin-de-siècle symbolists and decadents; and Leonid Andreev's popular stories of tormented individuals, alienation, deceit, disease, nightmares, violence, demonic sexual drives, and death. Russian folk culture—in less baroque form and less influenced by European modernism (though by no means locked, as some have imagined, in an insular and unchanging tradition)—also provided workers with a rich body of treatments of suffering: the narratives of the lives of martyr-saints; the evolving traditions of women's laments (especially the ritualized funeral laments or *plachi*); and the sorrow songs[24] of workers, soldiers, and exiles.[25]

All of these (and many other) images of suffering and sorrow expressed and evoked, often in uneasy combination, different meanings: a romantic infatuation with the sorrowing self; an empathetic (and often penitential) sympathy for the downtrodden; a melancholic "philosophy of despair," which, some argued—as part of a growing critique of traditional and especially popular culture—was typically Russian;[26] an appreciation of

---

A History of Russian Poetry (New York and Oxford, 1991).

[22] A phrase, often used in describing his writings, adapted from the opening lines of Ivan Nikitin, *Portnoi* (1860).

[23] Ovsianiko-Kulikovskii, *Istoriia*, 3: 400.

[24] I borrow the phrase from W. E. B. Du Bois, *The Souls of Black Folk: Essays and Sketches* (Chicago, 1903), chap. 14. The Russian, *skorbnye pesni*, was also the title of a 1915 collection of poems by the self-taught author L. Ia. Bystrov. See interview and discussion in N. Vlasov-Okskii, "Ogon'ki v stepi (iz vstrech c pistateliami-samouchkami)," *Griadushchee* 1–3 (1921): 41–44.

[25] See Roberta Reeder, ed. and trans., with an introductory essay by V. Ja. Propp, *Russian Folk Lyrics* (Bloomington, 1992); *Pesni russkikh rabochikh* (Moscow and Leningrad, 1962); N. V. Os'makov, *Russkaia proletarskaia poeziia, 1896-1917* (Moscow, 1968), 50–51. For an eloquent contemporary description of the mournful spirit of Russian workers' songs, see Maxim Gorky's story "Twenty-Six Men and a Girl" (1899).

[26] Ovsianiko-Kulikovskii, "Itogi russkoi khudozhestvennoi literatury XIX veka" (prodolzhenie), *Vestnik vospitaniia* 22, no. 6 (September 1911): 12, 22–24. See Maxim Gorky's praise of these observations (written in response to Gorky's story "Toska" [Melancholy]) in *Maxim Gorky: Selected Letters*, Andrew Barratt and Barry Scherr,

the transcendent spiritual significance of world suffering; a metaphysical faith in redemption and salvation through suffering; a complex sense of the uplifting experience of the tragic; a way of voicing moral outrage at humiliating social conditions; a way of recognizing and elevating the self as the experiential and moral site of suffering. All of this was part of the cultural terrain on which worker-writers tried to make sense of their experiences, articulate ideas about selfhood, and voice criticism.

Indeed, when literate Russian workers wrote about their lives, typically first in emotive lyric verse, they filled their writings with stories and images of suffering, and of individual suffering in particular. A rich vocabulary of personal suffering saturated the poetry (as well as stories and essays) of the growing numbers of worker-writers: *grust'*, *pechal'* (sadness); *unynie* (hopeless sadness, depression); *gore* (misery, grief); *skorb'* (sorrow); *muka, muchenie* (torment); *stradanie* (suffering); *slezy* (tears); *bol'* (pain); and, most frequently, *toska* (a mixture of anguish, melancholy, sadness, and languor). Images of the suffering self of the worker filled the pages of the trade union press, popular and populist journals, and numerous pamphlets and books containing the creative works of lower-class writers (and not only during the years of political repression and economic recession from 1907 to 1911, but also during the subsequent years of "revolutionary advance"—including after 1917). The images and tales of suffering—in poems, stories, and critical essays—were many, diverse, and imbued with an insistent critical pathos: childhoods ruined and lost (part of a growing view of childhood as the time when the personality is nurtured and which should be a happy time);[27] childhoods recalled (or represented) as painful memories of lost joy;[28] sleepless nights yielding only to dreams "tortured by exhaustion" (it would seem that even the most private moments alone with one's self—and away from the "nightmare" of waking life—offered no escape);[29] the frustrated sexuality of male workers from the village who could not afford to keep their wives with them in the city (showing, again, the intimately personal dimen-

---

eds. (Oxford, 1997), 160.

[27] Nechaev, "Moia pesnia" (1906), in *Vecherniia pesni*, 79–80; (also in *U istokov*, 92); idem, "Sirota," *Dolia bedniaka* (19 July 1909) (issue of journal confiscated due to this and another poem, see *U istokov*, 406.)

[28] Mariia Chernysheva, "Ne prigliadite kartiny...," *Balalaika* 18 (1910): 2.

[29] F. Gavrilov, "Son," in *Proletarskie poety*, 1 (1935): 197–201; Nechaev, "V bessonnitsu" (1906), *Vecherniia pesni*, 98; S. Obradovich, "Bezsonnoiu noch'iu," *Severnoe utro* (Archangelsk) 52 (6 March 1913): 2 (a cutting in Rossiiskii gosudarstvennyi arkhiv literatury i iskusstva (hereafter RGALI), f. 1874, op. 1, d. 2, l. 8); Gerasimov, "Zavodskii gudok," *Pervyi sbornik proletarskikh pisatelei* (St. Petersburg, 1914), 91–92.

sion of social suffering);[30] the anguish of a mother watching her children starve;[31] drunkenness as a way to "obliterate this hell on earth";[32] the beatings, work-related maiming, and death that often occurred in factories;[33] nature itself—especially damp, windy, and melancholy fall—echoing and framing the harsh lives and dark moods of workers; [34] or the beauties of awakened nature becoming inaccessible due to the "anguish, pain and bitterness / in my weary soul."[35] Above all, these writings were filled with constant assertions that "the life of a worker is a chain of suffering / A river of sweat, a sea of tears."[36]

The insults and injuries that women suffered—though still a relatively rare theme before 1917—were treated with particular moral pathos. At the same time, images of women's suffering complicate these arguments. Women's suffering was treated as exemplifying violation and injury to both the universal ethical ideal of human dignity and the particular virtues associated with women's gender, with women's difference. Thus, in a speech in 1916, G. D. Deev-Khomiakovskii, a leader of the Moscow Surikov circle of "writers from the people," argued that women's "majestic" potential as "a force of love and good" was suppressed by the actual social and legal position of women in Russia.[37] Similar was a once well-known poem by Aleksandr Pomorskii (first published in 1913 in the anthology of writings by worker-poets associated with Countess Panina's "People's House" [*Narodnyi dom*] in St. Petersburg and then again the following year in the journal of the Petersburg Metalworkers' Union) on the lives of women working in factories. Innocent and pure country girls were corrupted by their lives as urban workers. They became "factory girls, doomed sacrifices / pale, tired, darkened by sadness." Seeking to escape factory work, they fell further as they "sold" their "pure bodies."[38]

---

[30] Mark Bich (Savin), "Tsentrovoi" (prodolzhenie), *Bulochnik* 2 (26 February 1906): 20–22.

[31] *Metallist* 4 (10 November 1911): 7–8; *Pechatnoe delo* 24 (11 September 1910): 3–4.

[32] G. D. Deev-Khomiakovskii, "Sorok let kak odin den'," *Rodnye vesti* 3 (1912): 4–5.

[33] *Metallist* 4 (10 November 1911): 7–8; *Pechatnoe delo* 24 (11 September 1910): 3–4.

[34] V. Aleksandrovskii, "Osen'iu," *Novaia rabochaia gazeta* 55 (13 August 1913): 2; Sergei Gan'shin, "Ne prikhodi vesna," *Zhivoe slovo* 10 (March 1913): 6; Il'ia Volodinskii, "Dumy naborshchika," *Nashe pechatnoe delo* (21 February 1915).

[35] Semen Popov, "Vesna," *Chelovek* 4 (24 April 1911): 32

[36] N. E. Dodaev, "Trud," *Zhizn' pekarei* 1(4) (10 March 1914): 2.

[37] Deev-Khomiakovskii, "I. Z. Surikov v pesniakh o zhenshchine i trude," *Drug naroda* 1 (October 1916): 13. See also comments on Surikov's work by L. Sergievskaia in *Drug naroda* 5-6-7 (1915): 4; and "Chitatel' iz naroda," in *Narodnaia sem'ia* 5 (4 March 1912): 13–14.

[38] A. Pomorskii, "Zhertvam goroda," *Nashi pesni: pervyi sbornik* (St. Petersburg,

This was a conventional and easily recognizable image: prostitutes as emblems of fallen innocence and debased purity, an image growing out of the larger convention of seeing women as (or, at least, having women represent) weaker but naturally purer creatures.[39]

At the same time, these images were sometimes used to speak about the universal ideal of the suffering human self. This was explicit, in a rather complex way, in the argument the printer Ivan Kubikov made that a "conscious worker," sensitive to the "human personality" of prostitutes, might have sex with a prostitute, but could never free himself from doubt and guilt for doing so.[40] It was implicit in complaints about viewing women as mere "sexual objects."[41] It was evident in a story published in the 1914 anthology of proletarian writers. Called "The Death of Agasha," it told the history of a young woman who came to the city from the village to find work. Agasha was not completely frail and innocent—hers was not entirely the conventional image of "terrible perfection": she coped well with the roughness of urban working-class life and as a waitress in a tearoom had learned to laugh off the degrading and insulting suggestions made so often by male customers. But when, one night, her employer raped her, this was an injury to self that she could not endure: she hanged herself—the ultimate answer to a moral (and, implicitly, mortal) assault on the self.[42]

In a growing number of writings, male workers explicitly insisted on the dignity of women as human beings. Especially in trade union papers, which nurtured these ideas, a number of worker-writers wrote of the "honor" and "moral dignity" of women as human beings.[43] But con-

---

1913), 9; and *Metallist* 5(29) (19 July 1913): 4.

[39] Engelstein, *The Keys to Happiness*; Laurie Bernstein, *Sonia's Daughters: Prostitutes and their Regulation in Imperial Russia* (Berkeley, CA 1995); Barbara Heldt, *Terrible Perfection: Women and Russian Literature* (Bloomington, IN 1987). See also discussions of comparable cultural usages in Judith Walkowitz, *Prostitution and Victorian Society: Women, Class, and the State* (New York, 1980); and idem, *City of Dreadful Delight: Narratives of Sexual Danger in Late-Victorian London* (Chicago, 1992).

[40] Kvadrat, "Propoved' khuliganstva v russkoi literature," *Pechatnoe delo* 33–34 (1 April 1910): 3–4.

[41] "Chitatel' iz naroda," in *Narodnaia sem'ia* 5 (4 March 1912): 13–14.

[42] Nikolai Ivanov, "Smert' Agashi," *Pervyi sbornik proletarskikh pisatelei* (St. Petersburg, 1914), 56–61.

[43] This was an early and common theme in writings in the union press of printers after 1905. For some early examples, see *Vestnik Pechatnikov* 5 (20 May 1906): 3; 6 (28 May 1906): 2; 8 (11 June 1906): 3; *Balda* 2 (9 January 1907): 1, 5–7. Similar articles, stories and poems can be found throughout the labor press. For example, *Golos portnogo* 1–2 (10 May 1910): 10; *Metallist* 13(37) (14 December 1913): 2–3.

cern with women's selves was most explicit in the few women's voices we hear. Mariia Chernysheva, a seamstress and salesgirl who wrote under the name "Baba Mar'ia," wrote exclusively about inner feelings—loss, sorrow, and tears—in exploring the hardships of her working class life.[44] A young woman working in a St. Petersburg tailoring shop, in a letter to a trade union journal, even more directly linked her experiences to the universalized moral ideal of the self. She spoke of the "humiliations" and "insults" suffered at the hands of foremen and employers by all of the female apprentices in her shop—"white slaves," she called them, using a term often used to describe young women forced into prostitution. And she condemned this treatment in the key words of the universalistic moral discourse about the self: "their feelings of human dignity" were "trampled in the dirt."[45] Most often, however, women were absent from these writings. If the self whose dignity and humiliation so passionately concerned these workers had a gender, it was implicitly assumed to be male. The occasional critiques of the neglect or denial of the equal dignity of women's selves are the exceptions reminding us of the rule.

Among the many images of the suffering self in these writings, death is perhaps the most important in illuminating meanings of this discourse on suffering. Images of premature death figured prominently in workers' writings. We see workers dying in factories when crushed by machines, dying of hunger and of diseases associated with poverty—especially tuberculosis (and, adding further insult, being cruelly treated in the public clinics where they sought care[46]), and dying young and innocent.[47] And when they died, one poet suggested, black blood would flow from their mouths, a sign of lifelong suffering.[48] These were complex images. Death was often portrayed also as an answer and an escape, a comfort and a way to freedom. Repeatedly, poems and stories pondered or described suicide—a phenomenon also reported with shocking regularity in the daily press in the prewar years—or voiced prayers that death would come, bringing a long sought "oblivion" and "rest."[49]

---

[44] Chernysheva, "Ne prigliadite kartiny..."; and idem, "Zaveshchanie," *Dumy narodnye* 7 (13 March 1910): 5.

[45] *Golos portnogo* 1–2 (10 May 1910): 10. See also ibid., 9; and An. Petrova, "Kul'tura i kooperatsiia," *Trud* 5 (October–November 1916): 23.

[46] *Zvezda utreniaia* 21 (20 June 1912): 7.

[47] In addition to references below, Chechenets, "Nevol'niki truda."

[48] Stepan Bruskov, "Smert' byvshago cheloveka," *Rodnye vesti* 3 (1912): 2–3.

[49] Chernysheva, "Zaveshchanie"; Shkulev, "Pil'shchik," *Narodnaia mysl'* 2 (February 1911): 107; Bruskov, "Smert' byvshago cheloveka," *Rodnye vesti* 3 (1912): 2–3; Obradovich, "Bezsonnoiu noch'iu"; Nechaev, "K ditiati," *Zhivoe slovo* 20 (May 1913): 6.

But intertwined with these traces of despondency was moral rage. And the suffering self was at the heart of this moral argument. For example, an "epidemic" of suicides around 1910 among tailoring workers was explained not by poverty and unemployment—since conditions were in fact relatively good—but by workers' feelings that life had become a "big, dark, empty and cold barn" in which there is "no one to whom they may tell of their insults."[50] Stories and images of suicide and death—especially of the young and innocent—were strong signs of how much the "spirit ached," of how deeply the self was wounded.[51] Death spoke loudly (as both discursive symbol and material proof) of the denial of the workers' "right to live as human beings."[52]

As may be noticed, this discourse of suffering held many and ambiguous meanings. Marxist and Soviet critics saw mainly peasant traditions of stoic passivity and fatalism in workers' preoccupation with the suffering self. They were not altogether wrong. Like traditional peasant funeral songs (*plachi*), these poems and stories were partly cathartic laments, songs of suffering that helped the writers and readers cope with hardship by voicing it. No doubt, too, these plebeian writers were influenced by familiar Christian teachings about the inevitability of human suffering in the sinful temporal world. As Mikhail Savin complained, for too long workers tended to see "fate" rather than the "bosses fist" as the cause of their misery.[53] Extending these arguments ideologically, Marxist critics insisted that the preoccupation with suffering was not truly "proletarian." Defining the proletarian worldview ideologically as expressing a certain view of life—bold, optimistic, and focused on collective experience and action—rather than sociologically as the views of actual workers, these critics could then more easily purge this grim aesthetic from the orthodox canon, or, at least, relegate such views and emotions to a backward stage in the development of a conscious working class. Preoccupation with suffering, they argued, was most common before the class awakening of the

---

[50] Syryi, "Pomnite o samoubiitsakh," *Golos portnogo* 3 (10 July 1910): 3–4, 8.

[51] Petr Zaitsev (a shoemaker who briefly published and did most of the writing for this magazine for the common reader), "Ot chego," *Kolotushka* 1 (1911): 3 and "Umru ia," ibid., 2 (1911): 4; Semen Popov (a waiter), "Iz pesen goria i nuzhdy," *Chelovek* 3 (27 March 1911): 11; Obradovich, "Na zavode," *Rabochii den'* (Moscow) 8 (11 June 1912): 1 (a cutting in RGALI, f. 1874, op. 1, d. 2, l. 6); Samobytnik, "Zdes' ...," *Voprosy strakhovaniia* (October 1915), quote in *Proletarshie poety*, 3 (1939): 25.

[52] For some early examples of this interpretive construction, see *Pechatnyi vestnik* 1 (12 February 1906): 2; *Pechatnik* 1 (23 April 1906): 12; and *Vestnik pechatnikov* 6 (28 May 1906): 3.

[53] Dedushka s Protivy (Savin), "Sovremennaia pesenka bulochnika," *Bulochnik* 1 (19 February 1906): 13.

1905 revolution and among workers of recent peasant background. When such themes persisted beyond these boundaries, as they undeniably did, they did so as false consciousness.[54] This political manipulation of the definition of proletarian perception reflected not only ideological clichés about what class consciousness should be, but also a greater blindness to the complexities of proletarian thought and emotion, and, in particular, to the range of meanings evident in workers' attention to the sorrowing self.

Articulated sorrow also had a critical, transgressive, and inspiring power. Of course, the same may be said for larger cultural traditions: even traditional folk laments blended themes of discontent into resignation before fate.[55] Sometimes, the fatalist argument was explicitly resisted (though such resistance, if the censor was alert, could block publication). For example, in Nechaev's poem "Na rabotu" ("To Work"), written in 1881 but denied publication until 1919, a young worker tries to convince a comrade who has suggested collective suicide that such a thought is the voice of the devil, and recalls the Christian teaching, "We are doomed to suffer unto death / for the sins of our fathers." But he is rebuffed bitterly: this is a "fairy tale" and a priestly deceit.[56] A similar lesson was implied in a story that appeared in 1911 about a homeless man who finds it painful to be reminded of "the usual philosophy" that "life is an unbroken chain of suffering" and "harsh duty."[57] Of course, denying such comfort could make the suffering only harder to bear—suicide, after all, as the daily press made abundantly clear, was not only a trope. We should also keep in mind that in the Christian tradition suffering was not only the necessary lot of sinful man, but was also (especially in the Eastern Church), part of a positive valorization of saintly emulation of Christ's passion and martyrdom, and a reminder of Christ's promise of redemption, resurrection, and salvation.[58] In Russia, this was further complicated by the influence of another familiar cultural current upon

---

[54] See, for example, Valerian Polianskii (P. I. Lebedev), "Motivy rabochei poezii" (1918), in his *Na literaturnom fronte* (Moscow, 1924), 23–28; L'vov-Rogachevskii, *Ocherki*, 14; A. M. Bikhter, "U istokov proletarskoi poezii," in *U istokov*, 6, 8, 10, 13; Os'makov, *Russkaia proletarskaia poeziia*, 50–51, 69–70, 100; "Proletarskaia poeziia," in *Istoriia russkoi literatury*, 4: 396–97.

[55] Christine D. Worobec, "Death Ritual among Russian and Ukrainian Peasants," in *Cultures in Flux: Lower-Class Values, Practices, and Resistance in Late Imperial Russia*, Stephen P. Frank and Mark D. Steinberg, eds. (Princeton, 1994), 24.

[56] Nechaev, "Na rabotu," in *U istokov*, 43. This argument was repeated in Nechaev's 1906 poem "Golos dushi."

[57] Mikhail Zaharov in *Rodnye vesti* 2(3) (1911): 5.

[58] See Steinberg, "Workers on the Cross."

which worker-writers drew: the empathetic and socially-critical tradition of Russian "civic poetry" and journalism, with its moving accounts of popular suffering. As an echo of this writing, plebeian songs of suffering evoked pity (even self-pity) as a critical device. Moreover, as lower-class writers, they transformed this tradition by becoming, as it were, speaking subjects in this civic intellectual tradition—active citizens in this discourse, rather than silent objects of attention and care.

It matters also that these writings were almost all public texts: written with audiences in mind and published in popular newspapers and in journals aimed at lower-class readers. In the face of state censorship, simply chronicling aloud the sufferings of the poor and the subordinate was an implicit challenge and protest. It is thus telling that a number of these authors took explicit pride in "singing of suffering," treating it as an act of moral witness to injustice and inequality and a reminder of the virtue of the poor.[59] "Don't expect from me joyful tunes / Friend, I cannot comfort you / I learned to sing in sinister times / With sorrow in my soul and mind."[60] "I am a bard of the working masses / No one envies my song / I sing not of flowers nor the sun / Of twilight I sing."[61] "Let others be joyful / And clink their glasses / ... We are not capable of joy /... We are dying as we work / And suffering without a word."[62]

At the intellectual heart of the moral anger in these writings was the self and its ethical value, and, more precisely, the modern ideal of the self as the seat of emotions, creative genius, spiritual worth, and individual dignity, and hence as fundamental moral measure. These writers seem to have found in suffering evidence not just of the hard lot of the poor but, even more, of the existence of an inner spirit in the persons of the poor that made their hard lot constitute spiritual injury and moral wrong. To gaze at the self was to say that it mattered ontologically and ethically, that it was a key to understanding and valuing the world. And to dwell on suffering was at once to "contract full intimacy with the Stranger within"[63] and to remind oneself and one's readers of the great evil of

---

[59] S. Stepanov (better known as Stepan Bruskov), the editor of the Moscow journal, *Rodnye vesti: zhurnal trudiashchagosia naroda*, chose in 1911 as this journal's motto lines from Nikolai Nekrasov, "One who lives without sorrow and anger / Is one who loves not his own native land."

[60] Nechaev, "Mne khotelos' by pesniu svobodnuiu pet'" (1906), in *U istokov*, 89.

[61] A. Pomorskii, "Pesnia," *Metallist* 4/28 (3 July 1913): 4. See also Neliudim (A. Solov'ev), "Grustny pesni tvoi, proletarskii baian..." (from *Sotsial Demokrat* (24 August 1917) in *Proletarskie poety*, 3 (1939): 185.

[62] P. Zaitsev, in *Kolotushka* 1 (1911): 2.

[63] Advice to beginning authors by Edward Young, *Conjectures in Original Composi-*

conditions that harmed the self. In other words, by casting the everyday brutalities of lower-class life in a language of the injured self, these writers were helping to craft a potent and very usable moral identity. Suffering simultaneously defined workers and the poor by an essential common experience, valorized these sufferings as signs of the worthy interior lives of the poor, and condemned poverty and social hardship as harm to the self and hence as violations of a universal ethical truth.

In one regard, Soviet critics were right, 1905 was a turning point. Not in the replacement of images of suffering by the mythic optimism of the "proletariat," but in the more explicit and systematic use of these images to condemn oppressive social conditions and relationships. However, to categorize these usages as expressions of a heightened "class consciousness"—as critical awareness of the social inequalities of capitalism and of the progressive historical mission of the working class—tells us rather little. To be sure, most of these writers would have identified themselves as class conscious and understood this to mean a social critique of capitalist oppression of the working class. But for our purposes of understanding them, this identification is both too sweeping and too anemic to convey the full weight and reach of their critique. This critique was built upon ideas of moral right (a universal category of judgment) much more than on ideas about the class structure (a relative and historical category). And at the core of this moral critique was the category of the self. Social anger, even when more explicit in 1905 and after, remained persistently constructed around a core of inward suffering and moral regard for the inner life of the individual. Although the suffering of workers and the poor was (and was acknowledged to be) shared with others in a similar social position, the notion of the injured self was at the very heart of how these writers understood social oppression and inequality and defined these as intolerable injustice. By the same token, this fueled a moral rage that was far more emotionally convincing and rhetorically powerful than ideas about the historical development of capitalist class relations or the extraction of surplus value.

At the same time, we must not dismiss the importance of the idea of class in this language. As they endeavored to make sense of their own lives and the lives of others, and to give public voice to their experiences, anger, and ideals, activist workers reworked the various ideas, metaphors, and images that came to hand, including the ethical idealization of the human self. Paradoxically, viewed through the prism of their own and other workers' lives, the universalized ideal of the individual person also

---

tion (1759), quoted in Cox, *The Stranger Within Thee*, 3.

encouraged class identity and commitment to class action. Heightened feelings of self-awareness and self-worth also stimulated workers to feel more intensely their class oppression. Indeed, this discovery of self may have been essential to the discovery of class. To become class conscious, workers did not need to be told that they were poor and exploited. This they already knew. What workers needed, as Jacques Rancière has described for nineteenth-century France, was "a knowledge of self" that would reveal "a being dedicated to something else besides exploitation."[64]

Culture and the Self

The moral anger fueled by these ideas about the human person was not limited to a critique of social inequities and oppressions—it was also directed against the weak or decayed selves of individuals. Just as the condition of the self was so central to their critique of society, so did the individual stand at the center of the solutions they envisioned to end the sufferings of the poor. Partly this entailed a cultural critique that reached beyond criticism of the structures of social inequality and even beyond the goal of overcoming capitalism. Partly, this entailed looking beyond "society's" humiliations of the selves of the poor to face workers' own failures to recognize, respect, and nurture their inward personalities and their autonomous wills. At the heart of these questions were ideas about culture as the key to recovering the self and nurturing its will.

Like many educated Russians of the time, worker authors were obsessed with the idea of "culture" as a universal moral ideal and goal. There was little debate over what it entailed—cultural relativism was still alien to their way of thinking—but there was much argument against violations of this norm. The parameters of "culture" were laid out mostly in this negative critique. There was much that offended them: the "journalistic cretinism" of the boulevard press with its obsessions with scandals, crime, sex, rape, murder, and suicide;[65] the shallow pointlessness of the cinema;[66] the growing popularity of horse racing, auto racing, and other diversions;[67] the modern "epicurianism" of the rich, echoing ancient Rome's "sated, perverted, and debauched" elites who degraded ideals about nature and beauty into their purely "animal and physical" form,[68]

---

[64] Jacques Rancière, *The Nights of Labor: The Workers' Dream in Nineteenth-Century France*, trans. John Drury (Philadelphia, 1989), 20.

[65] *Nadezhda* 2 (26 September 1908): 6; M. Volkov, "Obzor pechati," *Narodnaia sem'ia* 4 (19 February 1912): 12–14.

[66] Kvadrat in *Pechatnoe delo* 11 (30 September 1909): 4.

[67] Loginov in *Dumy narodnye* 3 (13 February 1913): 1–2.

[68] Mikhail Tikhoplesets (Loginov), "Epikuritsy," *Zvezda iasnaia (Zvezda utreniaia)*

the spread of "pornographic" literature;[69] and the "sexual hooliganism" of popular literary writing that preached unrestrained sexual expression and fulfillment.[70] A notion of what the English Victorians called "respectability" pervades these constructions of violations of morality and culture. And like many other rhetorics of respectability, this ideal was inseparable from arguments about the dignity of the self. But it was also, in the hands of these plebeian writers, a challenging rhetoric.

This criticism was directed not only at society. Worker-writers focused a steady stream of criticism against the weak, undeveloped, and "fallen" personalities of the majority of lower-class Russians, for which they blamed, at least in part, individuals themselves. A huge outpouring of published criticism targeted drunkenness, swearing, cruelty, and lowbrow cultural tastes. Such criticisms obviously echoed the "culturalist" arguments of many elite Russians worried about the dangerous backwardness of the poor.[71] The difference, though not absolute, was telling: when worker critics of popular culture talked of raising the culture of the poor and nurturing the self and the will, the logic was defiant and transgressive more than integrative. In other words, the goal was to make the poor more dangerous to an unequal social order, not less.

In essays, feuilletons, satirical writings, and other forms in both Marxist-oriented trade union papers and in the more populist papers of "writers from the people"—these writers tried persistently to shame their fellow workers away from behaviors and mentalities that were said to degrade the personality and weaken the will. This list was long: drunkenness, thievery, superstition, bigotry, fighting, crass tastes in entertainment, male sexual harassment, female prostitution, dishonesty, and passivity. The Russian vocabulary used was richly moralistic (and difficult to translate directly for it was grounded in a cultural language of moral judgment): *poshlost'* (self-satisfied crassness), *nravstvennaia padenie* (moral fall), *raznuzdannost'* (licentiousness), *razvrat* (debauchery), *nechesnost'* (dishonesty, dishonor), *durnye instinkty* (low instincts), *skandal* (scandalous behavior), *pakosti* (trash, depravities, obscenities), and more.

Drunkenness was a particularly common target, and it was generally treated as both a sign and an aggravation of a weak self, as a practice that

---

6 (29 February 1912): 5–6.

[69] *Balalaika* 12 (1910): 1; *Metallist* 10 (11 February 1912): 4.

[70] Kvadrat, "Propoved' khuliganstva v russkoi literature," *Pechatnoe delo* 33–34 (1 April 1910): 3–7. See also *Narodnaia sem'ia* 5 (4 March 1912): 13–14.

[71] Stephen Frank, "Confronting the Domestic Other," *Cultures in Flux*, 74-107; Brooks, *When Russia Learned to Read*, chap. 9.

"defaces the image of man" (*obezlichivaet obraz cheloveka*), and leads to immorality and depravity.[72] But drunkenness was only the most obvious sin, only one piece of a larger story of the common people's degraded cultural selves. M. A. Loginov, writing in the "people's" journals he edited, regularly wrote of the "darkness and chaos" he saw in the life of the common people: the fall in morals, breakdown of families, wasteful and harmful time spent in taverns and café chantants, inhuman crimes, cruelty, ignorance, superstition, and fatalism.[73] He described with disgust, for example, "laboring people" resting along the shore of the Volga near Moscow on summer evenings: "coarse swearing, arguments, and fights," "drunkenness, violence, and depravity."[74] The printer Ivan Kubikov similarly castigated the "tavern civilization" that threatened urban workers, and complained, as others did, of workers escaping to the crass diversions of the movie house, the fair booth (*balagan*), or the gramophone.[75] A waiter complained that his fellows wasted their free time on nothing but degrading "buffoonery": "as soon as a few comrades get together, right away they start in with stupid witticisms, obscenities, card games, drunkenness, and other such trash [*pakosti*]."[76]

In hundreds of essays, stories, and poems, plebeian authors wrote of the "savage manners" and crass tastes of ordinary lower-class Russians,[77] of workers' "moral and physical fall" and troubling "indifference" to "self-betterment,"[78] and of superstition and bigotry (especially anti-Semitic prejudice).[79] The Bolshevik miner and poet Aleksei Chizhikov wrote of the majority of "working folk" (*rabochii liud*) as only just beginning to wake up from a "long and heavy nightmarish sleep."[80] Others were less confident and wrote with undisguised contempt for "backward" workers

---

[72] *Pechatnik* 2–3 (6 August 1917): 6. For a few other typical examples, see *Dumy narodnye* 2 (February 1910): 1, 6–8; *Balalaika* 8 (1910): 6–7.

[73] *Dumy narodye* 2 (February 1910): 1; *Zvezda iasnaia (Zvezda utreniaia)* 6 (29 February 1912): 2–4; *Zvezda utreniaia*, 17 (23 May 1912): 2.

[74] M. T-ts (Loginov), *Dumy narodye* 1 (February 1910): 2.

[75] Kvadrat, "Kul′tura i prosveshchenie," *Pechatnoe delo* 8 (27 June 1909): 5, and reprinted in the paper of the metalworkers' union, *Edinstvo* 7 (10 July 1909): 7–8; *Pechatnoe delo* 11 (30 September 1909): 4–6; Sinebluznik, "Grammofon i soiuz," *Nash put′* 6 (30 August 1910): 3; letter from a reader, Odinokii, "O razvlecheniiakh dlia rabochikh," *Edinstvo* 15 (12 March 1910): 11–12.

[76] I. Shch-v (probably I. I. Shcherbakov, a leader of the Mutual Aid Society of Waiters), "Budem rabotat′," *Chelovek* 3 (27 March 1911): 12.

[77] For example, the writings by Savin and Chernysheva in *Balalaika* (1910–11).

[78] Blizhnyi, "Prosvetimsia liudi," *Rodnye vesti* 4 (Easter 1912): 3.

[79] *Trud* 5 (October–November 1912): 24–25.

[80] Aleksei Chizhikov, letter to *Pravda* (4 March 1914), RGASPI, f. 364, op. 1, d. 315, ll. 1-3 (quote from original p. 3).

who seemed not to care that they were living "the life of an animal."[81] Many wrote about the popular reading tastes, especially the ill effects on the "nerves" and on the moral "taste" of reading boulevard newspapers like *Kopeika*. Long-term reading of such papers might, it was feared, cause a reader to grow so accustomed to "the smell of scandal and rowdy disorder [*deboshirstvo*]" that he would lose his natural "taste for that which is clean and bright."[82] Aleksei Bibik translated these perceptions and concerns into literary form in his novel of the popular life he grew up with, painting a hellish scene of a drunken father philosophizing about patience and endurance, a drunken mother neglected her hungry and crying baby, and all around the sounds of swearing, weeping, crass arguing, and the baying of a dog.[83]

These writers saw weakness and disintegration deep in the very selves of most workers. For example, an essay in the paper of the Petersburg Metalworkers' Union in 1908 gloomily noted the irony that just at the moment when employers' assaults on labor were reaching the most "crude and inhuman forms," workers exhibited a "growing shallowness [*izmel'chanie*] of proletarian thinking [and] the manifestation of base instincts."[84] A year later, Aleksei Gastev described the world of workers harshly, but not untypically as the "realm of the unconscious, the realm of dark melancholy, impenetrable unbelief, stagnating inertia."[85] In 1910, the prominent worker-leader of the Metalworkers' Union, Fedor Bulkin, wrote a stinging indictment of workers' "moral nonchalance" (*nravstennyi khalatnost'*), dishonesty, crass literary tastes (*Pinkertonovshchina*), and generally the "flourishing of low instincts" among workers.[86] Similarly, the printer Ivan Kubikov complained of finding in many workplaces an "abyss of self-satisfied crassness [*poshlost'*] and apathy" and "philistine indolence."[87]

The deeply rhetorical nature of these accusations should be kept in mind. As these workers no doubt knew, and as historians of Russian la-

---

[81] Kirill Babich (worker at the Nevskii textile factory), poem "Ostavshemu tovarishchu," sent May 1914 to *Pravda*, RGASPI, f. 364, op. 1, d. 324, l. 4.

[82] *Nadezhda* 2 (26 September 1908): 6.

[83] Bibik, *K shirokoi doroge*, 23–28.

[84] *Metallist*, "K karakteristike nastroenii v rabochei srede," *Nadezhda* 2 (26 September 1908): 10.

[85] A. Zorin (Aleksei Gastev), "Sredi tramvaishchikov" (nabrosok), *Edinstvo* 12 (21 December 1909): 11.

[86] Fedor Bulkin, "Bol'noi vopros (upadok nravov v rabochei srede)," *Nash put'* 11 (20 December 1910): 7–8.

[87] Kvadrat, "Vpechatleniia zhizni," *Pechatnoe delo* 24 (11 September 1910): 6.

bor have extensively documented,[88] the number of literate, cultured, and socially conscious workers was in fact greater than ever before and could be found by the hundreds in trade unions, workers' clubs, religious movements, and other organizations which featured cultural programming for workers. So, just as we should not mistake for simple factual reporting on popular culture the widespread rhetoric of "culturalist" intellectuals, church missionaries, temperance activists and others about the dark and savage ignorance of the poor, we must also not misapprehend the testimonies of worker intellectuals. These too were pieces of rhetoric, but not different ones: the message they conveyed was a particular and complex one.

Like other Marxists, Bulkin blamed society and especially the autocratic state for "dehumanizing" workers.[89] Others similarly complained that workers were purposefully excluded from "real culture." As one worker wrote, in a letter to the paper of the Petersburg Metalworkers' Union, borrowing the familiar Biblical metaphor chastising the rich, "it is easier for a camel to go through the eye of a needle than for the working man to enter a good theater."[90] Others similarly noted the lack of availability of good books and healthy entertainment.[91] But most of these writers also argued that workers, and especially workers' leaders, must take responsibility for these effects. This was Bulkin's argument.[92] Similarly, August Tens, a compositor well known for his writings in trade union papers and for his years of leadership in the Petersburg Printers' Union, insisted that drunkenness cannot be dismissed as simply a product of social conditions: "Drunkenness is a disease of the will, and the will depends on reason. It is necessary to develop reason. It is all about culture."[93] And, one might add, for this was implicit the self.

Drunkenness, indiscipline, crude manners, ignorance, and a general lack of culture were condemned partly as practical obstacles hindering workers' collective struggle, as making workers "passive," "apathetic," "undisciplined," and unable to "stand up for their interests."[94] Con-

---

[88] For example, Zelnik, "Russian Bebels"; Bonnell, *Roots of Rebellion*, McDaniel, *Autocracy, Capitalism, and Revolution in Russia*; Steinberg, *Moral Communities*;
[89] Bulkin, "Bol'noi vopros."
[90] Odinokii, "O razvlecheniiakh dlia rabochikh," *Edinstvo* 15 (12 March 1910): 11–12
[91] For example, K. T-ts, "Russkie rabochie," *Zvezda utrenniaia* 10 (4 April 1910): 2.
[92] Bulkin, "Bol'noi vopros."
[93] *Pechatnoe delo* 13 (24 November 1909): 10–11.
[94] *Pechatnik* 1 (23 April 1906): 11–12; *Pechatnoe delo* 15 (9 February 1907): 7; *Protokoly pervoi vserossiiskoi konferentsii soiuzov rabochikh pechatnogo dela* (St. Petersburg, 1907), 80, 82, 109.

cretely, attention was paid to certain "moral" faults that had particular significance for class solidarity and militance: groveling and deference before employers, stealing from other workers, selling jobs to the unemployed, fighting and beatings, overtime work, and strikebreaking.[95] Taking a longer but still largely practical view, some worker-authors, like Ivan Kubikov—writing in 1909, when he was chair of the Petersburg printers' union—insisted that workers needed to be culturally and morally prepared for their future historical role. Quoting Ferdinand Lassalle, Kubikov maintained that since workers were the "stone upon which the church of the future will be built," that foundation needed to be strong and polished. More immediately, Kubikov argued, echoing a view held by many activists, workers' "class consciousness" was closely connected with their "cultural consciousness": every lecture on science and every reading of a classic work of literature led workers to "understand the order of things."[96]

Especially noteworthy is the logical dependence of the collective on the individual in these arguments. Individual development was essential for effective class struggle. Sometimes the argument was mainly individualistic. As this was put by one essayist, we need to "worry about our own moral and intellectual condition" for, in order to solve our problems, "we must rely on our own individual abilities."[97] But even when the focus was on class struggle, the individual stood at the logical center. Just as personal culture was seen to aid the class struggle, so was class struggle seen as serving the development of the individual self, of emancipating workers' human selves, and creating a society, as it was so often said, where people could "live like human beings." Moral and cultural backwardness were denounced not only as evidence of social oppression or on the pragmatic grounds of the needs of the class struggle, but also as inherent evils, for the harm they inflicted on the individual self.

Strangers

Paradoxically, the inspiration driving most of these worker authors to articulate social activism was a profound sense of being strangers, outsiders and wanderers, in their own world. Estrangement strongly inflected their own sense of themselves as individuals and their practices as self-proclaimed voices of popular feeling and will. In memoirs, these writ-

---

[95] *Protokoly*, 80, 82, 109.

[96] Kvadrat, "Alkogolizm i usloviia bor'by s nim," *Professional'nyi vestnik* 26 (31 October 1909): 6–8. This essay also appeared in *Pechatnoe delo* 13 (24 November 1909): 4–5.

[97] Blizhnyi, "Prosvetimsia liudi," *Rodnye vesti* 4 (Easter 1912): 3.

ers very often recalled feeling alienated from the crass everyday worlds around them, looking for truth and meaning in isolated searching, reading, wandering and thinking. Mikhail Savin, writing in 1909, claimed to have spent his youth feeling so out of place "amidst the prose of everyday life" that he preferred "living in dreams, drunk with poetry and the thirst for light."[98] We know from the biographies of these worker-writers that many in fact took to the road as wanderers and pilgrims: some went on religious pilgrimages; others "wandered" (*peredvizhit'*) and "tramped" (*brodiazhit'*) around the country (seeking happiness or truth, they would later often claim); a few even journeyed about Europe and on the high seas to America and back.[99] This sojourning and seeking was part of a familiar cultural tradition in Russian culture: that of roaming religious mystics (*stranniki*), lay preachers, holy fools (*iurodivye*), pilgrims, tramping peasants and workers, wandering artists (*peredvizhniki*), literary wanderers like Gorky and Tolstoy, and the vast genre of popular literary and folk tales of questing heroes, sympathetic bandits, saints, and vagabonds.

In the lives and writings of these workers, wandering had particular meaning and pathos. The writings of proletarian authors elaborated endlessly on feelings of cultural and moral isolation—feelings that bordered on a sort of moral and social nausea. As we have seen, the labor press was filled with writings by workers voicing contempt (ranging from condescending sympathy to open disgust and loathing) for the ordinary sort of lower-class Russian. Many were quite explicit about the significance for their own selves of living in this environment. "Thinking workers," Ivan Kubikov wrote, found it a constant struggle to "defend their inner world from being spit upon"—whether by bosses or by fellow workers. If anything, workers were worse, for the debased cultural personalities of workers increased the dangers that might pull a "thinking worker" back into the common corruption all around. In any case, the depravity of their fellow workers most disturbed "thinking workers": commenting on a recent story by Maxim Gorky, Kubikov commented, "How well Gorky portrays the thinking workers' feelings of being alone [*odinochestvo*]... amidst the gray and backward mass." Seeing "in what filth the soul of man is stewing," he feels like "an alien creature among these people."[100]

---

[98] *Gallereia sovremennykh poetov*, ed. Tiulenev, 11.

[99] See autobiographical sketches in *Sovremennye raboche-krest'ianskie poety*, ed. P. Ia. Zavolikin (Ivanovo-Voznesensk, 1925).

[100] Kvadrat in *Novaia rabochaia gazeta* 5 (13 August 1913): 2. This is a review (begun in the preceding issue), of Gorky's story, "The Boss: Pages from an Autobiography," (Khoziain: stranitsy avtobiografii), published in *Sovremennik* 3–5 (1913).

In the poetry and fiction of these writers—most of which, of course, had a strong autobiographical element—a major theme was the awakened and sensitive individual, estranged from the crass ordinary people all around. They were, in the language of the time, "cultural loners" (*kul'turnye odinochki*),[101] and sometimes adopted noms de plume that reflected this spirit, such as Gastev's "Odinokii" (unique, peerless, solitary), Mashirov's "Samobytnik" (unique, self-made, autonomous), Solov'ev's "Neliudim" (which may be loosely translated as "one who is not like ordinary people"). To borrow Savin's autobiographical remarks quoted above, these writers tended to dwell on the anguish of the "poetic" self mired in "the prose of everyday life." One fictionalized life-story of a sensitive, high-minded, and lonely young worker described the hero's distaste for "the scarcely cultured or literate environment that surrounded him since childhood." As an adult, he had to "always hold himself apart from his co-workers, among whom he noticed many vices." This was not an easy stance. When he refused to join his fellow workers in stealing from the shop, he was ostracized.[102] Another author described the derisive laughter of workers against one who was obsessed with reading. He was repelled by the "fighting, swearing, and reproaches" of these fellow workers, who, in turn, dubbed him a "Pharisee."[103] This sort of conflict had become a cliché in writing about worker-intellectuals, but one that was painfully true to life. At the same time, these authors occasionally suggested even more tragic results whenever such workers tried to fit in by joining their fellows in drink and revelry (and beating their wives) and giving up the reading and search for truth that had set them painfully apart: one such worker, briefly back in the mainstream, ended by throwing himself beneath the wheels of a train.[104] Sometimes, this estrangement from the workers' milieu extended to an even more painful alienation from one's own social self. The miner and poet Aleksei Chizhikov wrote in 1914 of the "workers' soul," no different in essence from the soul of a tsar or a prince, "imprisoned in a rough worker's hide" (*zakliuchena v grubuiu rabochuiu kozhu*).[105]

---

[101] Deev-Khomiakovskii, "Kul'turnye ugolki i kul'turnye odinochki," *Drug naroda* 2 (31 January 1915): 11.

[102] A-ch, "Ternistyi put," *Samopomoshch'* 2, no. 1 (December 1911): 6.

[103] Deev-Khomiakovskii, "Prozrel," *Drug naroda* 1 (1 January 1915): 7–8.

[104] D. I. Semenov (a metalworker on the railroad), "Kto vinovat," *Melitopol'skaia vedomosti* 83 (25 December 1911): 2. This story, the author's first, was sent to Maxim Gorky. Arkhiv Gor'kogo, KG-np/a, 22-4-2.

[105] Aleksei Chizhikov, letter accompanying verses submitted to *Pravda* by the miner (4 March 1914). RGASPI, f. 364, op. 1, d. 315, l. 1–3 (original quote from p. 4).

What did these stories of alienation mean? For some of these writers, the image of the sensitive plebeian as stranger was an expression of a neo-romantic fascination with sensibility, and, more precisely, an extension of the suffering self into the stance of the "exquisitely depressed" stranger. Julia Kristeva (whose phrase this is) has written eloquently of the stranger (though she had in mind primarily the actual foreigner) as very often nurturing a "precious exquisite pain," even a pleasurably bruised personality, as a proud but also anguished outsider.[106] A comparable ambivalent mix of pain and pleasure can be seen in a number of poems that appeared in journals created by and for "writers from the people"—typically with titles like "Mood" ("Nastroenie") and "Solitude" or "Loneliness" ("Odinochestvo"). Typical is Sergei Gan'shin's 1912 poem "Odinochestvo"—placed on the first page of *Rodnye vesti* under a drawing of a man who appears to be a homeless wanderer, leaning against an old fence at the edge of a frozen road, his eyes downcast. "I stand alone / Heart gnawed by anguish / Oppressed, tired, and troubled. / I glance to heaven, where stars burn clearly / Bright stars of a far away world."[107] Similarly, the poetry of the worker L. Bystrov, whose poems were collected in 1915 (after his death in the war) in "Songs of Sorrow" (*Skorbnye pesni*), was replete with images of human weakness, of his own alienation from human society ("I bear the heavy cross of exile," he told an interviewer), and of suicide (especially of young women).[108] Vladimir Aleksandrovskii, a young worker-socialist, mused on the ennui of solitude.[109] Even trade union papers featured such writings, such as the waiter Semen Popov's lament, "I wander each night without refuge / Having neither family nor friends."[110] Petr Zaitsev, long associated with the Yaroslavl' printers' union, frequently imagined dying alone, "forgotten by all," crushed by "sorrow and adversity," and disappointed by the failure to find "light and truth," welcoming the peaceful oblivion of death.[111]

More common than these sentimental and pathetic images of the thinking worker as stranger, was a critically edged alienation: a representation of estrangement as part of the ideal of the awakened and moral self.

---

[106] Julia Kristeva, *Strangers to Ourselves* (New York, 1991), 5, 10, 21, 29, 38, 135–36.
[107] Gan'shin, "Odinochestvo," *Rodnye vesti* 3 (1913): 1.
[108] N. Vlasov-Okskii, "Ogon'ki v stepi (iz vstrech s pistateliami-samouchkami)," *Griadushchee* 1–3 (1912): 41–44.
[109] V. Aleksandrovskii, "Odinochestvo," *Zhivoe slovo* 30 (July 1913): 4.
[110] Semen Popov, "Iz pesen goria i nuzhdy," *Chelovek* 3 (27 March 1911): 11.
[111] Petr Zaitsev, "Umru ia," *Kolotushka* 2 (1911): 4. See other poems by him in this and other issues of *Kolotushka*. See also Vladimir Korolev, *Lazurnye prakhi* (Yalta, 1912), and *Vsem skorbiashchim* (Yaroslavl, 1915).

Although Egor Nechaev felt as if the world around him was a "prison," filled with "the noise of machines and the talk of people" (barely differentiated), he found comfort in an inner fire, his "best friend"—calling him to an unknown future.[112] Dmitrii Odintsev similarly wrote of reading in the lonely dark of night and of distracted thoughts amidst the noises of factory work as secret moment when he nurtured his inner fires.[113] Likewise, Aleksei Mashirov ("Samobytnik") described a worker sitting alone in his cramped room after work, reading by the "pale light of a lamp," trying to ignore the "laughter and tears of carefree fellows" in an adjoining room.[114]

Although the point, as we have seen, was to enlighten one's fellows, ambivalence about them persisted even among the most politically committed. Radicalized workers like Odintsev and Mashirov portray themselves as improving their minds in order to bring a message back to their fellows. Mashirov, for example, is reading about workers' hardships and struggles. And when he finally "gives in to his exhaustion," he "quietly lays down, full of thoughts and dreams," determined, the next day at work, to "tell his friends all about them." As a Bolshevik and as a worker-intelligent, Mashirov resolved to share his enlightenment with others—at least with his "friends." But, as this last hesitancy may suggest, this was not a simple matter of a conscious worker committed to his backward class fellows. As an intellectually developed worker—an *intelligentnyi rabochii*—he remained a cultural loner (*kul'turnaia odinochka*) in everyday life, sitting alone in his room reading (even if partly for others), feeling himself a stranger to the laughter and tears "beyond the wall."[115]

Such ambivalence was common and "tragic," thought the Marxist literary critic L'vov-Rogachevskii, commenting on the writings of Aleksei Bibik, especially his popular 1912 autobiographical novel "To the Open Road." For a person to be simultaneously a "proletarian" and to be "cut off from the masses" was wrong, though unfortunately all too common. This was certainly the existential situation of Bibik's worker-heroes. Once awakened to "culture" by reading and seeking answers, they were repelled by the smell of beer, herring and tobacco in their working-class homes, by the passivity and drunkenness of ordinary workers (including

---

[112] Nechaev, "Moia pesnia."
[113] D. Odintsev, "Vpered," *Pravda* 156 (31 October 1912): 2, and in *Pervyi sbornik proletarskikh pisatelei* (St. Petersburg, 1914), 166.
[114] Mashirov, "Posle raboty," *Pravda* 163 (8 November 1912): 2; and *Pervyi sbornik*, 160.
[115] Mashirov, "Posle raboty."

their own parents), and by the hostility of other workers toward "worker-philosophers."[116] The novel's two protagonists (a duality that represented some of the ambivalence in the minds of awakened workers, though much of the tension remained within each character) seek different paths from this degraded everyday to a higher truth and hope. They discussed these paths, toward the end of the novel, in a prison cell where both are awaiting their likely sentence of exile for leadership of a strike. The more politicized and militant Artem insists that one must go "among people... into humanity." But Ignat—the character closest to the author, the central figure in the novel and the most ambivalent—seeks truth more complexly. He looks to nature and to "the inner world," and proposes that they become wanderers. The phrase he uses is *idti v odinochku*—meaning literally "to go into [a state of being] singular and alone," or, more loosely, "to withdraw from society, to drop out." "You know what, Artem, let's go into *odinochka*! Come on! It's not so terrible there. It's easier there to get into one's self, to sort things out." And if one must be among people, Ignat argues, Siberia is the place to go ("harsh semi-mythical Siberia," Bibik calls it): "There are real people there—strong, great souls!"[117]

As the critic L'vov-Rogachevskii recognized, there was a certain tragedy in the painful ambivalence that so many worker-intellectuals felt in being simultaneously class-conscious activists and alienated from "the masses." A vanguard mentality, dedicated to sharing thoughts and ideals with others, competed and often mixed with contempt for those same others. Sentimental pride in the richness of soul that could feel exquisite torments of solitude competed and often mixed with anguish over lonely isolation.

The Poetics of Genius

When these worker-writers felt confident that resistance to the injuries the self was worth the effort—a confidence most common in periods of social mobilization such as 1905–07 and 1912–17 (and in the first years after 1917)—they penned vigorous protests and calls for struggle. But their focus was typically less on collective action than on the inner will and power of awakened individuals to challenge inequalities, lead others, and change society. Marxist and Soviet critics have argued, often convincingly, that this was not conventional individualism—i.e., that it was not "petty-bourgeois," "philistine" individualism.[118] We see this distinctiveness in

---

[116] L'vov-Rogachevskii, *Ocherki*, 217–18; Bibik, *K shirokoi doroge*, 23–30, 39, 49, 74.

[117] Bibik, *K shirokoi doroge*, 104–05.

[118] Kleinbort, "Ocherki," part 1, *Sovremennyi mir* (March 1913): 34, 40.

the ethical commitment to others articulated in the ideas of the dignity of all people and of the need to struggle against the social causes and the agents of humiliation and insult. In practice, many worker-writers joined unions (and sometimes led them) and socialist parties and participated in strikes, demonstrations, and revolution. In writing, they made these distinctions between individualisms themselves. A few did so explicitly, criticizing, for example, "worker aristocrats" who believed that individual self-cultivation and virtue was means enough to change conditions.[119] More commonly they implied as much by writing—in the well-established language of socialist collectivism (which would flourish after 1917)—of "we," "our sufferings," "workers," the "proletariat," and "humanity."[120] Most commonly, and most complexly, they resisted "philistine" individualism by articulating a more poetic and inspired individualism, built around romantic ideals of inward genius and heroic will—especially their own.

Writing itself was seen as a heroic act, grounded in inward genius— in the Renaissance and romantic senses of each person's unique inward personality and capacities, of their inward, and perhaps divine, guiding spirit. Invariably, these writers portrayed their will to write as reflecting a deep personal need—even a sacred inspiration—and as marking them as special individuals with a special mission. Egor Nechaev, for example, described responding to a semi-mystical call that came to him when he was seventeen years old. His mother, a domestic, brought home leftovers from her employer's dinner wrapped in the pages of an old magazine that happened to contain the autobiography, portrait, and verses of the self-taught shopkeeper-poet Ivan Surikov. After feverishly reading these texts, Nechaev reported, an "inner voice" advised him that he too could become a writer.[121] Nikolai Kuznetsov, whose parents were textile workers near Moscow, recalled that as a child left to wander the streets he found himself uncontrollably drawn to book kiosks where he would stand and stare at the books behind the windows even before he had learned to read.[122]

---

[119] For example, Baikov, "Kakoi put' vernee (zametki rabochii)," *Rabochii po metallu* 18 (26 July 1907): 3–5.

[120] Soviet collections of proletarian poetry (some of it, of course, written by educated radicals who never held working-class jobs, but much of it by workers and former workers) highlights this collectivist spirit in their selections. See especially *Proletarskie poety* 2 (1936).

[121] *Proletarskie pisateli*, ed. Semen Rodov (Moscow, 1924): 434.

[122] Maksim Gorky, "O pisateliakh-samouchkakh" (1911), in A. M. Gor'kii, *Sobranie sochinenii* (Moscow, 1953), 24: 105–08. See also Arkhiv A. M. Gor'kogo, KG-NP/A 22–24: 1–2.

Maxim Gorky, who corresponded with hundreds of beginning writers, reported in 1911 that many of the workers and peasants who wrote to him similarly described a higher or inner force driving them to read and write. One worker, a turner, told Gorky that he could not sleep nights because he was so tortured by the thoughts that were inside of him trying to get out. A metalworker claimed—and Gorky reported that such expressions were typical—that a "mysterious force" (*nevedomaia sila*) drove him to write. Many spoke of "fires" burning within them.[123] Others spoke, more traditionally, of "a divine spark."[124] Works of fiction similarly featured protagonists inexplicably driven to read,[125] and of moments of bright inspiration (like lightening or a meteor) when reading.[126]

Workers typically viewed themselves not only as inspired to write but as sanctified as individuals by their sufferings in service to this calling. Many recalled being beaten when they were caught reading or writing at work or even by their parents at home. Il'ia Sadof'ev, for example, wrote that at the age of ten he was given an "exemplary thrashing" by his father for "the shame of wanting to be a scribbler," so severe that he was confined to bed for two weeks. Sergei Obradovich, a stereotyper in a printshop, was repeatedly tormented by his foreman for writing poems on scraps of paper. Some workers even claimed to torture themselves out of devotion—denying themselves food, for example, in order to save money to buy books.[127] The suffering continued for those who managed to persist in writing and become "writers from the people." They carried the "heavy cross" of "torturous poverty and oppressive labor." And they suffered from conditions that suppressed their creativity: "I think that everyone knows how shining thoughts and the tormenting and caressing sounds of the proletarian muse perish and consume the soul when they are unable to see the light."[128]

These autobiographical representations of inspired, striving, and suffering selves were mixtures of memory and conscious myth-making. The memory reminds us that these individuals were, indeed, different in their

---

[123] See, for example, V. Friche, *Proletarskaia poeziia* (Moscow, 1919), 59 (Shkulev); Savin, "Bor'ba," *Bulochnik* 1 (19 February 1906): 5; Nechaev, "Moia pesnia."

[124] Deev-Khomiakovskii on Surikov in *Drug naroda* nos. 5–7 (1915): 2–3.

[125] For example, A-ch, "Ternistyi put'," *Samopomoshch'* 2, no. 1 (18 December 1911): 6.

[126] For example, Bibik, *K shirokoi doroge*, 46–47.

[127] Avolikin, *Sovremennye raboche-krest'ianskie poety*, 53–54, 76, 107; Gorky, "O pisateliakh-samouchkakh," 106, 108; Deev-Khomiakovskii on Surikov.

[128] S. Drozhzhin in *Drug naroda* nos. 5–7 (1915): 13; Sergei Gremiacheskii, K pisateliam iz naroda, *Drug naroda*, nos. 8–10 (October 1915): 2.

selves, that they were responding to a rare drive to create. But it is the elaboration of these memories into meaningful stories of self-awakening and self-expression that is the most revealing. While framing their stories in devotion to the common good, the heart of these tales was about striving and heroic individuals. The prevailing self-identities they described were of heroes and outsiders, agents inspired by an inward genius, not as common members of the popular community, proud working-class creators of material value, or even rank-and-file soldiers in the class struggle. In part, we recognize in their life-stories images refracted from literature: the self-assertive, superior, and rebellious individuals of bandit tales and adventure sagas;[129] Nietzschean rebels against convention and slavishness; even echoes of the lives of saints—often the first literature that workers encountered—with their inspiring accounts of exceptional individual suffering in the pursuit and in the service of truth.

This particular self-idealization—and its boundary-breaking implications—was linked strongly to the glorification of the printed word and the writer in Russian civic culture. Since the nineteenth century, it had become a familiar intellectual tradition for writers and critics to speak of writers as moral witnesses, prophets, and inspired voices of truth. Pushkin, Gogol, Dostoevsky, Tolstoy, and others were often spoken of in this way, and themselves often aspired to this role. Although, by the early 1900s, this tradition was resisted by modernists, who countered with the ideal of pure and autonomous art, this myth of the writer was strongly felt in the self-perceptions of lower-class writers. Memoirs and letters workers sent to political and trade union papers repeatedly expressed a reverence for the printed word and for those who wrote. N. Liashko, using a hyperbolic vocabulary that was not unusual, declared that our "national literature is our sanctum sanctorum—the only place where every one of us enters with reverence." Most important, in the face of oppression and passivity, it is literature that has struggled for change: "It has fought for faith and freedom, for the humiliated and the insulted, and for the rights and dignity of man. Like a nanny over a sleeping child, it has fought against all of the monsters of the nightmarish night. For the life of the Russian common people... has been one continuous nightmare."[130]

Writers were the agents of this sacred cause. For Aleksei Mashirov, the "proud word 'poet'" evoked "the joy of the first breath, / the emer-

---

[129] See Brooks, *When Russia Learned to Read*, esp. chap. 5.
[130] N. Nikolaev (N. Liashko), "O narodnom pisatele, pisateliakh, i 'pisateliakh'," *Ogni*, 3 (January 1913): 27.

gence in spring of the first growth." In particular, workers' poets were the "people's leader" arriving like "a peal of joyous thunder."[131] Poets, it was said, cared not about money or a full table: they loved only "the high ideal of thought," only the "sun of truth."[132] Others wrote similarly and often of the power of their songs to inspire others.[133] The Russian writer, it was argued, was "prophet and leader," and "rebel" against the evils of "bureaucratism, the bourgeoisie, and aristocratism."[134] The lower-class writer was especially honored. As Nikolai Liashko put this in 1913: "Is there a more brilliant name than the name people's writer [*narodnyi pisatel'*]?"[135]

Indeed, plebeian authorship had especially important symbolic power in the self-images of these writers and in their ideas about the individual. When subalterns write—especially when they write literature or criticism—this is an inherently transgressive act. Like black slaves and former slaves for whom writing stood as a complex "certificate of humanity," a political gesture that implicitly criticized the European social chain of being and their own low place on it by seizing hold of "Europe's fundamental sign of domination, the commodity of writing, the text and technology of reason,"[136] when workers wrote, they implicitly challenged their ascription as lower-class. When Russian workers wrote and published poems, stories, and essays, they violated the conventional divisions between manual and intellectual labor and between popular culture and the literary high culture. It was significant that Russian worker-writers almost invariably adopted an established literary style rather than a folk or plebeian style. Instead of echoing the rhythms and vocabulary of peasant songs and rhymes, worker-poets typically imitated popular established writers, notably Alexander Pushkin, Aleksei Kol'tsov, Nikolai Nekrasov, Ivan Nikitin, and Semyon Nadson, also foreign writers like Walt Whitman and Emile Verhaeren, and occasionally, though rarely, contemporary poets like Alexander Blok and Valerii Briusov. And instead of telling stories in the manner of the folktale—a style often adopted by radical

---

[131] Samobytnik (Aleksei Mashirov), "Ne govori v zhivom priznan'e," *Pervyi sbornik proletarskikh pisatelei*, 13. See also his "Ia ne odin, nas v mire mnogo," *Nashi pesni: pervyi sbornik* (St. Petersburg, 1913): 7.

[132] Savin in *Gallereia sovremennykh poetov*, 12.

[133] For example, Nechaev, "Mne khotelos' by pesniu svobodnuiu spet'."

[134] Loginov, "Uznavaitae po plodam," Zvezda utrenniaia 17 (23 May 1912): 2.

[135] Nikolaev, "O narodnom pisatele."

[136] Henry Louis Gates, Jr., "Editor's Introduction: Writing 'Race' and the Difference It Makes," in *Race, Writing, and Difference*, Henry Louis Gates, Jr. ed. (Chicago, 1986), 12.

intellectuals who sought to appeal to the common people—worker prosewriters were more likely to emulate Ivan Turgenev, Vladimir Korolenko, Leo Tolstoy, Maxim Gorky, or Anton Chekhov. High literary style was an emblem of the culture from which workers were excluded. Thus, in Russia as elsewhere, "workers' poetry was not at first an echo of popular speech but an initiation into the sacred language, the forbidden and fascinating language of others."[137] Its fascination and power derived precisely from its sanctified position in the established culture. Its otherness made it a symbol of workers' subordination and exclusion, making cultural imitation also appropriation, a half-conscious act of self-assertion and social rebellion. Sometimes this was fully conscious and deliberate. The appearance in Russia of "people's writers" (*narodnye pisateli*), Nikolai Liashko argued in 1913 (as one of them), was part of a "breaking down of centuries-old structures of popular life," of a "striving to change that which not long ago seemed immovable," and of a "revaluation of cultural values" (*pereotsenka dukhovnykh tsennostei*). And it was an answer to "those who imagine the common people to be wild beasts."[138] This challenge defied boundaries that defined social groups, but it remained rooted in acts of individual will. Reading and writing remained individual acts even when cast as part of a scenario of social protest.

We return to the problem of sorting out the complex relationship in the thought of worker-writers between the self and others—especially other workers. These writers mythologized their own individual inspiration and heroic role and sought to nurture their genius. At the same time—and fully in the tradition of the Russian intelligentsia—they sought to realize their selves by looking beyond themselves and attaching themselves to others. Thus, for M. A. Loginov, a true intelligent is defined not by social rank or profession, but by the "work for the well-being of their native people and for all humanity."[139] But it is the image of the inspired and heroic individual—typically a masculine hero—that remains most prominent and persistent. The pronoun "I" fills even the most militant poems of protest and struggle. Worker-authors wrote of their refusal to "bow down" before anyone,[140] and of their desire to "become one of the most daring of heroes" such as they read about in popular tales of bandits, heroes, and adventurers—"ruthlessly wreak vengeance on the

---

[137] Jacques Rancière, "Ronds de fumée (Les poètes ouvriers dans la France de Louis-Philippe)," *Revue des sciences humaines* 190 (April–June 1983): 33.
[138] Nikolaev, "O narodnom pisatele," 25.
[139] Loginov, "Uznavaitae po plodam," 2.
[140] For example, M. Zakharov, "Romans," *Rodnye vesti* 3 (1912): 5–6.

powerful and especially on their lackey-parasites."[141] They dreamed of imitating heroic rebels like Spartacus or Stenka Razin,[142] or the mighty heroism of legendary giants and warriors (*giganty, bogatyri*).[143] In the paper of the baker's union, Mikhail Savin offered this self-portrait:

> I go onto the road And meet evil.
> I am anger and vengeance!
> I am the terror of the enemy!
> Sacred honor
> Is my way.
> Where is darkness and lies?
> I am their scourge
> I am a sharp knife...
> I am a warrior
> With a pen in my hand
> Fire in my breast
> Poetry on my lips.[144]

Others vividly imagined themselves appearing before the suffering people as saviors. Sometimes relatively modestly: with words and verses starting "fires" in people's hearts.[145] Sometimes not so modestly: though a Marxist, the young factory worker Vasilii Aleksandrovskii represented himself as a god-like savior:

> I will be there, where backs are bent
> Where labor is profaned and defiled
> Where the cries of grief are heard
> And the noise and roar of machines.
> I will be there, where children perish
> In the grasp of rough labor....
> I will give them new thoughts
> And instinctual distant desires.
> Each is within me, and I am in everyone.[146]

Worker-poets often even envisioned themselves in flight, typically as ea-

---

[141] Zavolikin, *Sovremennye raboche-krest'ianskie poety*, 115, 214.

[142] Bibik. *K shirokoi doroge*, 36; Gerasimov, RGALI, f. 1374, op. 1, d. 6.

[143] Gerasimov, RGALI, f. 1374, op. 1, d. 6; Aleksei Chizhikov, Letter to *Pravda* (4 March 1914), RGASPI, f. 364, op. 1, d. 315, l. 1–3 (original p. 5).

[144] Savin, "Bor'ba."

[145] Gorelyi, "Rabochemu-poetu," *Novoe pechatnoe delo* (27 February 1916), in *Proletarskie poety*, 3 (1939): 71; Gan'shin, "V godinu bed," *Vpered!* 148 (2/15 September 1917): 2.

[146] V. Aleksandrovskii, "Novye pesni," *Nashi pesni* (Moscow, 1913), 1: 11.

gles and falcons. For some, flight was an escape. A provincial metalworker wrote to Gorky that he wished he was a "free bird" and could escape his life and fly to Gorky on the island of Capri in Italy or that he could be an airplane pilot and soar away from the earth into the sky.[147] Mariia Chernysheva dreamed of "light, swift wings" with which she could fly toward freedom, toward the expanse."[148] More politicized workers wished to use flight to serve others. Egor Nechaev wished that he were an eagle or the sun, bringing happiness and freedom to the world.[149] Sergei Gan'shin, a frequent contributor to *Pravda* in 1913–14, described himself as "an eagle from the skies... from which my mighty voice like a tocsin" rings out for victory "in the great and sacred struggle."[150] Aleksei Mashirov portrayed himself coming to the people in sacrificial but inspiring flight as a "meteor falling into the deep abyss."[151] Ivan Kubikov was even attracted by Gleb Uspensky's self-fantasy (apparently stimulated by his mental illness) that he could fly and that the sight of him soaring above the world would shame the oppressors and inspire the oppressed.[152] In each case, these were heroic acts of inspired, indeed transcendent, individuals, but acting not for themselves alone. In the tradition of the Russian intelligentsia, individualistic self-realization was linked to an identity and a purpose that went beyond self. Individual exaltation and devotion to the collective were said to be intertwined.

As here, activist worker-writers made every effort to link the individual and the collective. In their minds, the linkage was partly philosophical: recognition of the equal worth of every person necessarily highlighted the discrimination against workers as a class. The linkage was also partly practical: class struggle would emancipate individuals from social and political constraints on their development, and the developed individual best

---

[147] D. I. Semenov, "Moe zhelanie" and "K nebesam," sent to Gorky 14 November 1910, Arkhiv A. M. Gor'kogo, KG-NP/A, 22-4-1.

[148] Chernysheva, "Daite mne kryl'ia!," *Dumy narodnye* 3 (13 February 1910): 5. See also poem by V. E. Miliaev in *Narodnaia mysl'* 2 (February 1911): 126.

[149] Nechaev, "Pesnia nevol'nika" (1907), *U istokov*, 98–99.

[150] Gan'shin, "Orel," a manuscript poem sent to Maxim Gorky, 1914, in Arkhiv A. M. Gor'kogo, RAV-PG 37-13-1; Chernysheva, "Daite mne kryl'ia!." See also poem by V. E. Miliaev in *Narodnaia mysl'* 2 (February 1911): 121; and ibid. (1/14 August 1917): 2.

[151] See especially Mashirov, "Moim sobrat'iam," *Prosnuvshaiasia zhizn. Rukopisnyi zhurnal* (1913), and "Zarnitsy," *Proletarskaia pravda* (18 September 1913), both reprinted in *Proletarskie poety*, 2 (1936): 89–90. See also *Grebtsy* (1912), 87. Sergei Gan'shin also imagined himself as a meteor bringing light to human darkness. Gan'shin, "Ia syn stepei," *Zhivoe slovo* 20 (May 1913): 6. Also printed in *Vpered!* 112 (21 July 1917).

[152] *Pechatnoe delo* 5 (11 May 1912): 9.

Ambiguous Identities and Emotions

Indeed, ambivalence and ambiguity were endemic, pervading the stories of self that these writers presented. The savior was both selfless and an exalted self. Inspired and inspiring "flight" above the harsh and common world was a sign of both alienation and devotion to others, of engagement and escape. The winged-worker was a god-like fighter for others, but also simply god-like. The ethics these writers articulated were similarly ambivalent: the moral primacy given to workers' identity as human beings undermined class identity even as it provided a powerful sense of class injury and reason to fight as a class. After all, the ultimate purpose of the workers' movement was presumed to be not to build a "proletarian" social and cultural order but to demolish the barriers that kept workers separate, that identified them as anything other than human, and that restricted their individualities. Class struggle, in this conception, was aimed less against a different and dominant class than against class difference and domination itself. At least implicitly, this view echoed the Marxist dialectic that saw the particularistic class outlook of the proletariat negating the very idea of class, thereby giving to the working class a messianic historical role as a "universal class" destined not only to save itself but to deliver all humanity. But the tidy reasoning of this dialectic did not erase the ambiguity in the self-identities of many workers. At the heart of the self-idea of most worker-writers remained, at a minimum, the desire to be treated as human beings, and thus as individuals rather than as workers. And sometimes this evolved into more radical ideals of individual genius and exaltation.

Recognizing and understanding these uncertainties and tensions in self-identity require that we look beyond these logical constructions and look at the important (if more elusive) question of emotional perception and judgment. Emotion was often on the minds of workers and on the minds of intellectual critics of the proletarian imagination. Contemporary Marxist cultural critics and later Soviet literary historians repeatedly insisted on the boldly optimistic spirit defining the "proletarian" worldview. "Optimism," "bold confidence," "enthusiasm," and a generally "life affirming" feeling were said to be the hallmarks of the proletarian mood.[153]

---

[153] For example, Gorky, "O pisateliakh-samouchkakh," 107; L. Kleinbort, "Rukopisnye zhurnaly rabochikh," *Vestnik Evropy* 52, no. 7–8 (July–August 1917): 285; L'vov-

These arguments were tendentious—part of the politics of inventing a proletarian culture—but not without basis. The moral recognition that all people are human beings with dignity and rights certainly helped inspire a certain boldness and optimism. And the 1905 revolution, when the ideal of natural human rights was openly and repeatedly deployed by various groups against social and political inequalities, particularly stimulated this positive and militant mood. Almost every worker-writer, especially in the years from 1905, produced verses, stories, or essays voicing bold and militant optimism. Fedor Gavrilov's 1905 "song of a workman" was typical in its ringing declarations of "boldness," "courage," and faith in the coming victory over "darkness."[154] In subsequent years—including during the repressive years from 1907 through 1910—hundreds of writings used a similar vocabulary of insistent and self-advertised optimism: "boldness" (*bodrost'*), "hope," "enthusiasm," "mass heroism," "strength of spirit," feelings of "youthful life," "faith," and certainty that all obstacles would be overcome.[155] As one worker-intellectual insisted: "man was created for happiness just as a bird was for flight."[156] Metaphorically, this spirit was conveyed with repeated images of approaching dawn, the rising sun, and coming spring, and, less often, more original images such as the bold might of the wind and the inexorable power of streams cutting though granite.[157] When suffering and tears were mentioned in such writings, it was in order to insist that they be put aside: "This is not the time, friend, for us to sing of anguish [*toska*] and sadness."[158]

Rogachevskii, *Ocherki*, 39–41; Bikhter, *U istokov*, 13, 23.

[154] F. Gavrilov, "Iz pesen truzhenika," *Na zare* (Moscow, 1905), reprinted in *Proletarskie poety*, 1 (1936): 194–95.

[155] Chechenets, "Pesnia rabov," *Rabochii po metallu* 22 (10 October 1907): 3; Zorin, in *Kuznets* 7 (14 February 1908): 4; Nik. R-tskii (Rybatskii), "Pesnia pariia," *Edinstvo* 8 (10 August 1909): 3; Kvadrat, *Pechatnoe delo* 12 (23 October 1909): 6; Obradovich, "K svetu," *Ekho* (March 1912): 2 (a cutting in RGALI, f. 1874, op. 1, d. 2, l. 1); Bibik, "Bor obrechennoi," *Novaia rabochaia gazeta* 56 (13 October 1913): 2; I. Cherdyntsev and N. Dodaev in *Pervyi sbornik proletarskikh pisatelei*, 132, 143. Many examples can be found in Soviet anthologies, such as the three volumes of *Proletarskie poety* (Leningrad, 1935–39) and *Poeziia v bol'shevistskikh izdaniiakh, 1901–1917* (Leningrad, 1967).

[156] Kvadrat, "V. G. Korolenko i rabochaia demokratiia," *Zhivaia zhizn'*, 1 (21 July 1913): 5.

[157] In addition to examples in works cited in the previous notes, see Mashirov, "Ruch'i," "Na rassvete vesennyi zori," "Grebtsy," and others that appeared in *Pravda* in 1912 and 1913, reprinted in *Poeziia v bol'shevistskikh izdaniiakh*, 218–19, 227; P. Zaitsev, "Sapozhnik ia," *Kolotushka* 4 (Easter 1911): 2; A. Pomorskii, "Vesennyi zvon," *Zhizn' pekarei* 2 (29 June 1913): 4; Aleksandrovskii, in *Novaia rabochaia gazeta* 31 (13 September 1913): 2.

[158] Gorelyi, "Rabochemu-poetu," *Nashe pechatnoe delo* 29 (27 February 1916): 4.

But this other voice was hard to silence—even within oneself. One needed great faith in human goodness not to lose hope, M. A. Loginov argued in an editorial in 1910, and he admitted that it was hard for many to sustain such faith and hope.[159] All too common was the mood Aleksei Gastev described among his fellow tram workers: "unenlightened melancholy [*bezprosvetnaia toska*], impenetrable skepticism, and stagnant inertia."[160] In subtle and complex ways—for often combined with opposite moods and shaped by more involved notions of self and its place—much the same could be said of the mood among the most intellectual active workers. As we have seen, when writing of suffering, these authors tended most often to construct their accounts of misery around socially critical and even defiant narratives of inequality and oppression. However, we must not ignore the moments (and there were many) when worker-writers, including those associated with trade unions and socialist parties, felt impelled to tell others about more intimate sorrows (and, sometimes, joys), which had more ambiguous social meanings. The printer-poet Vladimir Korolev, for example, wrote of dying without ever finding love, tears of "blue longing" (*golubaia toska*), and the "hate in people's gaze."[161] Aleksei Gastev's first published work was an anguished tale of sexual passion, fear, and guilt. The hero of this tale is horrified at the sight of his own "elemental, animal passions," "weakening will" and "unhealthy and aroused imagination." When he succumbs to these drives, he experiences "a sensation of nausea and loathing, his hands seemed to be stained with blood—for several days he could not let them near food. His own self repelled him.... For a long time he could not even read his favorite authors."[162] The young socialist metalworker Vladimir Aleksandrovskii explored difficult feelings and thoughts while sitting beside a dying friend: where death appeared not a symbol of an unjust social order but the final marker of life's grim and meaningless course: "dark, faceless dread / concealed somewhere, beyond the gloom."[163]

This poem was addressed to a *compositor-poet* who had submitted a poem on misery (*gore*) to *Nashe pechatnoe delo*. Ironically, this author's pseudonym was constructed out of the word misery.

[159] *Dumy narodnye* 2 (February 1910): 1.

[160] Zorin, "Sredi tramvaishchikov" (nabrosok), *Edinstvo* 12 (21 December 1909): 11.

[161] Vladimir Korolev, *Vsem skorbiashchim* (Iaroslavl, 1915). Like many of Korolev's collections, this was printed and distributed by the local printers' union.

[162] A. Odinokii (Aleksei Gastev), *Prokliatyi vopros* (Geneva, 1904).

[163] Aleksandrovskii, "Pered razsvetom" (M.E.K.), *Novaia rabochaia gazeta* 9 (18 August 1913): 2.

Often, these reflections expanded into more explicitly existential despair over life's meaning. The awakening of nature in springtime, for example, was sometimes viewed not as a sign of hope but as only a reminder of the "melancholy, pain, and bitterness" in one's "weary soul," or of the truth that life's hardships "have no reason."[164] Many of these writers described lost hopes for a "bright life," growing feelings of anguished melancholy and depression (the term *toska* recurs constantly), and a deepening sense of the pointlessness of life.[165] Like so many of these proletarians, Sergei Obradovich, a socialist worker whose poems appeared in many labor journals, shared with readers dark thoughts about self and existence:

> I thought to myself: in this world of vanities
> I am a hollow and superfluous thing,
> Nothing and unnoticed
> Beneath the weight of suffering and misfortune...
> Loving all that the soulless world despised,
> I called upon death as if it were joy,
> And, in that indifferent darkness, in anguished doubt,
> I sought an answer to my question:
> Is there a place where life shimmers,
> Or are we fated to suffer forever.
> There was no answer.[166]

Perhaps there was one answer, however. Even within these troubled thoughts, the importance and value of speaking aloud about the inner life of the self remained clear. As a great deal of modern social and political history makes evident, this was a discourse with powerful critical and subversive potential. At the very least, even when despair lurked around the corner, there was a certain pleasure and pride even a "precious exquisite pain" in the ability to feel and express one's inner torments. It demonstrated the sensitivity and hence worth of one's inner self and creative powers. In profoundly unequal societies like prerevolutionary Russia, this was a dangerous discourse.

---

[164] Popov, "Vesna," *Chelovek* 4 (24 April 1911): 32.
[165] For example, the many poems by V. Vegenov that were the featured literary works in *Novoe pechatnoe delo* in 1911 and 1912; Kvadrat, "V. G. Korolenko i rabochaia demokratiia"; Obradovich, "Zhizn'," *Sever Rossii* (Arkhangel'sk) 1 (23 August 1913): 3 (a cutting in RGALI, f. 1874, op. 1, d. 2, l. 10); S. Gan'shin, "Tiazhelo na dushe," a manuscript poem sent to Maxim Gorky, 1914, in Arkhiv A. M. Gor'kogo, RAV–PG 37-13-1.
[166] Obradovich, "Bezsonnoiu noch'iu."

Some Observations on the Question of "Hegemonic Discourse": Language and Experience in the Scripting of Labor Roles*

William G. Rosenberg

By now the analytic implications of the "linguistic turn" have seeped deeply into the Russian backwater, even if labor history in our part of the geographic world still struggles to hold its head against the wash of post-Soviet (and other post-) critiques. Even a soft Marxist approach that emphasizes the agency of organized and self-conscious social formations— one dares not use the word "class" with less than four pages of preliminary exegesis—has to defend itself nowadays against the notion that language alone has constitutive power in social organization and development. For the moment, at least, "class" is academically respectable almost exclusively as a concept whose use creates certain kinds of (contested) social meanings, rather than identifies any objectifiable social formations.

Society-centered explanations of change in Russian and Soviet history have not only suffered displacement in these circumstances, but in some quarters, at least, have been rejected with contempt because of their imputed resemblance to reductive "Soviet" and "Marxist" historical visions. After all, did not the end of History in 1989 completely remake the past? Even a very intelligent and constructive recent effort by Geoff Eley and Keith Nield to renegotiate the analytical utility of class was dismissed by an eminent younger member of our field as the work of unsophisticated "Brezhnevites."[1] Those of us who have spent what some regard as

---

*This essay was originally prepared as an informal talk for the Roundtable on "Hegemonic Discourse" at the 1997 meeting of the American Society for the Advancement of Slavic Studies. The Roundtable was organized by the Allan K. Wildman Group for the Study of Russian Workers in Society.

[1] Geoff Eley and Keith Nield, "Farewell to the Working Class?," *International Labour and Working-Class History* 57 (Spring 2000): 1-30, and response by S. Kotkin, 48-52.

an unconscionable part of our scholarly lives explaining what used to be called "revolutionary situations" (before this discursive bath water was also thrown out with the baby) are at times scolded by our friends for imagining that anything as prosaic as social activism might actually be construed as an autonomous element in determining change.

As it affects Russian and Soviet labor history, there is a disturbing and appropriating presentism in this post-everything critique. In my view, "revisioning" the Russian or Soviet past, to use the modish neologism, cannot in any serious way be *necessitated* by the collapse of the Soviet order, since no current event in itself can fundamentally alter what was historically significant in the past. It can only prompt us to look at the past more carefully, something serious scholars do in any event (so to speak). The revising of historical understanding can only properly come from new evidence or new theoretical paradigms, like those introduced by gender and cultural studies. Historians studying Russian and Soviet workers need only engage the rich literature in West European labor history that has appeared since 1991 to shed whatever inhibitions (and resist whatever calumnies) that may have affected their work. As the new research in this volume amply testifies, the beliefs, mentalities, politics, institutions, social roles, self-images, cultures, and everyday experiences of those whose identity papers labelled them "*rabochie*" (workers) remain fertile grounds indeed for exploring the complex processes of Russian and Soviet historical development.

As we know, the critique of social history is hardly new. In West European historiography, it emerged in the 1970s and early 1980s around the interrelated issues of gender, discourse, and power, partly in response to E. P. Thompson and stimulated especially by the imaginative work of Habermas and Foucault. The question of power and politics also lay at the center of the assault by American Russianists on Russian and Soviet social history, but whereas the impetus here was to revalidate some version of the totalitarian paradigm, Europeanists broadened an understanding of power itself. Various forms and sites of social relations previously understood as distinct from the realm of politics, like the family, neighborhood, tavern, and factory workplace, were explored not simply as objects of political policy or control, but in terms of the ways they reflected hitherto unrealized forms and effects of power itself. In the broadest sense, power and politics were reconceptualized as a fundamental part of "the social," a move which led naturally to its equally complicated and important corollary: the effects of various social realms on political authority and institutions.[2]

The role of the state and the implications of culture have also been an important part of rethinking power and politics, the first in terms of an extended but de-institutionalized understanding of the ways in which the state is "present" in social spaces and relations, the second through a new appreciation of the ways that various cultural practices themselves create and reconstruct political forms and the affects of power.[3] What has become most interesting here, however, is not the efforts in some quarters to reassert the distinction between "culture" and "politics" but a fuller understanding of their apposition. Thus, it seems increasingly clear that while state institutions or policies can be usefully explored as if they were autonomous expressions of power (and useful work is clearly being done in the Russian and Soviet fields from this perspective), the diachronic effects of institutions and policies are invariably mediated by the cultural practices in which they are necessarily embedded. Similarly, the effects of autonomous cultural forms and practices on political meaning may be as consequential to policy outcomes as the political forms through which they are implemented. The currently fashionable issue of "unintended consequences" in state and public policy studies is, at its core, precisely about the power of culture, however rarely it is recognized as such or adequately described in these terms.[4]

Gender has also proven to be an extraordinarily "useful category of analysis", one that has come to expand greatly the reach of social history even as its use also sharply critiqued certain aspects of the social history approach.[5] Here the most powerful contributions, in my view,

---

[2] Geoff Eley and Keith Nield were also at the forefront of this effort with their stimulating and constructively provocative essay "Why Does Social History Ignore Politics?" *Social History* 5 (May 1980): 249–71. By now the literature is extensive. See esp. *Work in France: Representations, Meaning, Organization and Practice* eds. Steven Laurence Kaplan and Cynthia J. Koepp (Ithaca, 1986); Eleanor Accampo, *Industrialization, Family Life, and Class Relations in Saint Chamond, 1915–1914* (Berkeley, 1989); Sonya Rose, *Limited Livelihoods: Gender and Class in Nineteenth-Century England* (Berkeley, 1992); Louise Tilly and Joan Scott, *Women, Work, and Family* (New York, 1979); and *Gender and Class in Modern Europe*, eds. Laura Frader and Sonya Rose (Ithaca, 1996), among others.

[3] Eley and Nield, "Farewell to the Working Class?"

[4] See, e.g., Raymond Boudon, *The Unintended Consequences of Social Action* (London, 1982); Steven M. Gillon, *"That's Not What We Meant to Do": Reform and its Unintended Consequences in Twentieth-Century America* (New York, 2000); Judith Klinghoffer, *Vietnam, Jews, and the Middle East: Unintended Consequences* (New York, 1999).

[5] The seminal phrase, of course, is Joan Scott's. See "Gender: A Useful Category

have focused on the ways in which socially constituted categories of class have obscured radical gender-based differences in outlooks, behaviors, work relations, family life and especially everyday experience *within* well-established and recognized class formations.[6] While there has been some fine work by Russian and Soviet historians related to women and gender more generally, and at least one important new study of masculinity in the imperial period,[7] social historians in our field have been somewhat slow in absorbing the implications of Western European work in this area. I suspect this may have to do with the broader assault against social history as a whole. Thus the very complexities of paternalism in factory relations or the competitive and multiple identities of gendered social locations in other workplaces have been recognized more in terms of their implications for our understanding of new and not so new Soviet men and women than for their effect on how those identified and categorized as "workers" behaved collectively as a social formation.[8] The very ways Soviet archives have been organized has impeded this process as well.

---

of Analysis," in *Gender and the Politics of History* (New York, 1988).

[6] Here some of the best work has been done by my Michigan colleagues Kathleen Canning, Sonya Rose, and Laura Downs, from whom I have learned so much. See esp. Kathleen Canning, *Languages of Labor and Gender: Female Factory Work in Germany, 1850–1914* (Ithaca, 1996); "Gender and the Politics of Class Formation: Rethinking German Labor History," in Geoff Eley, ed., *Society, Culture, and the State in Germany 1870–1930* (Ann Arbor, 1996); Sonya Rose, *Limited Livelihoods: Gender and Class in 19th Century England* (Berkeley, 1992); *Gender and Class in Modern Europe*, eds. Laura Frader and Sonya Rose (Ithaca, 1996); Laura Lee Downs, *Manufacturing Inequalities: Gender Divisions in the French and British Metalworking Industries, 1914–1939* (Ithaca, 1995).

[7] See, e.g., Christine Ruane, *Gender, Class, and the Professionalization of Russian City Teachers* (Pittsburgh, 199); Elizabeth Wood, *Baba and Comrade: Gender and Politics in Revolutionary Russia* (Bloomington, 1997); Wendy Z. Goldman, *Women, the State, and Revolution* (Cambridge, 1993); Laurie Bernstein, *Sonia's Daughters: Prostitutes and their Regulation in Imperial Russia* (Berkeley, 1995); Mary Buckley, *Women and Ideology in the Soviet Union* (Ann Arbor, 1989); and Christine Worobec, *Possessed: Women, Witches and Demons in Imperial Russia* (DeKalb, Il, 2001), among others. Rebecca Friedman is examining constructions of masculinity in the early 19th century.

[8] But see Diane Koenker's beautifully integrated exploration, "Men against Women on the Shop Floor in Early Soviet Russia," *American Historical Review* 100 (December 1995): 1438–64; as well as Barbara Engel, *Between the Fields and the City: Women, Work, and Family in Russia, 1861–1914* (New York, 1994); Anne Bobroff-Hajal, *Working Women in Russia under the Hunger Tsars: Political Activism and Daily Life* (Brooklyn, N.Y., 1994); and Jane McDermid, *Women and Work in Russia, 1880–1930: A Study in Continuity and Change* (New York, 1998). Mary Buckley has also just completed an impressive study of women stakhanovites in rural Russia during the 1930s.

Here the embedded patterns of gendered relations and behaviors are often obscured because these subjects have never had a "categorical" life of their own. The most interesting materials are buried, often irretrievably, in records catalogued by dominant notions of "class" or "women", and within well set institutional subjects. Although the situation is changing, even Russian and Soviet labor history is still poorly integrated with gender studies, as is the field of Russian and Soviet social history as a whole.

Why the new (and actually not so new) paradigms of discourse analysis have had a relatively stronger impact on Russian and Soviet social history is an interesting question in itself. Part of the explanation may lie with the ways in which issues of language are much more readily understood in the existing documentation than questions of gender or the locations of power. Discourse analysis also links easily with traditional understandings of ideology, propaganda, and well-worn Orwellian notions of thought control. Another likely reason is that the paramount issues of social identity that engaged social historians even before the Soviet Union's collapse are also necessarily linked to forms and languages of representation. Thus, some of the most original thinking in this area was presented as early as 1988 by Leopold Haimson, whose seminal work on social stability more than two decades earlier had set the stage for Russian and Soviet social history itself.[9] And despite Ronald Suny's efforts to "offer a new way out" of the social history "problem" in his 1995 *Russian Review* article,[10] the degree to which discourse has historically been constitutive of Russian and Soviet social relations has been part of the literature as far back as Chernyshevskii's *What is to be Done?*, as Trotsky famously reaffirmed in his 1922 *Izvestiia* essay on "'You' and 'Thou' in the Red Army". Indeed, much of the effort at creating a radically new Soviet society focused precisely on issues of discourse, from forms of individual and collective address to the deadly forms of social labeling so essential to Leninist and Stalinist politics. As Jochen Hellbeck has demonstrated, a highly stylized confessional language characterized Stalinism, especially as regards the purges. It was also critical to the construction of Stalinist identities.[11] Among all forms of social and cultural representation, in

---

[9] Leopold Haimson, "The Problem of Social Identities in Early Twentieth Century Russia," *Slavic Review* 47, no. 1 (1988): 1–20. This issue also includes my commentary on Haimson's piece, "Identities, Power, and Social Interaction in Revolutionary Russia," 21–28.

[10] Ronald G. Suny, "Revision and Retreat in the Historiography of 1917: Social History and Its Critics," *Russian Review* 54 (1995): 260–64.

[11] See Jochen Hellbeck, "Fashioning the Stalinist Soul: The Diary of Stepan Podlub-

fact, language was consistently understood by Bolshevik leaders to be a central element in the complex of structures that created and replicated Soviet values, cultures, social relations, and the frameworks of political practice.

The ways that power and language conjoin are now widely recognized. The Gramscian concept of hegemony references socially dispersed patterns of power and authority, of course, but like Marx and Engels in *The German Ideology*, Gramsci himself understood language as a totality of notions and concepts within any given social order, and therefore a "hegemonic instrument" in and of itself. As such, however, it is a very tricky instrument indeed. If, as Foucault has argued famously and persuasively (and James Scott has neatly elaborated), the very exercise of power invariably produces resistance, even if only in the subtle but highly subversive form of "hidden transcripts,"[12] language also incorporates the possibility of "arming" potential resistance with a powerful "counter-hegemonic" weapon of its own. I am not thinking here so much of the well signified dissident movements of the 1960s and 1970s that played such an important role in undermining late Soviet authority, nor of the centrality of *glasnost'* to its ultimate collapse, although both illustrate the point. I have in mind rather two even more portentous ways in which power located within dominant or "hegemonic discourses" can provoke resistance: one, by structuring practices at odds with understandings of individual or collective well-being; the second, by failing to provide a vocabulary adequate to give convincing meaning to lived experience itself.

The connections I am trying to identify here might be described, with apology, by the jargony phrase "ascriptive linkages"—that is, the complex ways in which certain kinds of discourses and representations act to create or ascribe certain kinds of social roles, and how the actual experience of these roles in turn ascribes certain kinds of meanings to discourse. What interests me in particular are the effects of these linkages when the ascribed roles turn out not to function as expected. In these circumstances, the experience of acting in ascribed ways can create its own sets of meanings, overtly (or more subtly) resistant to those embedded in the discourse. While there may no longer be any real question among

---

dyi (1921–1939)," *Jahrbücher für Geschichte Osteuropas* 44 (1966): 344–73; "Writing the Self in the Time of Terror: Alexander Afinogenov's Diary of 1937," in *Self and Story in Russian History*, eds. Laura Engelstein and Stephanie Sandler (Ithaca, NY, 2000), 69–93.

[12] Michel Foucault, *Power/Knowledge: Selected Interviews and Other Writings, 1972–77* (New York, 1980); James Scott, *Domination and the Arts of Resistance. Hidden Transcripts* (New Haven, CT, 1990).

labor historians about the constitutive authority of language in forming social meaning or prefiguring social behavior, I want to suggest that an exploration of these "ascriptive linkages" can also show the *limitations* of discourse itself in this respect, especially in its ability to give meaning to the experience it may, at the same time, condition.

My point of entry into these complex matters is two very interesting sets of texts: the transcripts and documents of the so-called Plekhanov Commission, organized in April 1917 "to improve the material situation" of Russia's railroad workers, which are held in the State Archive of the Russian Federation (GARF);[13] and the protocols of the June 1917 All-Russian Conference of Factory Inspectors, which are part of the RGIA collection in St. Petersburg.[14] The Plekhanov Commission was a bilateral body composed initially of an equal number of representatives from the Executive Committee of the Petrograd Soviet and officials of the Ministry of Transport. It held its first formal session on 24 April 1917 under Plekhanov's chairmanship, and with an expanded membership of observers and technical advisors, worked actively through the spring. One of its goals was to provide a bonus from state resources to the "most needy" railroaders as a means to increase productivity and help resolve the transport snarl. On 8 May, the Commission sent a telegram to all private and state lines over the signatures of Plekhanov and N. V. Nekrasov, the Kadet minister of transport, setting up a differential system of bonus payments and new apartment allowances retroactive to 1 April. The opening sentence of the telegram stated that while the Commission could not immediately resolve the question of the general fairness of railroad wages, it had the "complete right" to come immediately to the assistance of the "most needy."[15]

There are several elements of interest in the language here. First, it effectively prefigured a responsive discussion among railroad workers themselves about the nature of "neediness." Railroaders were being "scripted," in other words, into a particular form of self-representation, one in which they identified and described themselves in terms of how and what it meant to be "needy." Responses in this form were not short in coming.

---

[13] Gosudarstvennyi arkhiv Rossiiskoi Federatsii (hereafter GARF), f. 1809 (*Kommissii Biuro Soveshchanii po uluchsheniiu material'nogo polozheniia zheleznodorozhnykh sluzhashchikh, masterovykh i rabochikh, 1917*). Related materials are in GARF, f. 5498.

[14] Rossiiskii gosudarstvennyi istoricheskii arkhiv (hereafter RGIA), f. 23 (Ministerstvo torgovli i promyshlennosti), op. 29, d. 1 (Stenograma S″ezda Fabrichnykh Inspektorov, June 1917), ll. 10–15.

[15] GARF, f. 1809, op. 1, d. 7, l. 14.

The telegram served to open a floodgate of petitions about the nature and degrees of "neediness," about the primacy of this experience in comparison to other aspects of revolutionary life, and about how this experience related to railroaders' "revolutionary expectations." Many of these petitions were hand carried to the Commission by special delegations. "Members of the railroad family," as many further described themselves, began to act out, in effect, the elements of supplication implicit in the Commission's formulation of its goals. In fact, the intense style and posture by which worker's delegations presented their "needs" soon prompted the Commission to decide unanimously to deny workers the right to address it, since otherwise it would "never get its work done."[16]

In addition, the emphasis on "most needy" also prefigured a sense of hierarchy with the worker community, one tinged with moral connotations. Some petitioners, for example, referred to themselves as "we little people," and described their conditions not only in terms of objective deprivation, but as "pitiful," one from which "we need to be saved." Others were somewhat more belligerent, lacing the language of their appeals with indignation. Indeed, one can identify in the petitions as a whole at least two competitive styles of presentation, one consistently beseeching, the other increasingly strident and belligerent. Appeals of the latter sort soon gave way to the articulation of clear "demands," especially as the Commission's work began to drag on.[17]

In both cases, it seems clear that the Commission encouraged a set of expectations among a very large number of railroad workers who readily deployed its language to consider, define, and represent themselves, that is, who used the Commission's official discourse to give particular kinds of meaning to the experience of "need." At the same time, however, the particular style of representation that the Commission's language structured reinforced the very patterns of domination and subordination that many railroad workers understood the revolutionary experience as bringing to an end. An alternative language of insistence or "demand," in other words, even against the receptive and supportive Plekhanov Commission, acquired a dignity that supplication lacked because its representations contrasted so sharply with the experience of pleading, i.e., the differing ascriptions of supplication.

In approaching its railroad worker subjects in these terms, scripting, in effect, a set of behaviors for those whose "needs" it appeared responsible, the Plekhanov Commission was also (discursively) constructing a

---

[16] GARF, f. 5498, op. 1, d. 80, l. 19.
[17] GARF, f. 1809, op. 1, dd. 3, 5, 6.

particular role for the new revolutionary state. Here was an extremely contentious "discursive field" in 1917, as we know, since representations of the state served, one might say, to construct its political and constitutional identity. The familiar points of conflict had to do, of course, with whether the institutions and value system of the state stood "above" particularistic social interests in support of universalizing "national ones," as Nekrasov and other liberal figures in the Provisional Government maintained, or necessarily reflected the particularistic interests of dominant social forces, the simplified socialist view. These contending representations clearly implied different roles for Russian labor in relation to the state, as they did for other social formations. In the first, the state was ideally an impartial adjudicator between contending social interests. Its principal function in this regard was one of mediation, itself a universal good. In the second, the state was represented as inherently partisan. Interest claims could thus be made appropriately by and through its institutions.

What is so interesting about the Plekhanov Commission in this regard is that with the goal of meeting revolutionary Russia's pressing "national" interests through a radical improvement in critical transport operations, the Commission—both a representative and a representation of the state—encouraged and even requested railroad workers both to take stock of their own grievances and to articulate them as forcefully as they could. In the language of these prominent agents, the state "spoke" (or was "prefigured") as a (paternal?) provider of bonuses and a (maternal?) reliever of want: caring, charitable, and capable, as was, by implication, the revolution it was leading. But the Commission postured the state in this way not because workers' interests were more deserving than those of other groups, and even less because some kinds of neediness were more deserving than others. Instead, it did so because the satisfaction of need and want was essential to a particular understanding of the national good, one that also assigned a particular meaning to the revolutionary experience as a whole. This possessively linked the state to a particular role for *its* (possessive form) railroad workers, whose labor was now further constructed around relations of dependency as well as the practices of supplication. Speaking as the revolutionary state, the Commission was saying, both literally and "in effect," that the satisfaction of legitimate grievances about wages, working, and living conditions was not to be gained, *nor could they be met*, by railroad workers taking matters into their own hands.

Yet it was precisely the call to take matters into their own hands that scripted the workers' roles more generally at the June 1917 Conference of Factory Inspectors, a group that as a whole prided itself for its professionalism in labor-management conflicts and its "supportive neutrality" with respect to workers' needs.[18] There was considerable division at this interesting conference on a number of issues: whether resuscitated and newly forming trade unions would be able to command the respect of their rank and file at such a politicized moment; the extent to which Russian industry was actually capable of responding even to workers' minimal demands; and the implications for all sorts of worker-management relations of what was described as the "revolutionary democratic climate," but which referred in fact to workers' day-to-day experiences in and outside their factories. But the state itself emerged clearly in the language of Conference discussions as an *independent* arbiter of conflict, not the provisioner of particular needs, as it did in the voice of the Plekhanov Commission. On the contrary, as more than one discussant put it, "the working class" was capable of defending its own interests and meeting its own needs in appropriate ways if the state could only provide sufficient institutional support through agencies like—hardly surprising—the Factory Inspectorate.

Here it was the ministries themselves, however, who were depriving the inspectors of this role and hence wrongly positioning the state, which meant of course the particular incumbents of specific ministerial positions and the various newly formed commissions and committees that were assuming what had historically been the Inspectorate's responsibilities. The Ministry of Trade and Industry was singled out in particular for no longer paying attention "to the need for labor protection," on the assumption that this whole sphere of attention was now the prerogative of the network of soviets.[19] The long-established authority of the Factory Inspectorate, recognized through "many turbulent years" as an institution that functioned to assure the state's social welfare prescriptions were both informed and enforced, was consequently being "destroyed." The newly formed Ministry of Labor was no better. Here there was interference everywhere in the settling of disputes in ways that encouraged confusion, occasioned misunderstanding, and ignored the Inspectorate altogether. As one speaker put it with some passion, to allow workers to *realize* their interests, the state had to offer appropriate counsel to *both* sides, assure informed and constructive negotiation, help chart effective outcomes, but

---

[18] RGIA, f. 23, op. 29, d. 1, esp. l. 110.
[19] RGIA, f. 23, op. 29, d. 2, l. 9.

at the same time remain strictly and unconditionally independent of partisan positions.

In the case of the Factory Inspectors Conference, in other words, the (discursive) configuring of the state thus ascribed a very activist role to Russian labor, both in terms of its self-organization (as opposed to its organization through state commissions or committees) and in terms of both state and non-state workers to act effectively in support of their self-defined interests. Insofar as the state in this particular construction failed to act through appropriately neutral institutions like the Factory Inspectorate, it was the state itself that was substantially to blame for the escalation of arbitrary and violent industrial conflict. Thus, the language of the Factory Inspectors also communicated the idea, however inadvertently, that workers activism might best be directed against the state, since it was the state itself, in the Inspectors' representation, that was bringing industry to the "brink of collapse" and Russia as a whole to the "edge of anarchy."[20]

This brings us back from several directions to the difficult issue of experience itself, and, more specifically, to the question of how something as ill defined and untidy as "living through the revolution" affected and related to these other linkages between the way the state was discursively constituted and what this constitution ascribed to the roles and behaviors of labor. The question of experience has, rightly enough, bothered critics of the linguistic turn from the day of creation, as the celebrated exchange between Joan Scott and Bryan Palmer in *ILWCH* testified so melodramatically.[21] I want to emphasize that I am not here essentializing experience in any way as some sort of foundation of historical reality or truth, but positioning its inchoate subjectivities instead as a source of memory and meaning, once they are remembered, told, ideologized, or otherwise given some discursive form. Historical experience, in other words, is more than simply the range of subjectivities one feels when living through a particular event. It constitutes instead the complex set of pre-discursive emotions or feelings whose meanings emerge through various interactions with the individuals, groups, institutions, and discourses that surround them.[22]

---

[20] RGIA, f 23, op. 29, d. 1, l. 14.

[21] Joan Scott, "On Language, Gender, and Working-Class History," and response by Bryan Palmer, *International Labor and Working-Class History* 31 (1987): 1–23.

[22] See, e.g., the discussion by Joan W. Scott and Thomas C. Holt on "The Evidence of Experience" in James Chandler et al., *Questions of Evidence: Proof, Practice and Persuasion across the Disciplines* (Chicago and London, 1994), 363–400; and the insightful piece by Kathleen Canning, "Feminist Theory after the Linguistic Turn: Historicizing

The analytical problems the concept of "experience" poses for historians—and it *is* very much a concept, as well as a set of subjectivities—are clustered around a basic epistemological issue: how to tease out of documents and other historical artifacts the meaning of lived events that shaped *contemporary* understanding and behaviors, and, even harder, how to understand *how* that contemporary meaning was created. This necessarily involves uncovering individual and collective subjectivities in some reasonably accurate way, an inherently problematic effort even with real life subjects. On one hand, the complexities of lived experience itself resists the reductions of representation; on the other, subjectivities that might clearly affect individual or collective behavior are rarely evidenced with any clarity. Their meanings are therefore often obscure not only for the historian, but even more problematically, sometimes for historical actors themselves. Behaviors that constitute "acting out," in other words, that are provoked by conflicts or emotions of which the actor is not fully aware (and thus not even recognized as "experienced"), can clearly influence social history as much as they affect individual biography, however difficult they are to evidence. Still, even in the case where subjectivities are unconsciously "acted out", abstractions, ideologies, commitments, and especially social institutions take on their own meanings largely in terms of the ways they link or *fail* to link to what historical actors understand they are experiencing.

Materiality, that is, social context, matters here as well. In my view, the Bryan Palmers have it just as wrong as the Patrick Joyces when they insist that what "matters" is simply the horse knocking over the demonstrator, not the way this experience was represented, or that "class" is simply a matter of language.[23] While the post-modernist position tends toward the assumption that *all* experience is reducible to representation, the literal materialist one implies that all pains are common, all brutalities provoke humiliation and anger, all experience, that is, is an essentialized part of socio-political life. Neither allows the possibility for a form of

---

Discourse and Experience," *Signs* 19 (1994): 368–404. I have also benefited from Geoff Eley's observations on this subject, and discussions I have had with other Michigan colleagues.

[23] In addition to Palmer, *International Labour and Working Class History*, see Patrick Joyce, *Industrial England and the Question of Class, 1840–1914* (Cambridge, 1991). Here and in the introduction to his edited volume *Class* (Oxford, 1995), Joyce substantially extends the argument initially laid out by Gareth Stedman Jones in his *Languages of Class* (New York, 1983). See the extended discussion by David Mayfield and Susan Thorne, "Social History and its Discontents: Gareth Stedman Jones and the Politics of Language," *Social History* 17, no. 2 (1992): 165–88.

experience—a realm of subjectivity—for which there is no readily available form of articulation, which can "defy" meaning, in other words, or go "begging for explanation." In these instances, experience may constitute in and of itself an ascriptive linkage to socially dominant discourses, shaping their meaning in unexpected and perhaps even unintended ways.

Both the Plekhanov Commission and the Factory Inspectors documents suggest, for instance, as do many other materials relating to those who thought of themselves as *rabochie* (workers) in 1917, that for many, the writing of letters and petitions, the formulation of demands, participation in demonstrations and negotiations with management, and especially involvement in strikes and more formal kinds of protests were all very much "reductive" experiences, if I can express it that way, in that they politicized subjectivities by giving them focused, "revolutionary" meaning. Activism itself, in other words, generated a sense of affiliation and collective attachment independently of how these affiliations and attachments were represented. Moreover, I would suggest that in the process, this experience in and of itself generated the need to find adequate descriptive and explanatory markers, that is, the need to find meaning that would "make sense" of what activists were feeling and help them find ways to express it.

Consider the case of the Petrograd laundry workers strike that began in May 1917, just as the new revolutionary state was reorganizing itself around a socialist-liberal political coalition. More than 5,500 women in nearly 200 Petrograd laundries left their jobs at this time to protest formally their working conditions and less formally the way they were being treated by men. Among their principal demands was the insistence on respectful address, a complaint that reflected the feelings of humiliation and indignity that women especially had woven tightly into Russian labor protests for years.

As the strike evolved (and the dirty laundry piled up), the quest for dignity provoked its opposite, at least according to contemporary accounts. Irons and other implements were thrown in some places both at and by the laundresses; nearby shop owners sympathetic to the owners threw boiling water at strikers; others angry that their laundry wasn't done went after the "damned vipers" and "filth" with revolvers. Newspapers with varying perspectives reported, however, that "working-class Petrograd" was rallying around the strikers. Mass meetings took place in both worker and non-worker neighborhoods where strikers were addressed by various political luminaries. In the Social Democratic and Bolshevik press, the strike was attached to a broader "working-class" protest against the "bourgeois" social and political regime, as Alexandra Kollontai and others encouraged the laundresses in their "solidarity."

But given the subjectivities that provoked the strike and the kinds of tensions it created, solidarity in this instance almost certainly made most sense in gendered terms: as loyalty among and between women, rather than simply unity within the "working class." Many other similar strikes in 1917 seemed to do the same, like the one shortly afterwards by sales clerks at Gostinnyi Dvor.[24] In these and other cases, it was not so much that a sense of affiliation as "workers" gave meaning to experience, but that experience reduced and clarified meaning, in the gendered case of the Petrograd laundresses, about what it meant to be a working woman. Thus, in more abstracted ways, one can also suggest that it is not so much that working class history is most of all the history of the *usage* of "class"—solely, or even largely, that is, the function of "hegemonic discourse"; rather, it is that labor history is also a history of the chain of experiences that *did* and *did not* find in "class" the set of meanings that explained them, the concept in Patrick Joyce's terminology "around which the meaning of being a worker could accrue."[25]

At the same time as experience reduces or focuses meaning, however, I would suggest that it can also amplify it in ways that tend to minimize differences and exaggerate commonalities. Mutual participation in events imposes commonalities that tend to blur difference; in large scale and dramatic events, in ways that tend to push difference to insignificance. The larger the scale of collective experiences, the greater this reductionist "experience curve," and hence the more appealing and powerful the common (reductive) signifiers that are sought to describe it, articulate its subjectivities, and attempt to give it meaning.

We learn further from Factory Inspectorate documents, for example, that industrial workers in revolutionary Russia became increasingly reluctant to accept the decisions of mediation boards even when they ruled in the workers' favor because their wide-spread experience with the boards generated feelings of distrust. Workers "solidified" around the feeling— the experience—of being taken advantage of, of not receiving what they could have even if they got most or all of what they said they wanted. In the case of the railroaders parading to the Plekhanov Commission, the documents suggest that the experience of subordination and supplication

---

[24] See the discussion and citations in Diane Koenker and William Rosenberg, *Strikes and Revolution in Russia, 1917* (Princeton, 1989), 3–4, 228–29, 314–16. The question of how strikes were represented generally is the subject of Chap. 7.

[25] Joyce, *Visions of the People*, 338.

was also a solidifying one. While this helped to further script their roles in relation to the Commission and its representation of the revolutionary state, it also created a new and relatively easy basis for a kind of mobilization around common and reductive identifiers quite different than the Commission members desired. Railroaders were soon being organized in far more militant fashion, leading to the paralyzing strike of the "railroad republic" in September.

Large-scale collective experiences may thus constitute in and of themselves a powerful scripting form of discourse—linking the meanings generated by smaller, more localized experiences and those projected onto larger narratives by the available repertoires of rhetoric, ideology, and action. The larger the scale, the more powerful this linkage may be, since large scale events seem to demand more urgent explanation and meaning than smaller ones. Like most other protagonists in the Russian revolutionary drama, the Factory Inspectors themselves also struggled to situate Russia's increasingly violent industrial conflict into a larger set of explanations and descriptions. Some at the June conference clearly understood that violence was becoming a discourse in itself. What was not clear (and which therefore "begged explanation") was what it signified? Hostility, anger, rejection, envy, longing, desperation? Frustration, impatience, fear, anxiety, or feelings of power? How this particular behavioral language—body language, if you will—was "read" clearly further scripted roles for both "workers" and the state, even if the meanings actually generated by the experience of violence did not necessarily correspond to those the factory inspectors and others ascribed to them.

This brings me to the final observation I want to make about the *limitations* of even hegemonic discourse in prefiguring social needs, behaviors, and identities. In a very few phrases, I would like to push our understanding of the relationship between experience and discourse in what might be called an "economic" or "materialist" direction, since I am interested in the way in which systems of exchange and the management of scarcity can themselves function both inaudibly and imperceptibly, and therefore in ways that are not readily susceptible to discursive representation, whether verbal or non-verbal. Language, after all, is essentially referential: hegemonic discourse is hegemonic because it references dominant social and political relations, even as the referencing itself composes and orchestrates these relations. But what happens when something like "economic necessity"—by which I mean the need to obtain essential goods and services—exposes someone who thinks of him or herself as a "worker" to conditions which are not readily susceptible to reference, i.e., to "unimaginable" difficulties? What happens, for example, when the evaporation of capital, a breakdown in transport, the devaluation of currency, and the absence of raw materials all create conditions that beg comprehension? Here the ascriptive power of experience *and* discourse—hegemonic or otherwise—is also likely to weaken, as individuals and groups both understand that neither "makes sense" (i.e., neither allows comprehensible interpretation) but also cannot easily find meanings that do.

In a way, this brings me full circle to my initial observations. Russian labor history may well have suffered from an overdetermined attitude of dismissal after the Soviet Union's collapse. Still, there is clearly an enormous amount of new and interesting work to be done about what should matter most to us all: understanding and giving *historical* meaning to that complex segment of imperial Russian and Soviet society whose lived experience, identity, behavior, and language were so much a part of what we can still properly understand, despite its many mis-appropriations, as Russia's momentous "revolutionary situations."

"Into the Hands of the Factory Committees":
The Petrograd Factory Committee Movement
and Discourses, February–June 1917

Michael Melancon

Factory committees arose quickly in the numerous industrial plants in Petrograd during and just after the February 1917 revolutionary crisis. Especially in state-owned enterprises, these committees from the outset wielded virtually decisive power within the factory walls. Committees in privately owned factories also exercised self-defined prerogatives that soon brought them into conflict with managers and owners. By their very nature, factory committee discourses and activities during 1917 represented an assertive vision of workers' roles in an industrialized economy, precisely as that vision interacted with the daunting wartime-revolutionary problems confronting workers and their factories. Faced with common crises and united by similar outlooks, factory committee leaders quickly contacted one another. Within weeks of the February Revolution, the committee activists had forged umbrella organizations for many of the capital's largest factory committees. By early summer, these same activists had summoned the first conference of Petrograd factory committees, which, in turn, lay the groundwork for an all-Russian factory committee structure. The events and strategies under discussion here therefore underlay the entire organized Russian factory committee movement, of such great (albeit ephemeral) note during 1917.

This study seeks to recapture the early experience of the Petrograd factory committees and their leading activists. Even as it lays out a chronological framework of principal events, the study will pay special attention to the discourses utilized by factory committee activists during the first half of 1917. These discourses—captured in speeches, resolutions, and programs—measure worker aspirations and outlooks on a series of

M. Melancon, A. Pate, *New Labor History*, Bloomington, IN: Slavica, 2002

central economic, social and political questions. The study proceeds on an assumption that the 1917 workers' movement exercised indisputable—but not exclusive—influence on the course of events that year. Its conclusions will suggest a fresh approach to analyzing the workers' movement in the revolution unobscured by adherence to any particular ideology or the prerogatives of any particular party. Examining factory committee experience during the movement's formative period will help recapture significant aspects of workers' thought and outlook on their own situation in the midst of revolution, on the basis of which much that workers did and much that occurred in general will become explicable. Since many factory committee activists and, to some degree the movement itself, had political involvements, one mode of analysis, among others, will concern the respective roles, such as they were, of parties in the ideational origins, rise, and functioning of the factory committee movement.

Published and unpublished worker memoirs, as well as various secondary studies, provide information about the rise of factory committees in the capital's plants beginning during the last days of February 1917. Well-attended workers' meetings elected committees to act as workers' spokespersons both within the respective plants, that is, with the managers and owners, and, if necessary, with whatever outside entities the plants came into contact.[1] Collective analysis of memoir accounts and other sources suggests that workers tended to elect to factory committees (and soviets) already trusted activists, mostly February crisis strike committee members.[2] Leiberov, a close student of the February Revolution's dynamics, emphasizes the workers' almost exclusive trust in the strike committees (rather than in individual party collectives) and confirms the close identity between the strike and early factory committees.[3] Voronkov, Arsenal strike and factory committee member and

---

[1] Descriptions of the process can be found in S. A. Smith, *Red Petrograd: Revolution in the factories 1917–1918* (Cambridge, MA, 1983), 80–86; Z. V. Stepanov, *Fabzavkomy Petrograda v 1917 godu* (Leningrad, 1985), 10–24; I. A. Baklanova, *Rabochie Petrograda v period mirnogo razvitiia revoliutsii (mart–iiun' 1917 g.)* (Leningrad, 1978), 88–114; and Gennady Shkliarevsky, *Labor in the Russian Revolution: Factory Committees and Trade Unions, 1917–1918* (New York, 1993), 1–19.

[2] Of most direct interest in this regard are worker memoirs in Rossiiskii gosudarstvennyi arkhiv sotsial'no-politicheskoi istorii (hereafter RGASPI), f. 70, Istpart TsK RKP(b), Vospominaniia o fevral'skoi revoliutsii, oktiabr'skoi revoliutsii i grazhdanskoi voine, Petrograd, dd. 546–627. See also comments in *Petrogradskii sovet rabochikh i soldatskikh deputatov v 1917 godu. Protokoly, stenogrammy* . . . 5 vols. (St. Petersburg, 1993), 1: 86–87.

[3] I. P. Leiberov, "Petrogradskii proletariat vo vseobshchei politicheskoi stachke 25 fevralia 1917 g.," in *Oktiabr' i grazhdanskaia voina v SSSR: Sbornik statei* (Moscow,

soviet deputy, recalled how this took place at his plant. At a general plant meeting early on 27 February, "we [members of the strike committee] were all elected" into the new factory committee, which also was mandated to choose soviet deputies. Members of the newly chosen factory committee repaired to a nearby tavern, "Stop-Signal," to discuss priorities and choose a soviet deputy (Voronkov). The new committee, continued Voronkov, contained none of the conservative (presumably pro-war, non-socialist) workers who had previously wielded some influence at Arsenal.[4] Not surprisingly, considerable continuity existed between pre- and post-February factory leadership groups (minus conservatives as of the latter), an interpretative turn that applies to the election of soviet deputies as well. Although the question of provenance will receive further attention below, a preliminary conclusion is that the factory committees that arose throughout the empire's industrial establishments reflected a natural, direct outgrowth of the pre-1917 factory level workers' movement.[5]

A notable aspect of the early factory committee movement is that questions of parties simply did not arise. In the factories, workers selected individuals known and trusted by them. As in most worker-oriented organizations during the first half of 1917, including the soviets, in the matter of electing factory committees this set of priorities favored Socialist Revolutionary (SR) and Menshevik cadres, the largest and most influential in most plants at the time. Regardless, an array of anarchists, Social Democrats (SDs), populists, and non-party workers became involved. Overt partisanship had no place. The movement had a generalized "socialist" cast, understood as including all forms of radical worker-oriented socialist, anarchist, and non-party activism.

From the outset, factory committees confronted a wide array of problems concerning the internal operations of individual plants. In general, they attempted to defend workers' rights, especially in terms of salaries and work hours. In privately-owned concerns, heavy factory committee intervention into matters of administration and production (as befit some workers' understanding of "workers' control") proved impossible because owners and managers blocked the way. Consequently, during March the

---

1966), 41.

[4]RGASPI, f. 70, op. 3, d. 559, Recollections of Voronkov, l. 23 ("none of the old conservatives were elected into the factory committee").

[5]Shkliarevsky's analysis of the rise of factory committees in various cities indicates the similarity of the movement everywhere. Shkliarevsky, *Labor in the Russian Revolution*, 1–63 passim.

Petrograd Soviet executive committee had found it necessary to carry out direct negotiations with the manufacturers' association to achieve the eight-hour day in private plants, whereas the factory committees in the state plants had simply proclaimed the shorter work day.[6]

Because of their nature as components of a state structure undergoing revolution, state plants offered—indeed necessitated—a wide scope for factory committee intervention. The two largest segments of the capital's state factories fell respectively under the categories of the artillery and naval administrations, each with primarily military officers as managers. Prior to February, the state plants' military administrators had applied harsh wartime discipline, a factor that doubtlessly explains their abrupt absence upon the old regime's fall. Thus when workers returned from the February strikes to the Arsenal, Izhorsk, Sestroretsk, Baltic Shipbuilding, Cartridge, Pipe, and other such plants (over twenty large defense plants belonged to the artillery and naval administrations), they found plants threatened with closure due to the lack of management personnel. In their speeches to the late May factory committee conference, prominent factory committee organizers N. Voronkov and V. M. Levin both emphasized the workers' dilemma. In Voronkov's words, when the workers returned "they saw that administrators had abandoned many of these plants to fate." Levin's remarks continued the story: "it was necessary to put these factories back into operation without the administrators. But how?... the plants quickly elected factory committees, with the help of which normal life was resumed at the plants and factories.... The plants fell into the hands of the factory committees."[7] The last comment, which symbolizes the 1917 factory committee experience and discourse, gives this study its title.

Some commentators have attributed the desire of the workers to keep their plants in operation to their alleged "defensist" or pro-war proclivities. In this interpretation, the primarily SR and Menshevik leadership in the big defense plants, now gathered in elected factory committees and not wishing to see war production cut off, actively intervened in their management.[8] Indeed, when a little later the bourgeois press, followed

---

[6]*Petrogradskii sovet . . . Protokoly*, 219, 224–25.

[7]Gosudarstvennyi arkhiv Rossiisskoi Federatsii (hereafter GARF), f. 472, *Fabrichno-zavodskaia konferentsiia Petrograda*, op. 1, d. 1, ll. 11–12, 30–31, 43–44; A. M. Pankratova, *Fabzavkomy Rossii v bor'be za sotsializatsiiu fabriki* (Moscow, 1923), 179; Baklanova, *Rabochie Petrograda*, 99.

[8]An example is Smith (*Red Petrograd*, 60), who states that "the crucial reason why factory committees took over the running of state enterprises was to ensure that production for the war effort was not jeopardized."

by indignant soldiers, leveled accusations at defense plant workers about their alleged slacking off in production to achieve the eight-hour workday, the state enterprise factory committees (as well as those in private plants) fended off the criticism. They proclaimed that, after achieving shorter work hours "in principle," they were not only perfectly willing to work overtime but were doing so, thereby fulfilling their patriotic duty in support of the soldiers at the front. On 30 March, the Cartridge plant (artillery administration) worker committee even issued the month's day-by-day production figures to demonstrate the effectiveness of the plant's workers, whom it called "true patriots of the motherland in the midst of war's travails."[9]

Regardless, ardent pro-war sentiment among workers in state-owned enterprises had little to do with worker intervention in the plants' operations. After all, they had just participated in stubborn anti-war and anti-tsar demonstrations that had brought down the regime. Refusing to return to work without the eight-hour day, they had simply decreed it "on their own" (*iavochnym poriadkom*), aided in this demarche by the fortuitous absence of the managers. Whatever verbal formulations these workers deployed to protect themselves from accusations, none of their activities remotely fit the profile of ardent defensism. Their first concern in keeping the factories running had been to avoid joblessness, a serious matter in inflation-ridden wartime Petrograd, although, of course, workers hardly wished to see German invasion of the homeland because of a collapse of military production. As noted above, in his remarks about factory committee formation, Voronkov, the Arsenal factory committee chair, later noted that the committee was completely bereft of conservative workers.[10] The history of the state factory committees during the first half of 1917 suggests something quite different from conservatism or ardent defensism. These very committees and their leaders forged the famous 1917 factory committee movement, with its radical associations and symbolism.

In any case, when workers returned to work at the big defense plants, usually around 8 March, their newly-elected factory committees found no choice but to take very broad action. In Smith's account, "in the absence of management, the factory committees took responsibility for running

---

[9]*Izvestiia* 33 (6 April 1917) published pronouncements to this effect from factory committees and worker meetings at the privately-owned Benua, Simens-Gal'ske, and Shetinin plants. See also *Fabrichno-zavodskie komitety Petrograda. Protokoly* (Moscow, 1982), 199–202.

[10]RGASPI, f. 70, op. 3, d. 559, l. 23; GARF, f. 472, op. 1, d.1, ll. 31–32.

the state enterprises by setting up 'executive committees,' comprising workers' representatives, engineers, technicians, and, in some cases, members of the old administration." Since no rules existed to guide the way, each committee created its own ad hoc regulations about administrative matters and workers' rights. For example, most plant committees quickly passed regulations establishing their right to "fire" objectionable administrators. In some cases, old managerial personnel began to reappear at their plants, only to find themselves subjected to entirely new worker-imposed regulations, including the possibility of being fired. So-called "mixed" administrations often arose, in many cases on an elective principle and with almost unlimited factory committee oversight and control.[11]

The enormous responsibilities assumed by the state enterprise factory committees, in the presence of no regulations or previous experience, naturally led the committees to consult with one another. For example, on 13 March the Arsenal factory committee sent three representatives (the SR Voronkov, the Menshevik Samodurov, and Kabanov) to a meeting of military plant managers scheduled at the Main Artillery Administration to discuss new operational procedures. At the meeting, a motley mixture of worker delegates and old-line managers, factory committee representatives received quick approval of a series of demands—the eight-hour day, pay for all workers during the recent revolutionary strikes, and, perhaps most notably for this study's purposes, funding for a unified factory committee organization. The factory committees' easy success in its various requests suggests the decisive power workers now wielded. Later that day the three Arsenal delegates attended a gathering of all artillery administration factory committees, now funded by the Main Artillery Administration. This was the first step toward the creation of an umbrella organization. The meeting opened with representatives from the Cartridge, Gun, Pipe, Porokhov, Sestroretsk, Arsenal, Small Arms, Optical, Nail, and several other plants. At the urging of the Cartridge plant delegates, the delegates discussed "organizing the administration of the plants." As noted, the factory committees were already doing just that. In some cases, the committees appointed factory directors, as occurred at the Cartridge and Sestroretsk plants. At others, such as the Pipe and Okhta plants, the committees themselves directly assumed all management functions. Unresolved debate among factory committee delegates on 13 March seems to have centered around a plan offered by the Cartridge plant delegates calling for "autonomous factory management" and

---

[11]Some examples are *Fabrichno-zavodskie komitety Petrograda. Protokoly* (Moscow, 1979), 104, 108, 112; and *Fabrichno-zavodskie komitety* (1982), 20–23, 189.

an alternative plan from the Arsenal delegates that involved coordinating management among various plants. Debate aside, both versions assumed the factory committees' command functions. The gathering also created an artillery administration bureau and elected Voronkov to chair it.[12]

These measures marked the factory committee movement's first organizational steps. Toward the end of the month, on 28 March, a second conference of artillery plant committees met, this time under altered conditions. The Provisional Government had by this time reformed and democratized the two military administrations, so that acceptable hierarchical managerial structures were in place. At the same time, the bourgeois press campaign had placed the military-oriented plant workers on the defensive. As a result, the factory committees decided to relinquish administrative control of the plants, the immediate assumption of which had never been a part of socialist programs. Having accomplished their task of keeping the plants open and achieving tolerable working conditions, the artillery factory committees resolved at their 28 March conference that "until the achievement of full socialization of the economy, state and private, workers will not undertake responsibility for the technical and administrative-economic organization of production and refuse to participate in the organization of production." The committee movement still maintained the right to fire unacceptable administrators and to work out regulations for an ongoing worker-elected factory committee movement on the basis of *"full democracy and collegiality"* (emphasis in original).[13] Regardless of their apparent step backward under pressure, the workers did not abandon the idea of full-blooded workers' control, toward which the factory committee movement was dedicated. This was a tactical retreat until "full socialization of the economy," semantically posed as not distant. In any case, in practice the factory committees' heady new interventionism proved difficult to put aside. By the time of the late May Petrograd factory committee conference, most factory committee activists were already pushing for the "full socialization of the economy" under a socialist-aligned government.

The 28 March committee conference noted that many plants were experiencing fuel and raw material shortages that were responsible for

---

[12] *Fabrichno-zavodskie komitety* (1982), 25–27, 30; *Izvestiia* 37 (11 April 1917); A. S. Gaponenko, *Rabochii klass Rossii v 1917 godu* (Moscow, 1970), 353; Smith, *Red Petrograd*, 61. Smith mistakenly attributes to 13 March the artillery administration factory committees' decision of 28 March, when conditions had changed, to refrain from heavy administrative intervention. The point of the 13 March meeting was to discuss plant management by factory committees in lieu of absent managers.

[13] *Izvestiia* 28 (30 March 1917), 33 (11 April 1917); Smith, *Red Petrograd*, 62–63.

production shortfalls, which "rumor mongers" were blaming on workers. Later, leaders of the factory committee movement such as Voronkov and Levin insisted that, in the face of scandal about worker motivations and even after overall control had passed back to the democratized artillery and naval administrations, the factory committees had often used their ties and influence to obtain needed fuel and materials to avoid collapses of production. Although the state factory committees now officially assumed responsibility only for matters of "internal regulation" (workers' rights and relations with administration, as well as the right to remove offending bosses), they exercised de facto involvement in production by, among other things, obtaining necessary materials. Smith concludes that, even after the re-establishment of conventional administration, the artillery (and other state) factory committees intruded themselves deeply in plant operations, with Arsenal and one or two others leading the way, whereas committees in private plants lagged behind.[14]

In tandem with the rise of the artillery administration committee movement, the naval administration plants underwent a similar process both in terms of chronology and substance. The first joint meeting of naval factory committee representatives occurred on 18 March and the first citywide conference took place on 27 March. During March the factory committees of the Admiralty and Baltic shipbuilding plants undertook responsibilities in the realm of hiring and firing of administrative personnel and continued to exercise considerable administrative control after management's return. (Smith suggests that other naval plant committees played a somewhat lesser role.) On 15 April, the naval and artillery committees held a joint conference. Thereafter, while maintaining separate organizations the two groups worked in unison.

The joint naval-artillery factory committee conference passed a set of resolutions in mid-April leaving no doubt as to the resolve of the committees to intervene in all aspects of factory life. Under a general formula that stated that "the all-plant committee [of a given plant]... controls the activities of factory management in the administrative, economic, and technical areas," the conference asserted the committees' right to organize the entire internal order of factories and pass on all hiring and firing, including of administrators. At the same time, the resolution repeated the late March artillery committee conference's determination "not to take responsibility... for production... until the accomplishment of the full socialization of the national economy." As a result, "the all-plant committee

---

[14] *Izvestiia* 28 (30 March 1917); GARF, f. 472, op. 1, d. 1, ll. 11–12, 30–31; Smith, *Red Petrograd*, 64.

enters factory administration with only an advisory voice." With these almost contradictory formulas, the committees asserted control over all individual aspects of internal factory life, while divesting themselves of overall responsibility for production shortfalls.[15]

The question of the political orientation of the state plant factory committee movement has received some comment in existing studies. About the artillery plant committee movement, Baklanova states forthrightly, that "it was organized by Bolsheviks," thus continuing an interpretational line developed quite early, as when one 1927 account described "the obvious influence of a Bolshevik kernel organized in the factories of the artillery administration." Shkliarevsky seconds this stance by calling the artillery administration factory committees a "Bolshevik stronghold." Somewhat less categorically, Smith claims that the members of the artillery plant organizational bureau "were moderate Bolsheviks and radical SRs, in the main." The only evidence about the naval committee movement's overall make-up is Baklanova's statement about the 20 June naval committee conference that it occurred "under the rather powerful influence" of the SR and Menshevik parties, a probably definitive evaluation.[16]

The already noted list of artillery administration plants and that of the naval administration (Admiralty, New Admiralty, Okhta, Baltic, Obukhov, Izhorsk, and several others) leaves no room for doubt that in both cases the factory committees were primarily SR and Menshevik, with a tilt toward the former. Bolsheviks had limited representation in the early factory committees of the Arsenal, Sestrorestk and Izhorsk plants. In all the others they had few or no representatives. Of the artillery organizational bureau members (Zov, Evseev, Voronkov, Levkin, and Tumpovskii), whom Baklanova characterized as "Bolsheviks" and Smith as "moderate Bolsheviks and radical SRs," only Zov can be identified as a Bolshevik. Voronkov and Levkin were SRs. Evseev and Tumpovskii were likely to have been Mensheviks, bringing the bureau into line with the actual make-up of artillery factory committees. In any case, this early organizational bureau reflected the existing artillery factory committees and fulfilled their desires. For example, the Arsenal plant chose

---

[15]GARF, f. 472, op. 1, d. 1, ll. 41–42; Baklanova, *Rabochie Petrograda*, 112; *Fabrichno-zavodskie komitety* (1979), 32–35, 41, 108–09, 190–98; Smith, *Red Petrograd*, 64–65; *Oktiabr'skaia revoliutsiia i fabzavkomy: Materialy po istorii fabrichno-zavodskikh komitetov*, 2 vols. (Moscow, 1927), 1: 30–32; N. P. Dmitriev, "Petrogradskie fabzavkomy v 1917 godu," *Krasnaia letopis'* 23 (1927): 71.

[16]Baklanova, *Rabochie Petrograda*, 99, 112; Smith, *Red Petrograd*, 61–62; Dmitriev, "Petrogradskie fabzavkomy," 72; Shkliarevsky, *Labor in the Russian Revolution*, 21. Shkliarevsky calls the naval plant committees "a stronghold of the moderate socialists."

the SR Voronkov, the Menshevik Samodurov and one non-party activist to represent the plant at the 15 April joint factory committee meeting. With its primarily SR-Menshevik make-up, the Sestroretsk committee chose, among others, the Bolshevik Zov to act as its liaison with other committees. Plant committees selected a range of representatives reflective of their general make-up and orientation, with no overt mention of party membership. As noted, the artillery organizational bureau chose the SR Voronkov as chair.[17] Throughout the first half of 1917 and even beyond most state factory committee activists, leaders, and representatives happened to be SR-Menshevik oriented. Although parties as such played no role in these affairs, to the limited extent that it is possible to speak of the movement's political orientation, it was SR and Menshevik, with a nod toward the former, in terms of activists.

Besides the activities of the state plants, the March–April period also witnessed mostly desultory attempts to create district level factory committee organizations. During March, an abortive plan arose in the Narva district to coordinate activities and functions of the various committees. In various parts of the city and environs, the Izhorsk, San-Galli, and other factory committees sent out feelers about establishing links with other factory committees, usually with no results. The first successful district organization arose when several Vasil′eostrov plant committees, including Baltic Shipbuilding, met together on 29 March to set up an ongoing organization. During May a similar "district factory committee council" arose in the Nevskii district, at the initiative of Nevskii Shipbuilding. During the famous April crisis about Miliukov's note to the Allies, contacts between the Arsenal and Old Lessner plants led to a meeting of Vyborg district factory committees to discuss appropriate responses. The meeting also laid down plans to create an ongoing district organization, for which purpose it scheduled a founding session for 2 May. Lacking further information, Baklanova and Stepanov reasonably conclude that a unified Vyborg factory committee organization did not develop, although, it should be noted, materials of the Arsenal and Cartridge committees indicate ongoing ad hoc contacts among Vyborg District factory committees.[18] Although factory committee councils functioned in some districts, only the Vasil′eostrov district council played a discernible role in convening the Petrograd factory committee conference of late May–June 1917.

---

[17] *Izvestiia*, no. 28 (30 March 1917), no. 33 (11 April 1917); *Fabrichno-zavodskie komitety* (1979), 607; RGASPI, f. 70, op. 3, g. 559, l. 25.

[18] Stepanov, *Fabzavkomy Petrograda*, 30–31; Baklanova, *Rabochie Petrograda*, 96–98; *Fabrichno-zavodskie komitety* (1979), 203, 613; (1982), 74, 78, 214, 218.

Nevertheless, factory committee materials suggest a constant round of gatherings during April, May, and June of the artillery and naval administration committees (both jointly and separately), as well as of various other subdivisions of the factory committee movement. Out of this collegial context, characterized by constant consultations among several movement leaders, came the first unification impulse. Specifically, at the 29 April session of the Putilov factory committee, V. M. Levin, committee secretary, suggested that it was "necessary to convene a conference of factory committees of all Petrograd." As a result, the Putilov factory committee, chaired by the Bolshevik A. Vasil'ev, with the Left Menshevik M. Rozenshtein as assistant and the Left SR Levin as secretary, resolved to "issue a call in the name of the Putilov factory committee" about creating an organizing bureau for this purpose. Although the Putilov plant, as a private concern, was not a member of the various state plant administrations, on several counts it was not accidental that it played an initiating role. For one thing, it was much the largest industry in the city and the country, with 34,000 wartime workers. Consequently, it had always loomed large in the various strike movements and demonstrations, including those that toppled the tsarist regime. Furthermore, Putilov was a military production enterprise par excellence, on the basis of which its committee had close ties with the artillery and naval committee movements.[19]

---

[19] *Raionnye sovety Petrograda v 1917 godu*, 3 vols. (Moscow and Leningrad, 1964–66), 2: 125–29; N. P Paialin, "Putilovskii zavod v gody imperialisticheskoi voiny," *Krasnaia letopis'* 46–47 (1932): 182–84; *Fabrichno-zavodskie komitety* (1979), 415, 437, 442; *Putilovtsy vo trekh revoliutsiiakh*, ed. S. D. Okun' (Moscow and Leningrad, 1933), xl. Oddities exist in the Soviet-era reportage about the Putilov factory committee and the role of V. M. Levin in the organization of the factory committee conference. For example, in the index to *Fabrichno-zavodskie komitety* (1979), 643, some references report Levin as V. Levin, whereas the crucial ones about the factory committee movement report him as "I. V. Levin." V. M. Levin was quite well-known in 1917 as the chief organizer of the factory committee conference and, as such, a familiar figure to Soviet-era historians of these matters, such as B. D. Gal'perina, the editor of the volume in question. The fictive birth of "I. V. Levin," who, as nonexistent, handily escaped identification as an SR, reflected the sensitivity of the factory committee movement in Soviet-era historiography. Consider in comparison N. Popov's statement in the the above-named *Putilovtsy vo trekh revoliutsiiakh*, xl: "Three representatives from Putilov went into the organizational bureau of the [factory committee] conference. The secretary of the Putilov zavkom, V. M. Levin, directed the work of the conference." Having reported the individual accurately, Popov omitted to mention that he was a Left SR. The Bolshevik alignment of the factory committee movement was a linchpin of Soviet era analysis of the 1917 workers' movement. Aspects of the factory committee movement's history had, therefore, to be retroactively "Bolshevized" or simply obscured. Western commentators often inadvertently repeat or even embroider upon the Soviet

On 4 May, Levin reported back to the Putilov committee about "negotiations with the... bureau of artillery factory committees regarding the organization of an all-Petrograd factory committee conference and about... the creation of an organizational bureau." At this point the Putilov committee appointed Levin, Rozenshtein, and the Bolshevik A. Bogdanov as representatives to the proposed bureau. The negotiations mentioned by Levin were with his fellow SR, Voronkov, who chaired the artillery administration bureau.

Whether or not the Putilov committee ever issued a "call" to all factory committees is not clear, since no such item appeared in the newspapers. Levin's contact with Voronkov sufficed since the artillery administration bureau had just arranged a joint conference with the naval administration committees. Between these two networks of over 21 large concerns, which had ties with numerous other defense-oriented concerns and which were located in every section of the city and environs, word could be spread everywhere. The conference's official organizational report stressed the Putilov-artillery bureau connection, with some input from private plants and the Vasil′eostrov district committee, as the origin of the Petrograd organizational bureau that summoned the late May conference. Thus it was that the two individuals who reported to the inaugural factory committee conference sessions about the development of the factory committee movement and the convening of the conference itself were Levin and Voronkov. Organizational committee and other materials also make quite clear that Rozenshtein played a very active role in the organization of the conference. The organizational bureau's records disclose no sign of a Bolshevik role in organizing the conference.[20] The Bolshevik Bogdanov, Putilov bureau delegate along with the SR Levin and the Menshevik Rozenshtein, dropped completely out of sight. As regards secondary Bolshevik roles, it might be recalled that Vasil′ev chaired the Putilov committee session that issued the initial call for the conference and Zov, as artillery administration bureau member, had some involvement.[21]

---

versions, as, for example, when Shkliarevsky (*Labor in the Russian Revolution*, 28–29, 105) describes Levin as a "radical Bolshevik labor leader."

[20] GARF, f. 472, op. 1, d. 2, Organizational Bureau materials, handwritten note of 31 May; *Pravda* 70 (14 [1] June 1917).

[21] *Fabrichno-zavodskie komitety* (1979), 443–44. At the 26 May session of the Putilov factory committee, one committeeman noted "the absence from today's session of the members of the [factory committee conference] organizational bureau Rozenshtein and Levin, who should report to us in detail about how the affairs of the organizational bureau are progressing . . . It would be interesting to know the contents of Levin's

At this point, the newly formed all-Petrograd organizational bureau elected Levin as chair, while the other two active members were Voronkov and Rozenshtein (only their names appear in the records). The organizational bureau took the next step in the convening of the Petrograd conference of factory committees by publishing an appeal in *Izvestiia* on 26 May. Addressed to "All worker factory committees, councils of worker elders, [and] railroad and transport workers," it urged them to prepare for the upcoming Petrograd conference and for an all-Russian congress thereafter. The appeal contained a number of questions proposed for discussion. These concerned the state of Petrograd industry, control and regulation of production, tasks of the factory committees, unemployment, the role of factory committees in labor unions, the creation of a "unified economic center" of factory committees and labor unions, and the obtaining of fuel and raw materials.[22] The organizers thus visualized an active and expanding role for factory committees, including a national center created in cooperation with the national labor union movement.

The Petrograd factory committee conference opened on 30 May at the Tauride Palace, continued its sometimes tumultuous deliberations until 3 June, and even witnessed one disgruntled group's temporary abandonment of the hall. The organizational bureau's handwritten notes of 31 May list the existing organizing collective, Levin, Voronkov, and Rozenshtein, as members of the mandate commission. Two other individuals mentioned, Samoilov and Rybakov (perhaps Bolsheviks or representatives of private factory committees), subsequently disappear from factory committee sources without a trace. In its conference reportage, *Pravda* characterized the organizing bureau as consisting of "besides Bolsheviks, two SRs and one Menshevik," a semantic exaggeration of the Bolsheviks' minimal role in leading the movement and organizing the conference.

Archival and newspaper reports elucidate the events of the conference. At the opening, Levin, as organizational bureau chair, suggested a conference presidium of A. Shliapnikov from the Metal-Workers' Union, N.

---

report [to the upcoming conference] since he is more or less the Putilov representative on the organizational bureau for the convening of the conference". GARF, f. 72, Tsentral′nyi sovet fabrichno-zavodskikh komitetov, op. 1, d. 1, ll. 1–3, "Report on convening of the conference" states: "a meeting of the Putilov factory committee invited factory committees of the state concerns and then private concerns to a general conference . . . An organizational bureau of the private, state and Putilov plants took shape" and so forth. V. M. Levin's address (ll. 11–12) and Voronkov's address (ll. 30–32) to the June conference also discuss these matters.

[22] GARF, f. 472, op. 1, d. 1, l. 10; *Volia naroda* 29 (2 June 1917); *Izvestiia* 75 (26 May 1917), 79 (31 May 1917), and 81 (2 June 1917).

Glebov-Avilov from the Central Bureau of Labor Unions, G. Fedorov from the executive committee of the Petrograd Soviet, as well as Voronkov, Rozenshtein and Ia. Sverdlov (see discussion below) from the organizational bureau. After approval of this list by the delegates, Fedorov greeted the delegates from the presidium. Levin then made the organizational bureau report (not G. Zinov'ev, as reported in one secondary source). Levin began his speech by noting that, just as the revolution had created its new political organization in the soviet, so the workers' movement had created a new form of organization in the factory committees. He ended with an appeal to "create a powerful factory committee center that would direct, help build up, and... attain the maximum influence of the working class on... the Russian national economy, [as well as] bring to an end the destructive imperialist war and the big bourgeoisie's rapaciousness."[23]

After this first of many militant speeches at the conference, Levin introduced a speakers' list that included the Minister of Labor M. Skobelev, Zinov'ev, Glebov-Avilov, V. I. Lenin (who spoke the next day), the anarchist worker Zhuk, the Right Menshevik F. Cherevanin, D. Riazanov, Voronkov, and a number of workers. Focusing on restoration of the national economy, the opening round of speeches delineated two fundamental points or view. The first (radical) alternative found its initial exposition in Levin's inaugural speech, subsequently defended and developed by Zinov'ev, Riazanov, Voronkov, Lenin, and, with some variations, the anarchist Zhuk. This position emphasized the role of the workers, through the auspices of the organized factory committee movement (in some versions, in coordination with the labor unions), in controlling the national industrial economy. The second (moderate) alternative was best captured by Skobelev's comment that "the regulation and control of industry... is not the affair of an individual class, it is a state matter." This latter viewpoint received support not only from right socialists such as Cherevanin and the worker Tkachenko ("we are living in the era of the bourgeois democratic revolution"), but from labor union activist Glebov-Avilov. Although he loudly proffered his "SD-Bolshevik" credentials, Glebov-Avilov insisted that the economy had to be run "in cooperation

---

[23]GARF, f. 472, op. 1, d. 1, ll. 10–12; *Pravda* 69 (13 [31 May] June 1917); *Izvestiia* 78 (30 May 1917), 79 (31 May 1917); Shkliarevsky, *Labor in the Russian Revolution*, 28–29. *Pravda*'s account of the presidium election differs from the account in *Izvestiia* and in the archival documents in that, as opposed to the latter two sources, it claimed a six-person presidium, including four Bolsheviks, a Left Menshevik, and the SR Voronkov. Shkliarevsky correctly notes that V. M. Levin made the "keynote report" at the conference but, as noted, misidentifies him as a Bolshevik.

with state power," as a result of which workers should go "hand in hand with the Provisional Government."[24]

Debate on this vast question continued into the second day, interrupted by a first (and only overt) round of partisan squabbling. The drama began when the Menshevik Dalin, seizing the floor out of order, vociferously objected to the exclusion of "Mensheviks" from the speakers' list. In view of Skobelev's and Cherevanin's prominent placing in the list, Dalin evidently implied that they had represented the Provisional Government rather than the Menshevik party. Indeed, Skobelev's and Cherevanin's views were much more moderate than those of most Mensheviks, although at this conference Dalin and most other Mensheviks also defended moderate positions. When the plenum declined on a 230–128 vote, Dalin, "together with SRs and Mensheviks," claimed the archival transcripts, "abandoned the meeting hall." In response to urgent appeals, Dalin returned a few minutes later to announce that his group would agree to participate further only if allowed to speak on each question and if the presidium were re-organized to reflect the "conference's participating groups," a matter we shall return to below. In any case, Dalin's tactics and their results indicate, among other things, some rank-and-file objections to the heavy (and artificial) Bolshevik overweighing of the conference's presidium. The sometimes confusing archival record indicates that re-elections then created a presidium of three Bolsheviks (Fedorov, Shliapnikov, and Sverdlov), two SRs (Voronkov and Cherniakov), and one Menshevik (Rozenshtein), with the only change being the replacement of the Bolshevik Glebov-Avilov by the SR Cherniakov. None of the presidium's Bolsheviks had any connection whatsoever with the factory committee movement. Of presidium members, Voronkov received the highest vote, followed by Sverdlov and the rest. For some reason, the organizational bureau and conference chair, the SR Levin, is not listed on the presidium or, at least, was not mentioned in the discussion. Perhaps his membership was assumed. Cherniakov apparently represented the moderate SR-Menshevik group who had earlier left the hall. Clearly wishing to avoid confrontation and potential dissolution, the conference also yielded on the speaker question, as a result of which Dalin and other Mensheviks took full part in the debates.[25]

Among others, Dalin, Lenin, Zinov'ev, Voronkov, and a number of worker-activists entered the fray about the question of economic collapse.

---

[24]GARF, f. 472, op. 1, d. 1, 13–38; *Izvestiia* 78 (30 May 1917), 79 (31 May 1917); *Pravda* 69 (13 June [31 May] 1917), 70 (14 [1] June 1917).
[25]GARF, f. 472, op. 1, d. 1, 1.30; d. 2, l. 5; *Izvestiia* 80 (1 June 1917).

Lenin polemicized sharply with fellow Bolshevik Avilov: "Why hasn't our coalitional ministry with socialists produced workers' control?" Voronkov outlined a militant case for workers' control in the struggle against "economic collapse" by explaining just what the artillery factory committees had accomplished "despite the howling of the bourgeois press." The SR factory committee activist also defended the committees from Zinov′ev's unfortunate quip that they were "errand-boys of the [factory] owners." To this, Voronkov quietly retorted that they had "not [acted] like errand-boys. If we hadn't supported these factories and plants, what would have happened?," a telling point in a discussion about economic collapse. (It must be said that Zinov′ev's rambling speech displayed utter ignorance of the factory committee movement.) The Bolshevik worker Naumov (New Parviainen) made a dubious debating point when he commented that "the guarantee of the Bolshevik position is their closeness to the workers, whereas the SRs-Mensheviks showed how cut-off they are from the masses." Riazanov objected to the scare tactics of Cherevanin and other moderates who: "always frighten us with anarchy, [their] every resolution has this phenomenon."

Finally, Zinov′ev read the organizational bureau's resolution on the workers' role in the economy, which espoused "the establishment of real workers' control in the areas of production and distribution" and, within individual industrial concerns, a preponderant weight for factory committees in administration. The resolution conceded that this system could best be fulfilled under certain conditions, to wit, "only with the transfer of all state power into the hands of the soviets of worker and soldier deputies." This measure, less than accurately reported in *Pravda* as a "resolution to pass all power into the hands of the soviet," won by 290 votes to 131. The latter total, quite similar to the 128 who earlier on had protested and temporarily abandoned the hall, can be said to represent the moderate weighting at the conference, whereas somewhat over two-thirds of the delegates regularly supported radical stances.[26]

The conference then moved on to the next (and last) major question proposed by the organizational bureau, that is, the tasks of factory committees. Levin read the organizational bureau's report and resolution on this issue, touching most closely on the concerns of this particular gathering. Originator of the concept of the unified factory committee movement and its chief organizer, Levin was also its poet. He prefaced his speech with a dithyramb to the factory committees as "the progeny of the revo-

---

[26] GARF, F. 472, op. 1, d. 1, ll. 31-38; *Izvestiia* 79 (31 May 1917), 80 (1 June 1917); *Pravda*, 70 (14 [1] June 1917).

lution, fruit of its fruit," and so forth. He again emphasized the positive role of state (and to a lesser degree private) factory committees, whose efforts to maintain industrial production demonstrated the workers' ability to participate in and, indeed, control the national economy through the united factory committee movement. He felt that the factory committees were not only performing many tasks previously undertaken by labor unions, but had gone far beyond them, creating new revolutionary forms, as a consequence of which the "Russian revolution has become the model of the [world] liberation movement."

Levin wanted to "end anarchy of production." Workers' control had been, until now, "simple and primitive" due to workers' lack of requisite statistical, commercial and other forms of experience and knowledge, but with the organization of an all-Russian central factory committee structure, this problem would be overcome. But, he continued,

> It goes without saying that without... genuine revolutionary state power... the committees cannot deal with such a huge, complex task.... We cannot delay! Old socialists used to say, "The liberation of the working class is the task of the working class." Even socialist ministers cannot accomplish this. What is necessary is the totality of all worker organizations, all revolutionary democracy, and total revolutionary state power.

Levin closed by offering a resolution—he modestly called it his "personal offering"—that summarized his positions. This resolution went to the editorial committee, of which he was a member, where it served as the basis for the final version.

Neither this issue, nor other lesser topics of discussion, such as the relationship between factory committees and labor unions, provoked the delegates' passion to anything like the extent witnessed during the first two days. The whole point of the factory committee movement and the conference itself was that the workers' committees would play a great role in the economy, both locally and nationally. Once disagreements about the role of workers' organizations in dealing with economic collapse had been settled in a radical manner, the delegates deliberated more calmly. Indeed, the vast majority of factory committee activists, including SRs, Mensheviks, Bolsheviks, and non-partisans, assumed a steady development toward socialism that would provide the opportunity for creating thoroughgoing workers' control in the foreseeable future. This again underscores the inadequacy of our usual mode of political analysis during 1917, with its exaggerated dichotomies.

The militant radicalism of Levin's (and other activists') speeches, as well as of the conference's various resolutions, closely fit most delegates' mood (as noted, over two-thirds voted for the radical resolutions). The speeches of Voronkov and a number of other less well-known worker delegates make this very clear. For example, in his speech on factory committee tasks, Voronkov unleashed a barrage of angry pronouncements. He wanted to "seize resources from marauders [i.e., big capitalists]" in order to transform and develop industry, rather than "begging the bourgeoisie for coins like starving artists . . . we must look at things as they are. . . we should not yield, but demand categorically [what we need]. Compromise will get us nowhere." In a similar vein, Tseitlin, a Bolshevik delegate sent by the Kersten textile factory committee (chaired and dominated by SRs) stated that "we must create that power that will prevent hunger, create a strong [factory committee] center that will be the minister of labor. It will, of course, act more decisively than Minister Skobelev." This last picked up on a theme uniting many worker-speakers—the inaction of Skobelev and the Provisional Government and the uselessness of moderate positions. In this regard, *Pravda*'s reportage emphasized "the especially interesting speeches of a whole series of worker-orators, not only Bolsheviks, but also non-partisans and SRs, that refuted the minister-socialist [Skobelev], reflecting not some sterile doctrine, but the actual situation."[27]

Toward the conference's end, some differences of opinion arose about factory committee-labor union relations. The conference itself had provided an open door and a big welcome to labor union activists, placing several such individuals with no factory committee experience on the conference presidium. But when the Menshevik Rubtsov from the metalworkers' union in effect called for the factory committees to subordinate themselves to the labor unions ("the strike and economic struggle should be led by the labor unions"), this hit a false note and brought a quick response from Levin. Although he had earlier on emphasized joint work with the central labor union bureau, Levin now spoke out for the autonomy of the factory committees. He still emphasized careful planning and close work with the labor unions, but wanted "the central factory committee [structure] to unify the workers' movement. Since the labor unions have not been strong enough [to do so], the factory committees have undertaken this task." He did promise that "no strikes would be carried out without informing the labor unions," a sop to labor union activists'

---

[27] GARF, F. 472, op. 1, d. 1, ll.40–59; d. 2, ll. 10–11; *Volia naroda* 29 (2 June 1917); *Izvestiia* 81 (2 June 1917); *Pravda* 71 (15 [2] June 1917).

feelings. Finally, at Riazanov's motion, the conference elected the factory committee center, an ongoing factory committee bureau, whose proposed creation had spurred many speakers' enthusiasm and high hopes.[28]

Before returning to the principal task of analyzing factory committee discourses (and their implications), let us address the political question. As noted, Bolshevik activists played a minor role in the entire movement up to the conference, whereas the primary organizers were of Menshevik-SR orientation, reflecting the make-up of most factory committees. As regards the parties themselves, none of them really played a role prior to the conference, whereas during the conference itself the Bolsheviks established a certain organizational physiognomy. This matter requires comment because it, as well as the radical nature of the conference's resolutions, has created the misleading impression that the whole affair was somehow associated with the Bolshevik Party.

The very first sign of any association between the conference organizers and the Bolsheviks arose when Levin, the organizational bureau's chair, recommended a presidium that contained several Bolshevik invitees, along with two of the actual conference organizers (Voronkov and Rozenshtein). The Bolshevik invitees were leaders of the labor union movement (Shliapnikov and Glebov-Avilov), a representative from the Petrograd Soviet Executive Committee (Fedorov), and Sverdlov, listed as from the conference organizational bureau and, it would seem, an actual representative of the Bolshevik Party. No organizational bureau records prior to the conference itself listed Sverdlov as a member. His membership was honorary, in effect, the status of all the Bolshevik invitees into the presidium. The original conference organizers, led by Levin, maintained complete control of the conference and its resolutions. *Izvestiia*'s daily coverage, replete as it was with such phrases as "Comrade Levin, as head of the organizational bureau" read this or that report or entered this or that resolution, clearly demonstrated this.[29] The materials of the conference also show that Levin introduced the most important conference resolution (on the role of the factory committees) and alone of all the prominent participants spoke on every question. Why then did the bureau, under the leadership of its chair Levin, a Left SR, seek a special relationship with the Bolsheviks, who had the least to do with factory committee activism?

---

[28] GARF, f. 472, op. 1, d. 1, ll. 60–68; *Volia naroda* 31 (4 June 1917); *Izvestiia* 82 (3 June 1917); *Pravda* 73 (17 [4] June 1917).
[29] *Izvestiia* 78–82 (30 May–3 June 1917). Perhaps some readers have mistaken V. Levin for V. Lenin.

In lieu of hard data (the archival files lack some materials), one may surmise that the conference organizers sought a connection with the Bolsheviks as the only party willing to accommodate itself publicly (some will say cynically) to workers' movement institutions and aspirations. For example, during late April and May, just prior to the summoning of the factory committee conference, the SR and Menshevik parties and their leaders in the soviet executive committee had rather abruptly condemned the worker militia-red guard movement, even forbidding party members to participate. At least in its public pronouncements, the Bolshevik party turned a kinder face toward the red guards, although Bolshevik activists had not been foremost in the movement and it is doubtful that the Bolshevik leadership welcomed red guard autonomy any more than did SR-Menshevik moderates.[30] In this interpretation, the factory committee movement leadership accommodated itself to a party ostensibly friendly to autonomous worker organizations. We should also recall that at the time of the factory committee conference the Bolsheviks, despite their pretensions, still lagged far behind the other major socialist parties in popular support. Association with them lacked the connotations of a later period. Indeed, the factory committee leaders may have wished to boost Bolshevik popularity. Noteworthy in this regard is that support for a radical outcome of the 1917 revolution cut across party lines, separating moderates from radicals within each party rather than acting as a division among them.

Confusion, not to say distortion, has also arisen about the political make-up of the twenty-five person factory committee bureau, which then organized the all-Russian factory committee conference of August 1917. Upon the conference's closing, Sverdlov wrote a letter to Antonov-Ovseenko that allegedly averred: "the factory committee conference . . . progressed under our almost exclusive influence. It ended yesterday with the election of a twenty-five person . . . center[:] nineteen Bolsheviks, two Mensheviks, two SRs, one Mezhraionets, one quasi-syndicalist."[31] Historians often simply repeat Sverdlov's convenient figure (nineteen Bolsheviks of twenty-five members). Regardless, these figures are quite unreliable. For instance, the historian Stepanov names all twenty-five, with

---

[30] For official SR and Menshevik bans on militia-red guards involvement, see *Zemlia i volia* 25 (23 April 1917), and *Rabochaia gazeta* (29 April 1917). For general discussions of these matters, see N. Rostov, "Vozniknovenie krasnoi gvardii," *Krasnaia nov'* 2 (1927): 168–70, and Rex Wade, *Red Guards and Workers' Militias in the Russian Revolution* (Stanford, 1984), 85–96.

[31] *Perepiska Sekretariata TsK RSDRP(b) s mestnymi partiinymi organizatsiiami (mart–oktiabr' 1917 g.)* (Moscow, 1957), 12.

party identifications where he can establish them. Various data, partially provided by Stepanov and partially from other sources, establishes that—besides ten (more or less reliably) identified Bolsheviks—the central bureau consisted of one anarcho-syndicalist, four Mensheviks, two Mezhraiontsy, two SRs, and six unidentified (and by this time evidently unidentifiable) worker activists. Furthermore, seven bureau members (three Bolsheviks, one anarcho-syndicalist, and three Mensheviks) were invitees from the central labor union bureau. When one looks at the bureau members elected from the factory committee movement itself, one finds two SRs, two Mezhraiontsy, one Menshevik, seven Bolsheviks (assuming that all Stepanov's identifications are reliable), and six unidentified persons.[32] Were it possible, identification of the six unknowns would doubtlessly further enhance the multi-voicedness of the factory committee bureau. Despite the Bolsheviks' obvious interest in extracting political mileage from the factory committee conference, *Pravda* observed silence on the question of the central bureau's composition.[33]

The make-up of the conference also requires comment. Conference mandate materials indicate a total representation of something over 500 voting delegates from metallurgical, textile, printing, electrical, tobacco, aviation, railroad, and other enterprises.[34] Historians sometimes imply that those voting for the organizational bureau's resolutions (from 230 to 290) reflected the number of Bolsheviks and Bolshevik-aligned delegates, whereas, supposedly, the roughly 130 who usually voted the other way were the SRs and Mensheviks.[35] The conference materials indeed characterize the moderate group of 128 accompanying Dalin in leaving the hall as "SRs and Mensheviks." This referred, however, only to moderate SRs and Mensheviks (and doubtlessly their moderate non-party supporters). Those who voted for radical resolutions (between 230 to 290 delegates) consisted of leftist socialists—Bolsheviks, Mezhraiontsy, Left Mensheviks, and Left SRs—as well as anarchists and radical non-party activists. What proportion of the conference's radical section (roughly two-thirds of the overall delegates) belonged to which parties is not clear. The archival records of the conference contain no information about party alignments. Stepanov opines that party fractions probably did not take shape.[36] Any claims would therefore be hazardous, except to state the

---

[32] GARF, f. 472, op. 1, d.1, l. 10; *Pravda* 70 (14 [1] June 1917); Baklanova, *Rabochie Petrograda*, 131; Stepanov, *Fabzavkomi Petrograda*, 37; Smith, *Red Petrograd*, 84.
[33] *Pravda* 70 (14 [1] June 1917).
[34] GARF, F. 472, op. 1, d. 1, ll.18–26b.
[35] See Baklanova, *Rabochie Petrograda*, 131 n. 166; Gaponenko, *Rabochii klass*, 373.
[36] Baklanova, *Rabochie Petrograda*, 131; Stepanov, *Fabzavkomi Petrograda*, 36;

obvious: the make-up of the conference roughly reflected the make-up of the capital's factory committees at that time.

We would hardly need to linger over these matters had not misleading claims been made about Bolshevik quantitative hegemony of the factory committee movement and had not historians, even non-Soviet ones, based all analysis of the conference's outlooks and resolutions on this alleged sweeping hegemony. For example, one early Soviet-era publication asserted that "of course, the main initiators [of the first factory committee conference] were the Bolsheviks, in the person of the Central Committee and, especially, the Petrograd Committee." More recently, Stepanov has asserted that "all preparations . . . for the first conference of factory committees developed with the direct involvement of the Bolshevik party." Smith follows suit: "to counterpose the factory committees to the Bolshevik party is incorrect, since most of the leading cadres of the factory committees were also members of the Bolshevik party" and "there is no authentic, spontaneous 'factory committee' discourse which can be counter-posed to official Bolshevik discourse. A majority of the delegates were Bolsheviks, and the conferences voted overwhelmingly for Bolshevik-inspired resolutions."[37]

How can we more accurately assess factory committee discourses? As noted, the practical origins of Petrograd (and presumably other) factory committees lay in strike committees which for the most part were re-elected at large factory-wide meetings to represent workers at the factory level in the new revolutionary situation. Simultaneously, workers were constructing armed worker militias to provide security and electing delegates to district and city soviets to deal with broader questions. Exactly what functions the factory committees would have may at first have been unclear. Workers must at least have expected their committees to repre-

---

GARF, f. 472, op. 1, d. 1. Given Soviet historiography's motivation to associate the factory committee movement with the Bolsheviks, extreme caution should be exercised as regards some of Stepanov's attributions. Several of the individuals mentioned by Stepanov are well-known as Bolsheviks, whereas others are quite obscure.

[37] A. M. Pankratova, *Fabzavkomy Rossii v bor'be za sotsialisticheskuiu fabriku* (Moscow, 1923), 195; *Oktiabr'skaia revoliutsiia i fabzavkomy: materialy po istorii fabrichno-zavodskikh komitetov*, 2 vols. (Moscow, 1927), 1: 58; Dmitriev, "Petrogradskie fabzavkomy," 82; D. A. Kovalenko, "Bor'ba fabrichno-zavodskikh komotetov Petrograda za rabochii kontrol' nad proizvodstvom (mart–oktiabr' 1917 g.)," *Istoricheskie zapiski* 61 (1957): 73–80; Stepanov, *Fabzavkomy Petrograda*, 34; Smith, *Red Petrograd*, 150, 156. In his "Factory Committees" in *Critical Companion to the Russian Revolution, 1914-1921*, Edward Acton, V. Iu. Cherniaev, and William Rosenberg, eds. (London, 1997), 352, Smith's generally nuanced account states that the majority of delegates at the first factory council "backed Bolshevik resolutions."

sent their collective cause to individual managers and owners. Ideational origins are even obscurer: delegates at later factory committee conferences and meetings devoted little time to abstractions.

Smith gives the most detailed discussion of this question. His study analyzes the ideological origins of factory committees in terms of socialist and anarchist programs and outlooks, especially as regards the concept of workers' control of industry, a matter intimately associated with Russia's 1917 factory committees. Smith argues that the "slogan of 'workers' control' arose spontaneously among the Petrograd workers during the spring of 1917" without the involvement of any particular party. He also accepts Stepanov's definition of workers' control as applying to "proletarian organizations and linked directly to intervention in the productive... activity of the [individual] industrial enterprise... and to the control of the whole of production."[38] Clearly, in 1917 the factory committees (purely proletarian organizations) undertook this type of intervention and control, as shown by discussions at all factory committee conferences.

Following other commentators, Smith links the ideology of workers' control most closely to European anarcho-syndicalism, with its espousal of producers' (i.e. workers') direct control of the economy through nonpolitical workers' associations. The main problem, he observes, is that in Russia the anarchist and anarcho-syndicalist movements were too small to bear direct responsibility. Further, Smith correctly disassociates the ideology of factory committees and workers' control from social-democracy in both its Menshevik and Bolshevik forms. For example, he argues that, prior to 1917, the Bolsheviks "had no position on the question of workers' control. They began to formulate a position [during 1917] in response to deepening turmoil in the economy. Because the party's ideas were in the process of formulation, there is no absolute clarity, still less uniformity, in its attempts to come to terms with the movement for workers' control." The eventually predominant Leninist view adopted the language of workers' control, but interpreted it as being exercised by the revolutionary workers' state. One might add that this outlook, as practice would reveal, left little room for factory committee or worker autonomy. As for the Mensheviks, Smith argues that they "utterly rejected 'workers' control' as a serious strategy for controlling the economy." In order to develop the economy, they wanted intervention of the existing state (for the moment, in the person of the Provisional Government) into all aspects of economic life. For workers, they espoused only "representation of all popular organizations in government organs of economic control."

---

[38] Smith, *Red Petrograd*, 139–45.

In effect, this position maintained intact the outlook of the 1903 Social Democratic (SD) program, which approved measures that, during the period of the democratic republic, simply called for worker representation in various governmental and entrepreneurial institutions concerned with factory life. The program outlined no basis for an independent worker role.[39] Thus the "spontaneity" of the 1917 idea of workers' control, which, contends Smith, Russian workers did not previously articulate.

Although formally correct, Smith omits aspects of the pre-1917 workers' movement that may bear on the problem. For example, his discussion of SR approaches to workers' control focuses on moderate SR attitudes during 1917 and concludes quite fairly that SR leaders, like the Mensheviks but with somewhat different motivations, rejected workers' control in favor of state economic planning and control.[40] While accurate for moderate SRs during 1917, this was not the traditional position of the SR worker-oriented program, which since 1906 had espoused the "progressively widening participation [of workers] in the establishment of the internal organization of labor within industrial establishments."[41] On the basis of this language—unique among Russian socialist parties— many SRs had long since pushed ideas analogous to workers' control. SR wartime (1915) agitational leaflets issued in Petrograd and Smolensk called for the workers "to seize factories and plants" and even "the means of production." During the spring of 1917, the SR Petrograd newspaper *Zemlia i volia* (*Land and Freedom*) more calmly explained that "the SR minimum program calls for the widening of the power of organized workers over industries, [as a consequence of which] the powers of the factory committees should be strengthened."[42] A justifiable conclusion is that many workers had been exposed to propaganda of the anarcho-syndicalists and even more so the SRs (as much the larger party) with the

---

[39] Smith, *Red Petrograd*, 151–56; P. Avrich, "The Bolsheviks and Workers' Control," *Slavic Review* 1(1963): 62; F. I. Kaplan, *Bolshevik Ideology and the Ethics of Soviet Labor* (London, 1969), 93; O. Anweiler, *The Soviets: The Russian Workers', Soldiers', and Peasants' Councils, 1905–1921* (New York, 1971), 127; *Vtoroi s"ezd RSDRP, iiul'-avgust 1903 goda. Protokoly* (Moscow, 1959), 421–23.

[40] Smith, *Red Petrograd*, 151–52. Smith claims that the SRs rejected workers' control because they held that no one class had the right to control the economy, whereas the state could best administer to the interests of all classes.

[41] *Protokoly pervogo s"ezda partii sotsialistov-revoliutsionerov*, ed. Maureen Perrie (London, 1983), 362–65.

[42] SR leaflets are in the special collections of the Gosudarstvennaia obshchestvenno-politicheskaia biblioteka, Moscow; M. Gannetskii, "Fabrichno-zavodskie komitety," in *Zemlia i volia*, no. 17 (15 April 1917); see also V. M. Levin, *Fabricho-zavodskie komitety* (Petrograd, 1917), published by the Petrograd city SR organization.

germ of the idea of workers' control. Even SD teachings about general worker empowerment, in part through worker organizations and parties, would have helped form the ideational background of the 1917 movement. For that matter, so would traditional peasant communal mores, keeping in mind that most workers were of recent village origins. Any more assertive statements on this question would outrun existing sources and be speculative.

Analyzed on their own terms, factory committee discourses reveal a clear continuity between the very earliest organized expressions during mid-March and the resolves of the factory committee conference during May–June 1917, as well as with those of later conferences. In summary, factory committee spokespersons insisted on a decisive role for workers in the economy, exercised through the factory committees, which should therefore have a central nation-wide organization. They also believed that these goals could best be achieved within the context of a genuinely revolutionary government (or soviet power). Smith's analysis suggests that the first assertions of workers' control during early 1917 were reactive and defensive on the part of the factory committee and by late summer and fall of the year had become much more assertive and interventionist.[43] What was the precise contextual background of the initial assertions and evolvement of these positions during the late winter and spring of 1917?

The reader will recall that when workers in the capital's large state-owned defense plants returned to work in the days after tsarism's fall, they found plants denuded of managerial personnel. The newly-elected factory committees took charge in order to keep the plants in operation. Theory and ideology aside, the purely practical concern was to operate the plants in order to avoid unemployment, hunger, and other travails, although civic and patriotic feeling doubtlessly arose. Life in the form of severe crisis had outrun any ideology or program, none of which had laid a basis for what these factory committees undertook. At the 13 March conference of artillery plants, the committees openly proclaimed their management of the plants, including the right to hire and fire all personnel and perform all other managerial tasks. The conference also elected an artillery plant committee bureau and agreed to coordinate functions among all plants united by the bureau. Meanwhile, the naval plant committees pursued roughly the same path.

Toward the end of the month, when the Provisional Government had democratized the artillery administration and the bourgeois press was

---

[43]Smith, *Red Petrograd*, 146–49.

laying down a barrage of criticism, the artillery committees abandoned, at least verbally, overall administrative responsibilities but retained substantial control over the internal operations of plants. Of interest here is that the artillery committee bureau characterized this modest step back as valid only until the full socialization of all private and state plants, in other words, until the advent of socialism. In principal and in practice, the committee movement still posited workers' rights to full workers' control of industry. When the artillery and naval plants (over twenty huge enterprises) coordinated their committee administrations by mid-April, their joint conference asserted the same set of priorities: no overall administrative responsibility but full internal rights, up to and including firing of all administrative personnel, until the creation of socialism. As Petrograd's state and private factory committees planned for their first joint conference, these priorities remained in place. The conference organizers proposed a set of veritably Herculean tasks for the conference. As noted, these included "control and regulation of production," the "acquiring of fuel and raw materials," working out methods of dealing with unemployment, and the overall "state of production," as well as the creation of a "unified economic center" of factory committees and labor unions. Clearly, the hundreds of delegates who gathered at the late May conference could have had few doubts about the enormous tasks, real and potential, they were preparing to address.

The conference's main resolution on the tasks of factory committees, written and read by Levin, is of primary interest. The resolution summarized and pressed home all the points previously made in the factory committee movement: each factory had its committee and these committees should operate in an organized fashion under a "center" or bureau. The idea of complete factory autonomy received short shrift from workers. Both within plants and in the realm of the industrial economy in general the organized factory committees were to exercise virtually unlimited rights of control and regulation of all spheres of industrial operation. These priorities, however, could best be realized under conditions of "total revolutionary state power," as Levin proclaimed in his proposal. The concept of the need for a revolutionary (socialist) government in order to fulfill factory committee movement prerogatives was repeated in several conference resolutions and numerous speeches. Voting results suggest that this represented the view of roughly two-thirds of the conference delegates.

This approach to factory committee functions—very assertive responsibilities in the present and full control under socialism (posited as looming in the near future)—characterized all the movement's official statements from 28 March on. From the outset then, the factory committee activists perceived the economic and political aspects as developing side by side. This was the central kernel of factory committee discourse about workers' control during the first half of 1917. For real factory committee activists, such as Levin, Voronkov, and Tseitlin (see speeches above), the right of the workers through their committees to assert control over the entire industrial economy reflected not an abstraction but a real earned right, necessitated and proven in practice. When the managers had abandoned the plants and workers to their fates, the workers had stepped in to organize production and had continued thereafter to intervene in matters vital to the operation of the plants. In practice, workers had created "new revolutionary forms" in industry just as laborers had created new revolutionary political forms in the person of the soviets. The new factory committees had been forced "to take the factories into their hands" in order to save them. While carrying out these enforced functions, workers had proven their ability to "control the economy." For workers imbued with socialist-anarchist ideas of empowerment, the obvious corollary was that workers had the ability and right to end exploitation by moving toward revolutionary power.

In other words, in Russia in 1917 the concept of workers' control—the central factory committee symbol—arose out of the actual (unsought) practice of organized workers' control in Petrograd's state plants (and perhaps elsewhere) during the very first weeks of the revolution. Far from representing any theory or the intervention or guidance of any particular party (and certainly not the Bolsheviks), the factory committee movement and its discourses represented conscious actions and decisions, tried and tested in real life on an ongoing basis during 1917. Naturally, when economic collapse threatened later in the year, the factory committee movement proffered its solutions in a more strident fashion in the public realm. In part, this included an association with the Bolshevik Party, which seemed most closely aligned to worker aspirations. Nevertheless, the basic elements of the predominant factory committee discourse on workers' control originated early, autonomously, with quite broad consensus, and in a multi-voiced mode. In effect, these elements reflected worker revolutionary culture.

What further can be said about this culture on the basis of factory committee discourses? Analysis of the workers' movement during 1917 often turns on questions of class consciousness and links proletarian consciousness to a narrative about the Bolsheviks' rise to influence and ultimate power. Certainly, the factory committee movement and its chief spokespersons displayed elements of militant worker consciousness. The speeches of Levin and Voronkov, among others, at the factory committee conference were replete with references to "the rapacious bourgeoisie." At one point, Voronkov noted that for the bourgeoisie the "concept of private property outweighs not only the interests of any one class in the state, but the interests [of the state] as a whole."[44] Even so, class consciousness and its concomitant, class conflict, are not the only analysis to which factory committee formulations are susceptible. Worker spokespersons also expressed themselves in terms of the "duties and responsibilities" that had fallen to workers after the revolution. Having helped bring down the tsarist regime, workers then found that they had to intervene in the operation of factories—both private and to a much greater degree state—in order to operate them in the face of various derelictions of duty on the part of administrators and entrepreneurs. Workers fulfilled these duties quietly and without any remuneration. Workers and their organizations, implied the discussions of factory committee activists, were better guardians of society's and the state's interests than those usually invested with these high responsibilities. For instance, when administrators returned to their plants, they realized that workers were not so "bloody minded" as they had thought and were able to operate with and even under worker direction. In other words, factory committee discourses expressed quiet confidence in workers' now proven ability to act in fulfillment of civic and state responsibilities.[45]

This was not millenarian but practical class consciousness. Russian workers' views of themselves and their status in the factory and in the state had perforce received shape and interpretational force through contact with socialist ideologies. But in the end, workers acted primarily out of hard pragmatism. Interpreting Russia's workers' movement through the prism of workers' actual experience, expectations, and expressions offers the potential for a new understanding of hitherto obscure or simply misunderstood developments.

In this light, a final area of discussion remains. As noted in this study's analysis, at the time of the June 1917 Petrograd factory committee conference the Bolsheviks achieved, by invitation one might say, a certain not entirely deserved organizational status in the factory committee movement. Although the post-June history of the factory committee movement is not within this article's scope, readers will be aware

---

[44] GARF, f. 472, op.1, d.1, ll. 31–32.
[45] GARF, f. 472, op. 1, speeches, resolutions, and other expressions in ll. 1–70.

that prior to 25 October 1917 the Bolshevik role increased within the organized factory committee movement, as in other aspects of the labor movement. The Bolsheviks seemed to come to power with the full backing of the empire's proletariat. Yet, worker support for the Communists in power was so evanescent that by mid-spring 1918 workers all over Russia were again voting heavily for Menshevik and SR deputies, the same voting priorities they had shown during the first half of 1917. Can the experience of the Petrograd factory committee movement up through the June 1917 conference reflect any light on this phenomenon?

If one interprets the organized factory committee's alignment with the Bolsheviks as a political tactic on the part of the factory committee's non-Bolshevik leadership, things begin to fall into place. The organizers of the first Petrograd factory committee conference invited Sverdlov, Lenin, Zinov'ev and other Bolsheviks into the leadership because at the time only the Bolshevik Party offered public support for the factory committee movement and, so it seemed, its vision of workers' control. Thus until October, the Bolsheviks won enhanced influence in the national factory committee movement. Analogous phenomena occurred within workers' soviets, labor unions, and other worker-oriented organizations. Even so, when the October crisis arrived, most labor unions, local soviets, and, most importantly for our purposes, factory committees supported the creation of an all-socialist government rather than a Bolshevik-aligned dictatorship. Lenin won the factory committee movement's endorsement of Bolshevik rule by guaranteeing independence to the factory committee movement and by aligning himself with factory committee goals as regards the economy.[46]

This is not the place for commentary about the intent of Lenin and other Bolshevik leaders during October 1917. Suffice it to say that within a few months of assuming power the Communists disappointed much of its labor constituency with predictable political results, that is, renewed support for SRs and Mensheviks. The Communists achieved this striking turnaround by ruthlessly asserting party and government control over the soviets and, it should be noted, by firmly subordinating factory committees to the labor unions already brought to heel by party and state. In the eyes of rank-and-file workers, these policies in effect repositioned (perhaps spuriously) the SR-Menshevik block as the chief defender of an

---

[46]Shkliarevsky and Smith provide commentaries about these events. Shkliarevsky, *Labor in the Russian Revolution*, 118–20; Smith, *Red Petrograd*, 209–23. Shkliarevsky criticizes Smith's ready acceptance of the sincerity of Lenin's stances towards workers' control during the October crisis.

independent role for workers in politics and the economy. If one understands original factory committee discourses and positions as reflections of workers' independent aspirations, as suggested by this study, rather than as aspects of "Bolshevik ideology," as suggested by most scholarship, then the ebb and flow of worker support for various parties and blocks makes perfect sense. Readers should note that the general line of analysis offered here fits quite well with recent studies of the 1917 revolutions such as those of Chris Read and, of special note, Rex Wade.[47]

Through their organizations, workers maneuvered for the best deal they could get at any particular time. As it turned out, none of the three main socialist parties (the SRs and the two Social Democratic wings) were willing to meet worker aspirations about managing the industrial economy. For that one would have had to turn to some of the radical Bolshevik and Menshevik groups, to the Left SRs and SR-Maximalists, and to various Anarchist alignments. Labor utopias seem fated to brief lives. Still, one cannot help but note that the political context most suited for the workers' views about their role in running an economy was the all-socialist soviet government that workers, peasants, and soldiers overwhelmingly supported during the fall of 1917 and for years thereafter. Was this a utopian vision?

---

[47] Chistopher Read, *From Tsar to Soviets: the Russian people and their revolution, 1917–1921* (New York, 1996); Rex Wade, *The Russian Revolutions, 1917* (Cambridge, UK, 2000).

Big Strike in a Small City: The Smolensk Metalworkers' Strike and Dynamics of Labor Conflict in 1917

Michael C. Hickey

Although there are several fine studies of workers' strike activity in Petrograd, Moscow, and a few other large industrial settlements during the 1917 Revolution, we know little about how strikes in smaller cities helped shape politics in the vastness of provincial Russia. A case in point is the September 1917 strike by metalworkers in Smolensk, which often appears in aggregate data simply as an unidentified month-long conflict.[1] Although this was Smolensk's most dramatic labor dispute and an important factor in local politics, and although prominent Bolsheviks led the metalworkers' union, local historians have virtually ignored this strike.

The State Archives of Smolensk Oblast contain two sets of records on the metalworkers' strike. Files on the Viliia metalworking plant contain the plant manager's correspondence, memorandums, and directives, as well as records of the plant committee and minutes of contract negotiations.[2] The files of the metalworkers' union contain minutes of union and strike committee meetings and arbitration sessions, documents on the Viliia plant committee, and official and private correspondence of the city's Menshevik labor commissar.[3] Looking at this strike from the perspective of the union leadership, management, and the labor commissar reveals dynamics that made such provincial labor conflicts politically explosive.

---

[1] See, for instance, *Revoliutsionnoe dvizhenie v Rossii v avguste 1917 g. Razgrom kornilovskogo miatezha*, Institut istorii AN SSSR (Moscow, 1959), 250–51. (The volume mistakenly refers to a month-long strike in Smolensk in August.) The strike is mentioned briefly in Merle Fainsod's *Smolensk Under Soviet Rule* (reissue, Boston, MA, 1989), 26–31.

[2] Gosudarstvennyi arkhiv Smolenskoi oblasti (hereafter GASO), f. 146, op. 1, d. 21.

[3] GASO, f. 1994, op. 1, d. 1.

M. Melancon, A. Pate, *New Labor History*, Bloomington, IN: Slavica, 2002

The basic issues in the strike are familiar: wages and work control. The union demanded raises to protect real wages against inflation, while management considered wage increases a threat to the viability of the enterprise. The union believed workers had a fundamental right to oversee decisions regarding hiring, firing, and work assignments, while management considered these its own fundamental prerogatives. Both sides conducted negotiations within the framework of well-established practices of labor-management relations. The strike itself was part of a "normal" repertoire of actions employed in labor disputes. But in the context of the Revolution, the failed negotiations and strike took on enormous political weight.

Part of that political weight came from the fact that both sides framed their positions as vital to the Revolution. For Bolshevik union secretary Vadim Aleksandrovich Smol′ianinov, consolidating the Revolution required implementing the union's demands. Iosif Georgievich Esaitis, director of the Viliia plant and chief negotiator for the Society of Plant and Factory Owners, argued that defending the Revolution required production of war goods and that the union's demands would undermine this cause. In a very real sense, the strike was a contest over who would define the meanings of the Revolution.

As the conflict became more intense, both Smol′ianinov and Estaitis framed their positions in the language of class and class struggle. In his speeches Smol′ianinov defined the metalworkers' union as a weapon of class struggle and warned that owners were trying to crush the workers' movement. Esaitis often grounded his position in arguments for the rights of property owners, and plant owners also depicted the strike as a skirmish in a larger class war that could be settled only by force. Such superheated rhetoric contributed to the growing polarization of local politics and helped render the position of the moderate socialists untenable.

The position taken by Solomon Pavlovich Shur, the labor commissar of Smolensk, also contributed to the strike's political importance, and suggests the sort of moderate socialist statism that Ziva Galili, William Rosenberg, and Michael Melancon have noted as a key feature of labor politics at the national level.[4] Throughout the conflict Shur, a leader

---

[4] See Ziva Galili and Albert P. Nenarokov, "The Mensheviks in 1917: From Democrats to Statists," in *Critical Companion to the Russian Revolution, 1914–1921*, eds. Edward Acton, Vladimir Iu. Cherniaev, and William G. Rosenberg (Bloomington, IN, 1997), 267–68; William G. Rosenberg, "Social Mediation and State Construction(s) in Revolutionary Russia," *Social History* 19 (1994): 169–88; and Michael Melancon, "The Socialist Revolutionary Party (SRs), 1917–1920," in *Critical Companion to the*

of the local Mensheviks, worked to protect state interests. Shur employed two very different rhetorical frames in his public statements and private correspondence. Publicly, Shur argued that state interests must take precedence over any particularistic class interests. For workers, this argument only seemed to confirm Bolshevik claims that the Mensheviks and Socialist Revolutionaries (SRs) would not defend their class interests. In private correspondence, Shur endorsed the union's demands and worried that a union defeat would undermine the labor movement. Like other moderate socialists in 1917, Shur found himself caught between the imperative to defend the revolutionary state and his dedication to the workers' cause.

Contours of Labor and Politics in Revolutionary Smolensk

Smolensk, on the upper reaches of the Dnepr River in western Russia, was the administrative and commercial center of a grain-poor agricultural province.[5] By the outbreak of World War I, its population had barely reached 75,000. The city could claim fewer than three dozen industrial enterprises; only a handful of these employed more than a dozen workers or made use of steam or electric power. Although half the city's population worked for wages, only twenty percent worked in manufacturing and only 1,500 of these worked in factories or plants. The great majority of Smolensk's wage earners were illiterate or semi-literate young single men from peasant backgrounds.[6] At first glance Smolensk might seem, as Stephen Kotkin has described it, little more than "an agricultural backwater."[7]

But the contrast between life for working people in Smolensk's poor neighborhoods and that of the city's elite was as stark as in Russia's great urban centers. The juxtaposition of these social spaces, as well as the notoriously miserable conditions and social relations in small workshops, warehouses, and stores, made the elite's economic and political power palpable in daily life. Many of Smolensk's skilled workers and artisans defined these social relations in class terms and saw the socialist parties

---

Russian Revolution, 281–90.

[5] Although Smolensk is often grouped with the Central Industrial Region, the province had only one large factory (a textile plant at Iarstevo that employed 5,000 workers).

[6] The labor force remained mostly young, male, and single in 1917: of the 192 workers who joined the bakers' trade union in spring 1917, for instance, 136 were male, 121 were age 25 or younger, and 117 were single. GASO, f. 1998, op. 1, d. 12.

[7] Stephen Kotkin, "1991 and the Russian Revolution: Sources, Conceptual Categories, Analytical Frameworks," *Journal of Modern History* 70 (1998): 388. See also Kotkin's *Magnetic Mountain: Stalinism as Civilization* (Berkeley, CA, 1995), 371.

and labor unions as their best means of fighting both class inequities and tsarist political repression.[8]

In the decade before the Great War the labor movement sank roots in Smolensk. By 1902 the city's printers had ties to the Social Democrats (SDs), Jewish garment workers supported the Bund, and both groups had formed clandestine unions and organized strikes.[9] In 1905, hundreds of local factory workers, artisans, shop clerks, and employees unionized (as did students). Among those who organized in 1905 were the city's metalworkers, most of them mechanics who struck for higher wages that spring. On 10 March 1905, for instance, the twelve workers at the Birin Metalworking Plant went on strike demanding a ten-hour work day, a twenty percent wage increase, and more respectful treatment from the owner.[10] In December 1905 and January 1906 local police smashed Smolensk's short-lived workers' soviet and arrested many of the city's socialist and labor organizers. But local activists redoubled their efforts in spring 1906. Smolensk's 120 metalworkers registered their "Union of Mechanical Shops" with authorities in late March 1906. The union included mechanics, smiths, locksmiths, engravers, watchmakers, and workers in shops like Birin's.[11] In the fall of that year, though, police began shutting down unions suspected of illegal political activities; local police disbanded the metalworkers' union in December 1906. Most of the metalworkers' union leaders were arrested (although a few did flee abroad).[12]

Local gendarme reports provide no evidence of labor unrest between 1907 and 1911. In 1911, however, as the tide of labor activism returned across the Empire, workers in local printing and garment shops reor-

---

[8]On conditions in pre-war Smolensk's metalworking shops, see GASO, f. 1994, op. 1, d. 1, l. 208; on conditions in commercial enterprises, see V. I. Grachev, *Byt torgovykh sluzhashchikh v Rossii* (Smolensk, 1905), 25–26, 35; Tsentr dokumentatsii noveishei istorii Smolenskoi oblasti (hereafter TsDNISO), f. 7, op. 1, d. 132, l. 5. On Smolensk's social geography and its role in fostering class and political tensions, see M. Hickey, "The Rise and Fall of Smolensk's Moderate Socialists: The Politics of Class and the Rhetoric of Crisis in 1917," *Provincial Landscapes: Local Dimensions of Soviet Power, 1917–1953*, ed. Donald Raleigh, (Pittsburgh, PA, 2001), 14–35.

[9]Young members of the Party of SRs in Smolensk had contacts with workers in several enterprises, but found more support from students than they did from workers. See Igor Kiprov, "Delo Borisa Vladimirovicha Podvitskogo, ili Smolenskaia terroristicheskaia gruppa Obedinennogo Biuro Partii Sotsialistov-Revoliutsionerov, 1937–1938 gg.," *Krai Smolenskii* 7–8 (1994): 84–115.

[10]GASO, f. 1994, op. 1, d. 1, ll. 218–218ob.

[11]For a summary of the union's meetings in 1906, see GASO, f. 1994, op. 1, d. 1, ll. 218ob–219.

[12]Even after the police crackdown, eight unions (with 870 members) remained active into early 1907. TsDNISO, f. 7, op. 1, d. 132, l. 12.

ganized their clandestine unions and gendarme officials fretted over the revival of underground political activism.[13] But there is no evidence any re-enlivened organizational activity among Smolensk's metalworkers.

It was the context of the war and the February 1917 Revolution that led to the rebirth of the metalworkers' union. The hardships of war had contributed significantly to the radicalization of Smolensk's workers. The city, strapped for funds even during peacetime, cut back on the minimal services it provided to workers' districts, and conditions in workers' districts declined rapidly. A flood of war refugees in 1915 aggravated problems of housing, sanitation, and food supply in the city's poorest districts. So did the growth of the local garrison, which mushroomed to almost 25,000 soldiers when Smolensk became a major staging center for the Western Front. The war brought longer hours, more draconian labor relations, and wage-eating inflation. It also cost the jobs of hundreds of workers in breweries closed by prohibition and in workshops left idle by want of materials or orders. And as the conflict dragged on, managers found it increasingly difficult to protect their experienced workers from conscription.[14]

Yet the war did bring new opportunities in the metalworking trades. Several of the city's established enterprises re-tooled and took on defense contracts: the British-owned Gergard bobbin factory, for instance, now produced shell cartridges. Expanded defense production required that plants take on more metalworkers. In addition, Smolensk gained a sizable "new" metalworking plant in 1915, the Viliia plant of Vilnius. Viliia had manufactured agricultural tools, but in 1914 began producing army field kitchens, which made it valuable to the war effort. To protect the plant during the German advance of 1915, the Minsk Military District Staff arranged to relocate Viliia's equipment, office staff, and nearly one hundred metalworkers on Smolensk's Petropavlovskaia Street. Viliia instantly became one of the city's largest employers. Its director, Iosif Esaitis, emerged as a leader in the local Lithuanian "colony" and among the business community. Several of its workers, like Stanislav Ivitskii, were Lithuanian Social Democrats who subsequently became important "local" labor activists (and, in many cases, joined the Bolsheviks).

---

[13] For gendarme reports on labor and socialist party activities during 1911–14, see TsDNISO, f. 7, op. 1, dd. 308–310, 320, 327.

[14] *Smolenskii vestnik* (hereafter *SV*) (1–3 January 1917); *Vestnik statistiki* 1–4 (1921): 210; I. D. Krolik, "Sila internationalizma," *Materialy po izucheniiu Smolenskoi oblasti* 8 (1974): 38; GASO, f. 1, op. 8, dd. 738a, 763, 906, 914; GASO, f. 65, op. 2, dd. 1805, 1812–13; GASO, f. 1289, op. 2, d. 499.

The expansion of the city garrison also brought more metalworkers to Smolensk. Among the technical units attached to the wartime garrison were two large mechanical workshops: the First Rear Automobile Repair Shop and the First Rear Aviation Park. Both units included skilled metalworkers, many of whom were veterans of the Empire's largest factories, and some of whom were SDs, SRs, or Bundists. First Rear Automobile Repair Shop soldier Vadim Smol'ianinov was born into a Sverdlovsk oblast' metalworker's family in 1890 and began his own apprenticeship in the trade at age fifteen. In 1905, Smol'ianinov became active in the revolutionary movement, and in 1908 he joined the Bolsheviks. He had been a leading party agitator in Ekaterinoslav before being conscripted.[15] Activists from the garrison units, together with workers at Viliia, formed the core of the revived Smolensk metalworkers' union after the February Revolution.

During Smolensk's February Revolution, which actually took place in the first week of March, the local edifice of the tsarist regime crumbled with remarkably little violence. Liberals from the city duma created a new city administration, and local SRs and SDs organized a city soviet. Smolensk became a stronghold of Menshevik and SR influence. SRs ran the local press, and together the SRs and Mensheviks dominated local unions and controlled the soviet of workers' and soldiers' deputies. By late April, SRs and Mensheviks played a major role in city administration, and by late June they dominated the Provincial Executive Committee (PEC).[16] In July, their Socialist Bloc electoral ticket swept elections to the city duma.[17] By comparison, Smolensk had no formal Bolshevik organization until late April, and even after that the local Bolsheviks had trouble coordinating their activities. The Bolsheviks, anarchists, and left

---

[15] Smol'ianinov had assumed his name in the Bolshevik underground. His birth name was Sergei Aleksandrovich Smol'nikov. He was a central figure in the Smolensk Sovnarkom during the Civil War then through the ranks of the Soviet government. Between 1921 and 1924 he served as head of administrative affairs for the Council of Labor and Defense. He is perhaps best known for his role as the official responsible for construction of the Magnitogorsk metallurgical complex in 1929–32. See Kotkin, *Magnetic Mountain*, 44.

[16] Michael Hickey, "Discourses of Public Identity and Liberalism in the February Revolution: Smolensk, 1917," *Russian Review* 55 (1996): 615–37 and idem, "Local Government and State Authority in the Provinces: Smolensk, February-June 1917," *Slavic Review* 55 (1996): 863–81.

[17] The bloc won 20,830 votes (the Kadets 5,820, the Bolsheviks 1,235) and did exceptionally well in the city center as well as in poorer neighborhoods. The Socialist Bloc took fifty-four places in the duma, compared to fifteen for the Kadets and three for the Bolsheviks. *SV* (25 July 1917); *Golos Bunda* (8, 19 August 1917).

SRs did not represent any serious challenge to moderate socialist political hegemony in Smolensk until late August. The month-long strike by the Bolshevik-led metalworkers' union would be a contributing factor in that challenge.

Strike activity in Smolensk loosely followed national patterns in 1917. The city experienced two major groups of strikes: from mid-April through early May, when workers and employees demanded higher wages and an eight-hour work day; and from late August through October, when conflicts focused on wages and work control issues.[18] These two strike clusters correlate strongly not only with national political crises (the April Crisis and the mounting political crisis of fall), but also with local inflationary spikes that forced up the cost of living and undermined workers' real wages. The price of rye flour, for example, doubled in the first two weeks of April, then after months of remaining stable, doubled again in late September and early October. The driving force behind the spring strikes came from unionized needle-shop workers, bakers, and pharmacists, most of them Jews with close ties to the moderate socialist parties. In late August through October, though, ethnic Russian leather and woodworkers and Russian and Lithuanian metalworkers with ties to the Bolsheviks and anarchists set the tone for labor conflict, which then spread to other unions. Fall strikes by unions close to the moderate socialists failed, while several strikes by unions with left socialist affiliations forced owners to grant concessions. The results of the fall strikes helped weaken support for the moderate socialists and boosted the authority of the left socialists. The success of left socialist unions, however, had less to do with their leadership than it did with structural factors related to the war: unlike the moderate socialist unions concentrated in service industries and consumable goods production, the left socialist unions struck against companies with defense contracts. The state had a greater interest in seeing such strikes settled.

The Viliia Plant Committee and the Plant Director

In Smolensk, as in larger cities, workers expected the Revolution to bring a new dispensation in the factories: a living wage, respectful treatment from employers, improved work conditions, and democratization of man-

---

[18] For an outstanding analysis of strike patterns and representations of strikes in 1917, see Diane P. Koenker and William G. Rosenberg, *Strikes and Revolution in Russia, 1917* (Princeton, NJ, 1991). On Smolensk, A. T. Abramovich, "Smolenskie professional'nye soiuzy do 1917 i v oktiab'rskie dni. Ocherk," TsDNISO, f. 7, op. 1, d. 132; Michael Hickey, "Revolution on the Jewish Street: Smolensk, 1917," *Journal of Social History* 31 (Summer 1998): 831, 835.

agerial decisions. The soviets and factory committees were means towards this end. The first plant committee in Smolensk was created on 18 March, when over one hundred Russian and Lithuanian workers at Viliia elected seven men to represent them in negotiations with management and to oversee work assignments. The meeting also elected two soviet deputies, Red'kin (first name unknown) and M. Liekne. Both would join the Bolshevik party later in the spring.

Viliia director Iosif Esaitis moved quickly to defend managerial authority from potential encroachments by the plant committee. On 20 March, Smolensk Soviet chairman V. V. Podvitskii (an SR Central Committee member) "ordered" the plant management to pay Red'kin and Liekne for time spent on soviet business.[19] Esaitis agreed to recognize the plant committee and to release workers for soviet tasks with pay. But on 24 March he fired off an angry memo to the plant committee complaining that its members had "improperly" argued with him over suspension of the plant's second shift. Management, Eisitis argued, had struggled for months with shortages and had cut back production only after requisition efforts had failed. He warned that Viliia's state contracts necessitated strict labor discipline and that "disorders, rumors, and improper or illegal demands by workers will disrupt production, with the result that the factory will close." [20]

Unlike other enterprises in the city, where wages and the eight-hour work day were the main points of contention in spring 1917, work control issues proved the flash point at Viliia. On 6 April, for instance, the plant committee proposed raises of ten and thirty-five percent (for specialists and other workers respectively), and Esaitis described the demand as reasonable. But he outright rejected the committee's request to oversee hiring and work assignments. When on 12 April the committee repeated these demands, Esaitis instructed them on the scope of their legal authority. The Revolution, he said, had provided plant committees with rights, but they must exercise these responsibly. He instructed the committee that it should give "serious attention" to workers' disruptive behavior and warned that excessive demands could lead to violence and undermine the new order. The committee persisted, though, and petitioned state and soviet authorities for intervention. On 20 April, it charged Esaitis before Smolensk's Labor Arbitration Commission with threatening defense

---

[19]GASO, f. 146, op. 1, d. 21, ll. 249–53. On factory and plant committees in 1917, see Steve Smith, "Factory Committees," in *Critical Companion to the Russian Revolution*, 346–58.

[20]GASO, f. 146, op. 1, d. 21, l. 248.

production by assigning under-skilled turners to skilled tasks. When the commission found in Esaitis' favor, the plant committee appealed to the PEC. On 22 April, the PEC announced that they would not intervene in matters that were ownership's prerogative. A few days later the soviet's SR- and Menshevik-controlled executive committee endorsed the metalworkers' pay demands but urged that the plant committee maintain proper labor discipline.[21]

In spring Esaitis and the plant committee both defined their positions as consonant with the interests of the Revolution. For the plant committee, greater control over work was a right won by workers in the February Revolution. Esaitis framed his rejection of the committee's demands in terms of revolutionary legality and defense of the Revolution. Esaitis' letters and memorandums reveal a remarkably disciplined and well-informed administrator who sincerely believed that the Revolution's survival depended upon the war effort and that the war effort depended upon factories like Viliia. In spring, Esaitis skillfully avoided any reference to managerial decisions as an extension of property rights or to the owners' class interests. In his rhetoric the interests of the plant were inseparable from the needs of the Revolution.

In May labor unrest in the city as a whole waned; most of Smolensk's employers had agreed (at least in principle) to raise wages and to recognize the eight-hour workday, and prices for food, fuel, and clothing stabilized. Labor relations at Viliia seemed to improve, too. When on 16 May the plant committee repeated its wage demands, Esaitis agreed (retroactive to 1 May). But no sooner had a wage agreement been reached than Esaitis found himself dealing with a new metalworkers' union.[22]

The Metalworkers' Union and the Plant Director

Workers in Smolensk's few large plants did not begin unionizing until nearly two months after workers and employees in smaller establishments. Unions of tailors, pharmacists, and other artisans and employees had been organized with the help of locally well-known Bundist, SR, and Menshevik activists in March and April. In contrast, the 1917 metalworkers' union began as a cohort of leftists at the Viliia, Gergard, and Markusa plants and the First Rear Automobile Repair Shop, most of whom had been brought to the city by the war. This included Vadim Smol'ianinov and

---

[21]GASO, f. 146, op. 1, d. 21, ll. 238–44, 246–47ob.
[22]GASO, f. 146, op. 1, d. 21, ll. 225–32ob., 234–36. New daily rates ranged from 2.5 rubles for female unskilled laborers to 9 rubles for specialist turners, stampers, and smiths.

several leaders of the local Bolshevik faction, which had grown from 12 to 250 members between April and June. Most of these new Bolsheviks, however, were soldiers, and the party made few inroads among the city's workers outside of metalworking and woodworking plants.

In spring the local Bolsheviks had made few efforts to mobilize support in the city's factories and left union organization entirely to the moderate socialists.[23] But on 13 June two Bolsheviks, Viliia plant committee member Red'kin and soldier Vadim Smol'ianinov led some four dozen metalworkers in a meeting aimed at forming a union. Smol'ianinov gave a fiercely Bolshevist speech rejecting the moderate socialists' policy of "class conciliation" and insisting that the metalworkers' union would be a weapon in the class struggle. The meeting appointed a nine-man organizational committee. Three of the nine were members of the Viliia plant committee (Red'kin, V. Andrzhevskii, and Stanislav Ivitskii, all of whom had recently joined the Bolsheviks); the rest were soldiers, including Bolshevik activists Ivan Pindak and Smol'ianinov, who was elected unanimously.[24]

The Bolshevik affiliation of the metalworkers' union was clear from its inception. The majority of organizational committee members were Bolsheviks. The union took space at the offices of the Bolshevik faction, chose for its banner the Bolshevik slogan "Long Live The Third Revolutionary International," and stocked its library with Bolshevik newspapers.[25] It grew quickly: on 15 June all forty-one workers at the Markusa metalworking plant and thirty of forty at the city electrical plant enrolled; by 26 June, one hundred soldiers at the First Rear Automobile Repair Shop

---

[23]V. S. Smol'ianinov, "Nezabyvaemyi 1917 god," in *Vospominaniia uchastnikov bor'by za vlast' sovetov v Smolenskoi gubernii*, Partiinyi arkhiv Smolenskogo obkoma KPSS (Smolensk, 1957), 10–11; Leivik Hodis, *Biografie und Schriften*, ed. Sophia Dubnov-Erlich (New York, NY, 1962), 17. On the creation of the local party organization, see *Ustanovlenie i uprochenie sovetskoi vlasti v Smolenskoi gubernii. Sbornik dokumentov*, Partiinyi arkhiv Smolenskogo obkoma KPSS (Smolensk, 1957), 42–43. On the local Bolsheviks' failure to organize union activities before June, see *Ustanovlenie i uprochenie sovetskoi vlasti*, 70–71, 77–78; *Revoliutsionnoe dvizhenie v Rossii v maeiiune 1917 g. Iiunskaia demonstratsiia. Dokumenty i materialy*, AN SSSR (Moscow, 1959), 70; *Bol'sheviki Smolenshchiny do oktiabria 1917 g. Sbornik dokumentov*, Partiinyi arkhiv Smolenskogo obkoma KPSS (Smolensk, 1961), 225.

[24]GASO, f. 1994, op. 1, d. 1, ll. 14–17, 219ob.

[25]The library subscribed to one hundred copies each of the Bolshevik papers *Pravda*, *Sotsial-Demokrat*, *Rabotnitsa*, and *Zhizn' rabotnitsy*, but to only one copy each of the SR daily *Delo Naroda*, the Petrograd Soviet's *Izvestiia* and the Kadet paper *Rech'*. It also subscribed to ten copies of *Voprosy strakhovaniia*. GASO, f. 1994, op. 1, d. 1, ll. 1–3ob.

and one hundred workers at Viliia had signed up.[26] At the union's first general meeting, on 28 June, Smol'ianinov delivered a thunderous speech on the union as a weapon of class struggle. Its first battle would be for a citywide wage scale. The meeting elected Smol'ianinov as union chairman (he stepped down in favor of Red'kin on 13 July, then took the post of union secretary) and Pindak as its soviet deputy.[27]

The metalworkers' leadership spent July working out the details of a citywide wage scale. After carefully reviewing wage rates in Petrograd and Moscow, it drew up a contract proposal that provided for raises, reduced but did not eliminate wage differentials, and gave the union and plant committees considerable control over managerial decisions. It divided union members into two groups on the basis of the type of plant in which they worked: "specialists" in metalworking shops, and metalworkers employed in other industries. It then subdivided both groups into two skill ratings. Skilled workers would receive a thirty-five percent wage increase, with skilled specialists at the top of the wage scale; nonskilled workers would receive a fifty percent wage increase. According to the proposal, plant committee members and managerial personnel at each enterprise would assign skill ratings and disputes over ratings would go before an arbitration commission that included union representatives. The proposal set the workday at eight hours, with shorter shifts and double overtime on weekends and holidays. It specified that managers could not assign overtime without approval from the factory committee and union. It also detailed the precise conditions under which workers' pay could be docked and gave the plant committee control over vacation assignments.[28]

Esaitis had also spent much of July assembling materials on wages and arbitration decisions in the metalworking trades. Smolensk's Society of Plant and Factory Owners had chosen him as its chief negotiator; Esaitis prepared by reading up on labor law and on contract negotiations in other cities.[29] He anticipated that the union would press demands that, from his perspective, threatened Viliia's economic viability. Defense orders had given the plant a modicum of protection from conscription of workers but

---

[26] GASO, f. 1994, op. 1, d. 1, ll. 19–20, 53–56.

[27] GASO, f. 1994, op. 1, d. 1, ll. 58–59.

[28] On 7 August the woodworkers' union (led by A. I. Egorev, a turner at Gergard who joined the Bolsheviks in fall) drew up demands based upon the metalworkers' proposal. GASO, f. 1994, op. 1, d. 1, ll. 4–6ob., 220ob., 221, 233–33ob.; *Ustanovlenie i uprochenie sovetskoi vlasti*, 85.

[29] GASO, f. 146, op. 1, d. 21, ll. 219–24 and unnumbered pages.

could not insulate it from Russia's rapid economic collapse.[30] The breakdown of rail traffic and shortages of fuel and raw materials meant that the plant was constantly in danger of closing. Esaitis worried that rising labor costs would bankrupt the plant, but he was more concerned that allowing the plant committee to determine job assignments, set skill ratings, or limit overtime would undermine labor discipline and productivity. He would not let this happen and was certain that state officials would take his side. Esaitis had come to expect state intervention whenever Viliia's production was at risk. He frequently petitioned local officials for help in obtaining supplies and had found an ally in Labor Commissar Shur, or so he thought. Shur did, in fact, come to Esaitis' aid when supply problems threatened productions: on 1 August he personally appealed to the Moscow Region Labor Commissar and the Moscow District Supply Committee for help in securing supplies for Viliia.[31] Esaitis expected that Shur would also intervene if union demands threatened the plant. Moreover, Esaitis, who kept a close eye on leftist politics in the city, knew well that there were tensions between Shur and metalworkers' leadership.[32]

The Labor Commissar and the Failure of Negotiation

Tensions between the metalworkers' union and management came to a head in August. At this point Esaitis' rhetoric shifted. Like many business leaders across Russia, he worried that the Provisional Government could not maintain order; like many of Smolensk's liberals, he feared that the moderate socialist local administration was not up to the task of preserving legality and protecting property. References to managerial prerogative and the rights of ownership now dominated Esaitis' memorandums. On 9 August Esaitis fired two workers who had violated his directives. When the plant committee objected, Esaitis reminded them that "the administration has the legal right to maintain factory order."[33]

---

[30] In late July the Smolensk *Uezd* (district) Military Administration ordered conscription of several Viliia workers and employees. The committee and Esaitis both protested, and all eventually received deferments. GASO, f. 146, op. 1, d. 21, ll. 218–18ob., 206. For a similar case involving leather workers, see GASO, f. 65, op. 2, d. 1819.

[31] GASO, f. 146, op. 1, d. 21, ll. 217–17ob.

[32] The metalworkers' union had endorsed Bolshevik printer Ivan Kondrat'ev for the labor commissar's post. GASO, f. 1994, op. 1, d. 1, ll. 5–5ob, 221. Ideological antagonism between left and moderate socialists in Smolensk had grown more intense due to their conflicting positions on the war. But the fact that many leftists were "outsiders" to well established local oppositionist social networks doubtless contributed to these tensions.

[33] GASO, f. 146, op. 1, d. 21, ll. 214, 213.

On that same day, 9 August, the metalworkers' union presented its contract proposal to factory administrators. A blunt cover letter attached to the proposal gave management one week to respond.[34] Esaitis waited until 17 August, then categorically rejected the union proposal. He argued that he had already given workers a substantial raise, and that, moreover, the union proposal violated owners' right to control their own property: job assignments, skill ratings, the assignment of overtime and vacations, and the punishment of infringements of work discipline were all managerial prerogatives. Under no circumstances would he agree to union demands. The union forwarded Esaitis' letter to the city's labor commissar and asked that he bring the two parties together for contract negotiations on 19 August.[35]

Shur found himself in a very difficult position. Esaitis made clear that he expected the commissar to take management's side, and the union was going to great lengths to put pressure on him as well. The union postponed negotiations until 26 August and used the intervening week to lobby for support in the city soviet. From 20 August the metalworkers held all of their meetings at the soviet building, and on 24 August they called on the soviet to endorse their contract demands. Moving to the soviet, the focal point of working class political life, symbolically reinforced the legitimacy of the metalworkers' demands and pushed Menshevik and SR leaders to take a public position on the dispute.

The timing could hardly have been worse for Shur and the city's moderate socialists. They had been trying to dissuade workers from striking and warned that strikes threatened to disrupt the Revolution. Workers at several lumber mills and leather plants, with whom the moderate socialists had little influence, were already embroiled in strikes in mid-August. But to the great frustration of the moderate socialist leadership, tailors, cooks and waiters, bakers, and pharmacists ignored their warnings and prepared to strike. Failure to support the metalworkers, one of the city's largest unions, ran the risk of amplifying the Bolshevik's charges that Menshevik and SR "conciliators" did not protect workers' class interests.[36]

---

[34] The woodworkers' union sent management their proposal on 14 August. GASO, f. 1994, op. 1, d. 1, ll. 7, 12–13; GASO, f. 146, op. 1, d, 21, ll. 209–9ob.; *WKP* 1, 95, 96, 99.

[35] GASO, f. 146, op. 1, d. 21, ll. 207–8, 200–3; GASO, f. 1994, op. 1, d. 1, ll. 8–8ob.; WKP 1, 95.

[36] *SV* (23, 26 August 1917); *Ustanovlenie i uprochenie sovetskoi vlasti*, 95–96. Metalworkers' union membership was 350 at the beginning of August. Tram workers then joined, as did a greater number of workers in small shops, raising membership to 472.

For Shur, one of the most vocal statists among the city's moderate socialist leaders, the metalworkers' conflict posed a fundamental problem.[37] Since early April he had insisted that workers obtain the soviet executive committee's approval before taking any direct action and called on workers to consider the "all-state significance" of strikes. When the moderate socialists assumed control over state institutions, Shur argued that they must defend the interests of the revolutionary state even when these clashed with the interests of the working class.[38] Upon "election" as labor commissar on 12 July, Shur immediately resigned from the soviet. In a letter to all "comrade workers," he explained that as an activist in the soviet he had represented the proletariat, but as labor commissar "I will represent the interests of the Provisional Revolutionary Government." This required that he put state interests before "personal, group, or class interests." [39]

Shur's tasks as labor commissar as a representative of state interests required playing the role of neutral arbitrator in disputes between labor and capital, which he did with considerable skill. Partisanship, he feared, would alienate one side or the other and undermine negotiations important to the state. But Shur fully understood that this statist position exposed him (and the moderate socialists) to criticism from both sides: the owners might accuse him of failing to control union radicalism, whereas the left socialists might accuse him of abandoning the workers' interests.

When Shur brought union and management representatives together on 26 August, each side denounced the other's position as unacceptable. Esaitis, representing owners, pointed to "egregious provisions" in the union proposal that "encroached on owners' rights" by giving the plant committees control over hiring and job assignments. Smol'ianinov, representing the union, argued that the owners had ignored reasonable wage demands. Under current rates, workers earned a daily minimum of

---

The bakers' union, by comparison, had around 200 members, the woodworkers' 400, the meatworkers', commercial employees', and postal-telegraph employees' each about 300, and the union of cooks and waiters just over 250 members. GASO, f. 1994, op. 1, d. 1, ll. 9–10ob., 221; f. 1988, op. 1, d. 12; TsDNISO, f. 1, op. 1, d. 384 and d. 132, l. 32.

[37] Other local moderate socialist leaders who found themselves caught between their faith in the revolutionary democracy and their desire to preserve the revolutionary state included Mensheviks Petr Gal'perin and Mikhail Davidovich and SRs Solomon Gurevich and Sergei Efimov.

[38] Shur aggressively defended this statist Menshevik position, for instance, at a 29 June mass meeting of soldiers committee and plant committees held at the local circus.

[39] *SV* (6 April, 16, 27 July 1917); GASO, f. 799, op. 1, d. 1, l. 200.

4 rubles per day. Owners would raise that to 7.5 rubles, but the union wanted a nine-ruble minimum. Shur proposed a commission to establish points of agreement, but Smol'ianinov declared that the difference over wages was so great as to make conciliation hopeless, and Esaitis called wages non-negotiable.[40] Shur ended the session with no basis for a compromise.

On 27 August the metalworkers' union announced that it would strike beginning the next day. The Kornilov rebellion, however, forced them to suspend this plan. The strike committee's Bolshevik leadership declared the threat of the Kornilovites of greater immediate importance than the contract dispute and called on union members to help defend the city. The Bolsheviks' role in the local Committee to Save the Revolution, which coordinated anti-Kornilov efforts, did much to boost their popular legitimacy. But the emergency also gave Shur another opportunity to forge a compromise and to ask again that workers consider the larger interests of the revolutionary state.[41] Shur argued in a 3 September appeal that the Revolution was still in danger. He called on "conscious workers" to "go to your benches and machines," and explained that "At the present grave moment I consider strikes impermissible, and I appeal to you, comrades, to settle all conflicts through arbitration."[42]

But Shur's appeals had little effect on contract negotiations. On 5 September he brought the two sides together for another meeting. Smol'ianinov offered some minor concessions on contract language regarding the arbitration of disputes, but insisted that the owners in return agree to changes that gave the union greater control over assignment of overtime. Esaitis said that this was impossible and that the contract must affirm the owners' complete control over hiring and job assignments. These, he argued, were the owners' "exclusive rights"; at most, workers' might have a consultative voice on labor conditions. (Esaitis' handwritten comments on the owners' counter-proposal make it very clear that he considered the union's demands a threat to enterprise viability and simply would not grant concessions on this issue.)[43] Smol'aininov responded by "categorically insisting" on workers' right to oversee hiring decisions. Shur adjourned the meeting until the next day.

---

[40]GASO, f. 1994, op. 1, d. 1, ll. 31–31ob.; *WKP* 1, 100.
[41]GASO, f. 1994, op. 1, d. 1, l. 11; *WKP* 1, 99; *Sotsial-Demokrat* (27 September 1917); I. V. Sidorov, "Iz vospominanii sviazista," in *Za vlast' sovetov! Vospominaniia uchastnikov oktiabr'skoi sotsialisticheskoi revoliutsii na Smolenshchine* (Smolensk, 1977), 91.
[42]*SV* (3 September 1917).
[43]GASO, f. 1994, ll. 43–47ob. and unnumbered pages.

When the parties gathered on 6 September, Shur proposed a compromise: the union would drop some of its work control demands and management would increase wages by forty and fifty percent. Both sides refused. Shur proposed that his compromise be adopted as the basic framework for arbitration. Smol'ianinov asked for a recess to consider this, but quickly returned and announced that the union stood by its earlier position.[44] A strike was now inevitable.

The Metalworkers' Strike, Class War Rhetoric, and the Collapse of the Center

The Smolensk metalworkers' strike began on 7 September and lasted for twenty-nine days. The strike committee asked that tram and electrical workers remain on the job. (The reason was three-fold: the union claimed to be concerned for public safety; it hoped to use the threat of a strike by tram and electrical workers as a bargaining tool in negotiations; and the tram and electrical workers were city employees and therefore not covered by negotiations with the Society of Plant and Factory Owners.) The remaining 403 of the union's 472 members went on strike.

The metalworkers' strike seemed to trigger a cascade of other strikes over wages and work control. Striking metalworkers were soon joined by the cooks and waiters, bakers, pharmacy employees, and workers and employees in nearly a dozen other trades (the wood and leather workers were already on strike). All had seen their real wages eroded by the fall's rapid inflation, and all ignored pleas from Shur and the moderate socialist leadership to refrain from striking. By the end of September there were over 1,500 workers and employees on strike in Smolensk, and several strikes lasted well into October.[45] Strikes completely shut down several large enterprises.

Smolensk's moderate socialist leaders, already distraught over the city's rising crime rate, worried that the strikes would lead to violence.[46] Several socialists openly speculated that workers were giving way to "anarchistic tendencies" and that their "consciousness" was "deteriorat-

---

[44]GASO, f. 1994, op. 1, d. 1, ll. 39–39ob.

[45]*SV* (23, 26 August); (23, 28, 30 September); (1, 4–6, 19–22, 24–25 October 1917); *Revoliutsionnoe dvizhenie v Rossii v avguste*, 250–51; GASO, f. 1994, op. 1, d. 1, l. 231; *WKP* 1, 87, 105, 108; *Ustanovlenie i uprochenie sovetskoi vlasti*, 109; *Rabochii put'* (6 May, 7 November 1922); and *Volia naroda* (30 September 1917).

[46]*SV* (23, 26 August; 23, 28, 30 September); (1, 4–6, 19–22, 24–25 October 1917); *Revoliutsionnoe dvizhenie v Rossii v avguste*, 250–51; GASO, f. 1994, op. 1, d. 1, l. 231; *WKP* 1, 87, 105, 108; *Ustanovlenie i uprochenie sovetskoi vlasti*, 109; *Rabochii put'* (6 May, 7 November 1922); and *Volia naroda* (30 September 1917).

ing."[47] The owners were clearly concerned about violence as well: on 9 September Esaitis closed Viliia and, fearful of reprisals, asked that the militia post a guard at the plant. In a letter to the Shur, Esaitis claimed that the plant committee and members of the soviet had "made threats." He asked that Shur use his influence with the soviet to assure the plant's safety.[48]

The dispute seemed intractable. Union and management negotiators viewed each other with growing hostility. Shur, though, saw settling the metalworkers' strike as the key to restoring order in the city, and called yet another negotiation meeting on 13 September. After nearly two hours in which neither side moved, Smol'ianinov suddenly announced that the union would compromise on wages if the owners agreed to put the issue of strike pay before an arbitrator. The union would then return to work during the arbitration process. But Esaitis protested that the union had just introduced yet another new demand, strike pay. The meeting quickly degraded into mutual recriminations and ended without a settlement.[49]

The metalworkers' strike proved costly for plant owners, who despite state contracts had barely sustained operations.[50] But it was much harder on union members. Their strike fund quickly ran dry and the help they received from the All-Russian Union of Metalworkers covered only a tiny fraction of regular wages. Commodities prices rose rapidly as the strike dragged on, further crippling strikers' ability to hold out.[51] On 29 September Smol'ianinov met with Shur to discuss ways of ending the strike. He reiterated that the union was willing to compromise on most issues and would resume work during arbitration. Shur passed this message to Esaitis, but a meeting of the Society of Plant and Factory Owners that day had already rejected the union's proposal and absolutely refused arbitration over strike pay.[52]

The owners, aware that the union was running out of resources, now pushed to break the strike. On 1 October, Esaitis appealed directly to Viliia workers in an open letter posted at the factory, hoping to hasten the strike's collapse. He dropped all reference to the rights of the owners and instead reverted to his earlier theme of protecting the Revolution.

---

[47] *SV* (6, 7 September 1917).
[48] GASO, f. 146, op. 1, d. 1, ll. 195–96.
[49] GASO, f. 1994, op. 1, d. 1, ll. 235–36ob.
[50] Besides the account books for the Villia plant in GASO, f. 146, see Paul Flenley, "Industrial Relations and the Economic Crisis of 1917," *Revolutionary Russia* 4 (1991): 184–209.
[51] *Sotsial-Demokrat* (27 September 1917).
[52] GASO, f. 1996, op. 1, d. 1, l. 33; f. 146, op. 1, d. 21, ll. 183–85.

Production, he wrote, must resume "for the interests of the country and the population." If the union cared for the Revolution it would return to work. Esaitis insisted that owners had abided by government policy and that the union's demands "amount to robbery." Since the union would not listen to reason, he concluded, the workers should return to their jobs.[53] But this tactic failed; not a single worker returned to the plant on 2 October.

On 3 October, though, Shur seemed to come close to achieving a negotiated settlement. He called both sides to his office and sternly reminded them "that in addition to the interests of both sides there is here a third interest, that of the state [*gosudarstvo*]." State interests mandated arbitration. Esaitis responded that owners would agree to arbitration on wages, but not on strike pay, as this would be conceding that they were at fault. Moreover, Esaitis insisted that "as a free citizen" he had the right to hire and fire whom he pleased; that was not a matter for arbitration. Smol'ianinov now revised his earlier offer: if the owners agreed to workers' control over hiring, then both wages and responsibility for the strike could be decided by arbitration. Esaitis repeated that owners simply would not accept union rates as basis for arbitration. But he, too, seemed to revise his earlier position, and now claimed that the owners might agree to strike pay at the equivalent of two hours' wages per day at pre-strike pay rates. Smol'ianinov countered by offering a revised version of Shur's 6 September compromise: the union's wage scale proposal and the owners' drafts on work control would serve as the basis for arbitration and the issue of strike pay would go before a special arbitration court (*treteiskii sud*). The union had given ground on work control issues.

Shur seized on this opening. The union, he told Esaitis, had finally compromised; now owners should do the same. Esaitis agreed to Smol'ianinov's first two points, but he again absolutely rejected arbitration on strike pay. At this point Smol'ianinov clearly lost his temper. He shouted that the owners had no interest in settling the strike and that Esaitis had "revealed the capitalists' motives"—to hold down wages and refuse workers their right to oversee production decisions. He repeated the union's final offer, demanded immediate arbitration, and stormed out.[54]

The metalworkers' leaders publicly had described the union as a weapon in the class struggle, but their contract demands had avoided all reference to class antagonisms. Despite his public criticisms of Menshevik-

---

[53] GASO, f. 146, op. 1, d. 1, l. 192.
[54] GASO, f. 1994, op. 1, d. 1, ll. 41–42; SV (5 October 1917).

SR "class conciliation," Smol'ianinov had conducted negotiations like a traditional "bread and butter" union representative. And the union was depending upon arbitration by a commission under the control of the city's Menshevik labor commissar. Until 3 October, Smol'ianinov had refrained completely from using class rhetoric during negotiations.

But Smol'ianinov's 3 October outburst marked a turning point; he now seemed completely certain that this strike amounted to class warfare. On 4 October Smol'ianinov warned a metalworkers' general assembly that the Society of Plant and Factory Owners wanted to "deliver a death blow" to the infant union. In a foreshadowing of later calls for the nationalization of industry, Smol'ianinov proposed that the union ask the Moscow Region Labor Commissar to impose state control over Viliia and Gergard. If owners did not agree to arbitration, Smol'ianinov further threatened, then the union should shut down the city's tram and electrical service. The meeting unanimously approved Smol'ianinov's resolution. It then called on Smolensk's workers for "moral and material support." The fate of the metalworkers in this struggle, the union declared, would be the fate of all workers' organizations, the fate of the Revolution.[55]

Factory owners also saw the metalworkers' strike as a battlefield in a larger class conflict, for which they held the moderate socialists largely responsible. Again, they framed their own position as a defense of the Revolution, legality, and property rights. A 6 October resolution by the Society of Plant and Factory Owners accused the metalworkers' union of disrupting defense production, attacking property rights, and causing financial hardship for the entire city.[56] Arbitration of the strike using the existing procedures was impossible, owners declared: the moderate socialists who controlled the current arbitration commission were biased towards the workers and could never render a fair decision. The owners would agree to arbitration only if the arbitration commission had a "public [obshchestvennyi] character." The owner's use of this term reflected the liberal conception of a supra-class public devoted to national rather than particularistic interests. It can only be read as a condemnation of Shur and the moderate socialists; the owners defined their own interests as indistinguishable from those of the greater public and of the Revolu-

---

[55] GASO, f. 1994, op. 1, d. 1, l. 33ob.; *Rabochii put'* (6 May 1922); *SV* (6 October 1917).

[56] The Gergard Brothers claimed that the strike had ruined them and, in an interesting parallel to the union's position, proposed that the state assume control over their bobbin factory. *Ustanovlenie i uprochenie sovetskoi vlasti*, 126; *Znamia Truda* (14 October 1917).

tion, while the moderate socialists could not rise above class interests. Moreover, for the owners strikes and rising crime proved the moderate socialists could not control the lower classes. In an echo of the Kornilov affair, the Society of Plant and Factory owners called on the Minsk Military District Commissar to declare martial law. They also called for creation of a "Commission for the Struggle Against Anarchy" to preserve order and protect property rights.[57]

Shur's statist, centrist position simply could not hold. Both the owners and the union had equated their own interests with those of the Revolution. No matter what Shur did, one side or the other would accuse him of turning his back on the Revolution. The Bolsheviks made Shur a symbol of the failures of Menshevik-SR conciliation at a time when many of Smolensk's workers and employees had rejected moderate calls for conciliation.[58] Workers now began to recall their Menshevik and SR deputies from the soviet. As the moderates lost influence, the Smolensk Bolsheviks (whom the party's central committee had criticized all year for poor organizational and agitational work), gained almost 50 new places in the local soviet.[59] The Bolsheviks still had only 80 of two hundred twenty places in the soviet, but with the large Left SR faction and the many non-party deputies they formed a voting block that constituted the soviet majority from early October. In a stunning admission of political impotence, on 21 October the Menshevik and SR members of the soviet's executive committee announced that they had lost authority among worker and soldier deputies and resigned their posts. Two weeks later Shur stepped down as labor commissar, also citing "the shift in the mood of Smolensk's working masses."[60]

One of the ironies of Shur's position was that he had, in fact, supported the metalworkers' demands. Shur's statist convictions prevented him from doing so publicly, as this would have jeopardized the neutrality of the labor commissariat. But he had done so "privately," in a 4 October memorandum to the Moscow Region Labor Commissar. On the same day that the union requested Moscow's intervention, Shur informed

---

[57] GASO, f. 146, op. 1, d. 21, ll. 170–71; *SV* (11 October 1917).

[58] In his 1935 unpublished "official" history of the labor movement in Smolensk, A. T. Abramovich argued that Shur did nothing to support the metalworkers during their strike. TsDNISO, f. 7, op. 1, d. 132, l. 37.

[59] For criticisms of the Smolensk Bolshevik's disorganization, see *Protokoly Tsentral'nogo komiteta RSDRP(b), avgust 1917–fevral' 1918* (Moscow, 1958), 40; *Ustanovlenie i uprochenie sovetskoi vlasti*, 94, 99–105; *Bol'sheviki Smolenshchiny*, 234–40.

[60] For statements by Menshevik leader S. E. Gal'perin and SR leader P. I. Bukhshtab, *SV* (25 October 1917); for statement by S. P. Shur, *SV* (9 November 1917).

Moscow's labor commissar that the metalworkers had "important" demands "directed towards improving the workers' condition." He blamed the strike on the factory owners, whom he described as intransigent, and argued that the owners' refusal to settle the strike had opened the potential for violence: "whether the rank and file of workers will remain peaceful and prudent is hard to say." He begged that Moscow send a delegation and force owners into arbitration. Moscow could do this while appearing impartial, whereas he could not. "What is at stake here," Shur warned, "is the authority of a workers' organization—the Trade Union of Metalworkers . . . it is impossible to refuse the workers this demand without striking a serious blow against our workers' organizations, their authority, and their strength."[61]

Over But Not Settled

Existing documents are (remarkably) mute on this matter, but it appears that the Moscow Region Labor Commissar did intervene. On 8 October the Society of Plant and Factory Owners suddenly agreed to arbitration on all issues, including strike pay.[62]

The strike was over but far from settled. Hostilities actually intensified when metalworkers returned to their benches at Viliia. Esaitis greeted union representatives with a list of workers to be laid off "because of shortages." The plant committee called Esaitis a liar; the layoffs, they argued, were retribution against workers who had struck. They accused him of hiring replacement workers and ordered that he obtain approval from the plant committee for all future managerial decisions.[63] Esaitis not only ignored this order but on 23 October announced that he no longer recognized the plant committee. Because the committee had violated legal procedures and behaved irresponsibly, workers must elect a new committee, which he then would recognize. Moreover, Esaitis now warned that any worker absent from his post without permission would be fired, including union and soviet deputies.[64]

Although metalworkers in plants returned to their benches, other members of the union now went out on strike. Electrical and tram workers (the latter of whom had joined the union in August), were city employees. They demanded wage increases parallel to the union scale for specialists and greater control over work assignments. The city adminis-

---

[61] GASO, f. 1994, op. 1, d. 1, ll. 33–34.
[62] GASO, f. 1994, op. 1, d. 1, ll. 32, 221ob.; TsDNISO, f. 7, op. 1, d. 132, l. 37; *SV* (7, 17 October 1917).
[63] GASO, f. 146, op. 1, d. 21, ll. 176–79.
[64] GASO, f. 146, op. 1, d. 21, ll. 172–73.

tration, which had been resistant to city workers' wage and work control demands throughout 1917, refused to negotiate.[65] Tram and electrical workers then struck and effectively shut down the city's electrical grid and all public transport from 19 to 24 October.[66] On 25 October the city agreed to arbitration over the tram and electrical workers' demands. But national events had already superceded developments in Smolensk.

The Metalworkers and the First Months of Soviet Power

News of the Bolshevik seizure of power in Petrograd led to armed confrontation between the soviet's left faction and the duma in Smolensk. After a brief and inconclusive battle for control of the city on 30–31 October, both sides agreed to form a Committee of Public Safety. For almost two months the Committee of Public Safety, the soviet, and the duma quietly wrestled for authority. Then, in late December, the soviet disbanded the Committee of Public Safety and declared itself the city's sole governmental authority. But in reality all duma and Provisional Government agencies in Smolensk continued to function until mid-February 1918.[67]

The Bolshevik Revolution did not weaken Esaitis' determination to control "his" factory. Esaitis remained Viliia's director for all of 1918—even after the Soviet government nationalized Viliia in fall—and continued fighting the plant committee whenever it attempted to shift decision-making authority away from management. On 9 November 1917, he even refused to grant the soviet's request to provide paid release time for Bolshevik metalworker G. L. Tsetlin, who had been elected as Smolensk's new labor commissar.[68] In November the plant committee pressed new demands for control over the factory, citing the Soviet regime's 14 November Decree on Workers' Control. Esaitis still refused to recognize the legitimacy of the plant committee. On 22 November the committee informed Esaitis that a new workers' commission would oversee all activities in the plant office. It formed a "Provisional Control Commission" to implement workers' control and assigned Bolshevik metalworker B. Klimovich to oversee all purchasing of materials for the plant. Esiatis ignored them.

---

[65] See, for instance, the discussion of the June strike in city-run bakeries in Hickey, "Local Government," 871–72.

[66] *WKP* 1, 106, 108, 109; SV (19, 20 October 1917).

[67] The local soviet began arresting Menshevik and SR activists in late December 1917. Shur was arrested on 23 December; there are no traces of him in the source material from that point, and his fate is unknown. *Smolensk. Kratkaia entsiklopediia* (Smolensk, 1994), 539–40.

[68] GASO, f. 146, op. 1, d. 21, 167.

Although Esaitis held the plant committee in disdain, he recognized that keeping Viliia open required cooperation with the new regime. By the first week of December the plant could neither purchase materials nor pay wages. It was simply out of funds, a fact recognized both by the management and by the plant committee. Esaitis worked with the plant committee and the soviet administration to obtain funds and materials. But he consistently rejected the committee's efforts to oversee plant operations, in part because he believed them incompetent. On 19 December the plant committee demanded that Esaitis comply with its requests and cooperate in implementing its production plan. This was, the committee argued, "in the state's interest."[69] Esaitis did not reply until 15 January, when in a long and detailed letter he argued that the plant committee had shown "the limits of its economic competence." He had studied all of the new regime's laws and regulations regarding workers' control and had concluded that there must be an agreement over the "balance of rights" between the manager and the committee for the plant to maintain production. "If the plant committee agrees to these points," Esaitis concluded, "then it is possible to hope that we will have harmonious cooperation and our work together will be easier." The next day Esaitis presented the committee with a list of issues to be settled in the interest of production. But he reminded them that according to the law "the activities of the plant committee are to be as a CONTROL ORGAN ONLY."[70]

The relationship between Esaitis, the plant committee, and Soviet authorities underwent a significant transformation in early spring 1918. Viliia's workers elected new leaders in mid-February, just as the plant demobilized and Esaitis called for layoffs. (Esaitis decided that the first to be laid off should be those who "spend their time conversing, reading newspapers, and so on": this list included some half of the members of the "old" plant committee.)[71] The new plant committee was composed almost entirely of non-party Lithuanian metalworkers, and repeatedly ran afoul of the city's Bolshevik-dominated Central Council of Plant and Factory Committees, which by mid-August was accusing the Viliia workers of counter-revolutionary activities. The council even charged that Viliia's workers were not really proletarians, but representatives of alien class

---

[69] For the plant committee's 19 December letter, see GASO, f. 146, op. 1, d. 21, ll. 128–128ob.

[70] Emphasis in the original. For Esaitis' 15 January letter to the plant committee, see GASO, f. 146, op. 1, d. 21, ll. 216–17. For his 16 January letter (and a copy sent to the Smolensk Sovnarkhoz), ll. 118–123.

[71] GASO, f. 146, op. 1, d. 21, ll. 96–96ob.

interests.[72] The plant committee's battles with Esaitis over work assignments and other control issues continued, but from the summer of 1918 Esaitis found Soviet authorities more eager to take his side than that of the plant committee.

The Bolshevik Revolution did not bring an end to the contract dispute between plant owners and the metalworkers' union. The Society of Plant and Factory Owners had agreed to arbitration, but on 24 November the union rejected this on the grounds that a member of the arbitration commission was related by marriage to one of the plant owners. Most likely the real issue was that the arbitration commission had been formed when the Mensheviks controlled the labor commissariat, and its members included moderate socialists. The union demanded that the Smolensk Soviet take decisive action to end the dispute. In the meantime, the union leadership changed: Smol'ianinov and Red'kin resigned their posts to devote themselves to soviet tasks, and Ivitskii became the union's new chairman. Ivitskii met with the owners' representatives to discuss implementing the new contract, but with no success. On 27 December the Smolensk Soviet ordered the owners to pay the metalworkers for strike time, but owners simply ignored the order. In January 1918 the plant owners agreed to a soviet-brokered settlement that raised wages, increased the union's participation in managerial decisions, and provided the workers with back pay for the period of the strike. But owners never implemented the agreement. In March 1918, during yet another sharp inflationary spike, the union placed a new set of new wage demands before the provincial Council of National Economy (Sovnarkhoz), of which Smol'ianinov was the chairman.[73] Smol'ianinov now found himself on the same side of the negotiating table as Esaitis and the Society of Plant and Factory Owners (which was not disbanded until June 1918), arguing that union wage demands undermined enterprise viability.[74]

Conclusions

In their seminal work on strikes in 1917, Diane Koenker and William Rosenberg argue that strikes functioned both as "routine tools of labor-management relations in a system with mutually acceptable rules" and "as instruments for revolutionary change." They further explain that "strikes and other forms of activism did not just reflect the way workers, managers, and political figures thought about social and economic

---

[72] See, for instance, GASO, f. 146, op. 1, d. 21, l. 39.
[73] GASO, f. 146, op. 1, d. 21, ll. 1–50; f. 1994, op. 1, d. 1, ll. 221–22.
[74] See, for instance, GASO, f. 1994, op. 1, d. 1, ll. 64–72, 221ob.

relationships. Much more powerfully, they changed the ways these participants perceived the political process."[75] This microhistory of one labor dispute in one small city supports both of these contentions.

Both Smol'ianinov and Esaitis took "routine" approaches to negotiating the metalworkers' contract dispute, and the strike itself fit well within the established boundaries of labor conflict. A collapsing economy and soaring inflation meant that neither side could objectively afford to grant significant concessions. And in the context of the Revolution, these volatile issues became politically explosive.

In fall 1917 in Smolensk, as in Russia's larger cities, workers interpreted failed negotiations as proof that management would not yield power over the work place unless forced to do so through revolutionary means. In the wake of the Kornilov rebellion, both workers and owners framed their positions in ways that implicitly rejected the Provisional government's legitimacy. Workers' disillusionment with the prospects of negotiated labor settlements contributed to their rejection of moderate socialists like Shur, who had argued that workers must seek negotiation and arbitration. The statist position that Shur and other moderate socialists took became untenable and, in fact, contributed to their political collapse.

While the above points are familiar from studies of labor politics in larger cities, there is another critical, and often overlooked, aspect of such conflicts that is revealed by events in Smolensk. All players, including the owners, framed their positions as vital to the Revolution. Esaitis could not agree to the union's demands not only because they infringed upon property rights, but because he fundamentally believed that such demands would cripple productivity and damage the Revolution. At this level, the strike was as much a contest over what the Revolution itself meant, which amplified its political significance and made compromise even more difficult.

Finally, the strike and its aftermath also highlight a contrast between moderate socialist and Bolshevik political practice. Shur and the moderate socialists had staked out ground that was impossible to hold; they could not at once represent the interests of the working class and the "objective" interests of the revolutionary state. When it became clear that they had lost the support of the city's workers, the moderate socialists interpreted workers' changing dispositions as a breakdown in "conscious-

---

[75] Both quoted passages are from Koenker and Rosenberg, *Strikes and Revolutions*, 326.

ness," but nevertheless stepped down. When in 1918 the left socialists faced the same dilemma, they defined workers' demands as "counter-revolutionary" and attributed them to alien class characteristics. Unlike the moderate socialists, the Bolsheviks would not voluntarily abandon power.

Afterword

In the introduction, the editors indicated ways that this collection's viewpoints about labor history differ from those of the past. Irretrievably lost are previous certitudes about the structural intertwining of the workers' economic plight and political repression, their alleged attainment of consciousness in association with certain parties or factions of parties, and the socialist revolution and rise to power of a proletarian state. Workers certainly bore economic, social, and political burdens. They certainly attained a consciousness of themselves as a collective with grievances and coupled this with a generally socialist, radical, and anti-capitalist outlook. Workers indisputably supported and participated in the 1905 and 1917 revolutions and, for a time, provided considerable, if not exclusive, support for the Bolshevik Party. Yet, as recent research emphasizes, their pre-1914 plight reflected rising expectations in an expanding economy and liberalizing political regime as much as outright deprivation and oppression. Workers were also not so isolated from the educated and middle classes as we have thought. As several pieces of this study suggest, the workers' collectivism did not exhaust their psychology. Nor was their socialism and radicalism monologic, exclusive, or brutal. Furthermore, workers quickly withdrew much of their support for the Bolsheviks (Communists) in power and, by mid-spring 1918, had largely reverted to their earlier preference for Mensheviks and Socialist Revolutionaries. The extraction of so many planks of our former interpretative structure has left the earlier decades' meticulously constructed edifice teetering on the brink of collapse.

Some scholarly commentators now seek novel methodologies and interpretations for the Russian Revolution. Deep flaws in Russian political culture, the "backwardness of the peasantry," and cycles of violence are offered as explanations of a revolution run awry. Hardly new in terms of attitudes towards Russian political culture and the peasantry, these interpretative twists, often expressed in state-of-the-art representational and linguistic modes, stand on their heads the predominant analytical tendencies of the 1960s, 1970s, and 1980s. During those decades, many scholars portrayed the revolution and the rise of the soviet state as real or potential solutions to the problems of Russia's backwardness, whereas now historians deploy the alleged backwardness to explain the revolutions' failures, even into the Stalinist era. This collection's authors, undismayed by the falling away of the past's over-certainties, wish to avoid constructing oversimplicities for the future. For example, we doubt that counter-posing the alleged backwardness of the Russian people or of Russian political culture to Communist efforts at modernization is a fruitful approach. The following analysis of these studies' chief findings may help suggest just where labor historiography, at least in the *New Labor History* collection, stands on these and other questions.

The articles of this collection stress worker experience, which raises interesting questions about the relationship between experience and language. Rosenberg's study, conceptually central to our investigation, directly addresses this problem. Although it locates its empirical basis in certain developments of 1917, the article's theoretical framework has a broader application. Rosenberg displays exquisite sensitivity to the centrality of language. He perhaps exceeds the perceptions of the editors when he asserts that he is "not essentializing experience . . . [as a] foundation of historical reality or truth but posits its inchoate subjectivity as a source of memory and meaning." Still, Rosenberg highlights the role of experience, with the crucial additions of the unexpected and the inexplicable. These uncertainties, Rosenberg avers, partially reflect underlying culture. The resulting behaviors and responses may lie outside the principals' awareness. In this formulation, long- and short-term experience, tempered by indefinable contingencies, ultimately coalesce with discourse to shape action—in not always predictable ways. Taking this point to its logical conclusion, we would like to add, with a bow to Bakhtin's thinking about speech's contextual, experiential specificity, that experience, with all its components, molds discourse as much as language molds action. Regardless, the question of workers' civic culture occupies a central place in this collection. Rosenberg's workers escape easy classification or control as he warns against abject "presentism" in too precipitously jettisoning all the frameworks and understandings of the past. The editors agree. Social, party, and political history, with a broader embrace and wider empirical bases than in the past and with reframed non-prescriptive and non-reductionist conceptualizations, offer our best hope to understand the revolutionary era in Russia.

The founders of the Wildman Group originally intended to promote the investigation of political and party activism at a time during the mid-1990s when interest in such topics had waned. Although interest has still not revived, several pieces in this collection turn upon questions about workers' political experiences and their relationships to parties. These analyses, however, avoid the overly structured ideological frameworks of past historiography. For example, Pate's study of Social Democracy elucidates the discursive struggle for control of the workers' movement between 1907 and 1914. Worker activists in legal associations offered broad support for a unified workers' movement that neither rejected nor identified exclusively with political parties. With this focus, Pate recovers a lost history (and a very important one) of the pre-1917 Social Democratic and labor movements, with, it should be noted, great explanatory value of hitherto perplexing developments. Melancon's investigation of the 1917 factory committee movement and Hickey's study of the 1917 revolution in Smolensk, likewise, shift focus from narrowly defined party analysis to the broader implications of worker and socialist activism. Parties or, at least, members of parties figure closely in the episodes of history but not always stereotypically. These studies and Rosenberg's remind us in a timely manner of the centrality of politics. The Russian revolutions were political events of vast national and international significance. Political parties, with deep roots in Russian experience, society, and culture, acted out their views in ways that still significantly escape accurate classification. The Russian State Archive of Socio-Political History (the former central party archive) has undertaken a massive project of publishing documents and histories of all Russia's parties. Russian historians abroad could follow this lead by delving into the lived experience, strivings, and contributions of the various political groups, even conservative or failed ones, without reflexive animus. The contributions of Pate, Melancon, Hickey, and, as we shall see, others of this collection have the potential to serve as suggestive templates for aspects of a new political history.

Interactions between state, society, and the individual are lively subjects of investigation in Russian history just now. As noted, Gorshkov's examination of child labor during Russian industrialization has the merit of elucidating an uninvestigated area of labor history. In doing so, it also reveals the unexpectedly great role and burden that laboring children had in Russia's early industrial growth. Additionally, Gorshkov suggests relationships between the late tsarist state and society, in particular as regards legislation, that escape traditional priorities. Melancon, Rosenberg, and Hickey direct our attention forward to the workers' relationship to the state during the transitory period between the fall of the tsarist regime and the establishment of Communist autocracy. In various ways, these four studies, and those of Pate and Mikhailov as well, call into question the time-honored autocratic approach to the study of late imperial Russia. In Gorshkov's analysis, legislation about child labor and related matters arose in a lengthy interaction between working populations, entrepreneurs and their associations, academics, and various levels of state bureaucracies. Many of the last, especially at the local level, responded directly to workers' complaints in bringing forward requests for legal amelioration. The laws that eventuated reflected society's public discourses and pressures. During the 1890s and early 1900s, on the basis of peasant family and communal psychologies and practices, the workers portrayed by Mikhailov consciously press for and bring to life their own institutions in urban and industrial environments. The phenomena detailed in Pate's study of the labor movement and Social Democracy between 1907 and 1914 become comprehensible in terms of Mikhailov's earlier workers and Melancon's factory committee activists after February 1917. Workers' control of their workplaces and lives, based upon communal responsibilities and moral outlooks, are the common thread throughout much of this collection. Russian toiler—worker and peasant—as actor is a potentially powerful theme. This approach de-emphasizes old style class consciousness, with its partisan connotations, in favor of a new version, firmly rooted in worker-peasant psychology and worker culture, experience, and aspirations.

Most strikingly, Steinberg's, Firsov's, and Herrlinger's articles stress the individual, the subjective, and the spiritual. In the past, worker-oriented analysis concerned itself with collective categories of class, party, and, later, gender. Workers were drunk or sober, literate or illiterate, men or women, urbanized or "recently arrived from the village," "conscious" or "unconscious" as judged by their relationship to valorized or despised occupations (metalworkers or printers versus all others) or to party. Within the context of these fierce binary antinomies, the worker as suffering, transgressing, morally striving, and assertive subject, simply did not enter the picture. The implications of the historiographical *volte-face* from the collective to the individual transcend Steinberg's comment about the "dangerous discourse" of the workers' newfound subjectivity, as accurate as that might be. The field requires an accounting for this transformation. Russian historiography is not accustomed to hearing that individualism constitutes a dangerous discourse. One approach might suggest that the new focus on the subjective and the spiritual, and on peasant psychologies and independently articulated worker aspirations adumbrates an unexpected worker culture—with political, religious, and other ramifications—quite distant from earlier elite-generated formulations.

Recent historical conferences have been replete with discussions of civil society and the public sphere in pre-1917 Russia, another veritable transformation of our field's discourse about that era. Although this collection focuses on labor, ostensibly a part of the old historiographical discourse, its findings place it firmly in the new discourse. A rock bottom sub-stratum of civil society is, after all, the individual, who, in pursuit of individually defined interests, seeks association with others of like mind or interest, initially against the overweening pretensions of autocracy and then in the establishment of the new open society and state. In the old discourse, workers found their "consciousness" within estate or class boundaries ascribed to them by elites, with political and economic tasks also neatly in place. In this volume, workers seek and find their own identities. They are individuals, whose psychology, if Mikhailov is correct, reflects peasant communal outlooks that interact with the urban, industrial environment in a positive way. The result is a group of people whose identities are various, fragmenting strict definitions of class boundaries, but who independently seek association on their own terms. The worker associations that arise are assertive, responsible, and capable of reaching out to other social groups and institutions. All of this begins within the boundaries of a formally autocratic state that long before the 1905–06 political reforms had responded to societal pressures and aspirations in its crucial legislative procedures. State and society engaged in a dialogue, a precondition of civil society, with workers as fledgling participants, as many of these studies suggest.

By 1917, workers had graduated from fledgling to full participants in a new dialogue between state and society. In the process of what they saw as building a socialist society, the workers expressed their vision of the state as reflective of their individual and collective demands and interests. Drawing from a rich revolutionary tradition of action rooted in the language and outlooks of socialism, workers aimed at the democratic future of their hopes, dreams, and aspirations. Rather than summarily and arbitrarily jettisoning that imagined future, strikingly real to workers and others at that time as motivation for and organizing principle of action, the authors of this collection reclaim it for the workers as chief analytical fulcrum. These studies narrate a workers' history on its own terms, without the monologics and implied and real violence of Bolshevism and the Soviet state.

This is not to paint this era's workers' question in roseate colors. Poverty, drunkenness, anger, and despair also wend their ways through worker narratives. Nor will it do to pretend that all analyses within this collection offer coinciding views on all points. One might note the contradiction between Herrlinger and Firsov about the vitality of Orthodoxy among workers; or unresolved oppositions between religious outlooks and socialist or secularist ones; or, above all, the clash between worker collectivism and individualism. Nor are all questions addressed here. Except for Herrlinger's comments about women's religion, these studies say little about gender (a question addressed by several historians in the Russian field). Insufficiently noted in Russian historiography in general and in these studies in specific is the positive side of worker relations with the intelligentsia and even the bourgeoisie, an insight that reflects the editors' own research concerns and findings. Nor do these studies comment enough about workers' culture, political and everyday, as a general phenomenon, although the contributions of Steinberg, Firsov, and Herrlinger, among others here, offer genuinely fresh insights into the turn-of-the-century proletarian way of life. These questions and problems suggest new research agendas for which, we are thankful, ample sources now exist.

New Labor History's findings, if accurate, also raise new sets of questions. For example, we might note that the independent roles of workers, their striving for cooperation, their individualism, and their religiosity seem to predict a very different state than the one that emerged by 1918 with its multiple oppressions. The new Soviet state persecuted the bourgeoisie, entrepreneurship, religion, and all non-Bolshevik political movements, not to mention the workers, the peasants, and even the eponymous soviets. During the pre-revolutionary years and in 1917, workers resisted any version of state (or party) formation that limited their control of the workplace, their daily lives, and politics. How did it come to pass that a revolution made in the name of workers and other toilers and with wide support from such groups developed with malign consequences for these very social elements? The general anti-capitalist attitudes among Russian workers previously noted by many commentators and by Mikhailov, Melancon, Pate, and Hickey here doubtlessly played a role, as did the harshly posed crises and class conflicts of late 1917 and 1918. Yet, these parts of the puzzle do not equal the whole in a predictive way. An anti-capitalist class consciousness does not equal a hierarchical one-party dictatorship over all society's elements, at least not in the democratic, cooperative, and associative views of Russia's worker-peasants. We are only unaware of this at this late date because we have never really examined and taken seriously worker-peasant discourses about social, economic, and political matters, preferring instead to denigrate and snidely dismiss, the bane of the high Russian intelligentsia and many commentators abroad.

This brings us back to the editors' call for fresh research. The Russian Revolutions, in the end, produced a dictatorship that laid claim to be a workers' state, yet hardly resembled what the workers had envisioned (a prime example of unintended consequences). This tragedy can hardly be swept under the rug of war and civil war, an old tactic with new adherents that constitutes an historical hypocrisy. The 1917 revolutions were to a great extent *about* ending Russia's involvement in the world war. The 1918–21 civil conflicts, properly understood, were in great measure a *protest* on the part of workers, peasants, soldiers, and intelligentsia against draconian Communist policies and measures. The worker-peasant, as this volume suggests, cannot be labeled as a contaminant of the revolution. Workers and peasants were not a hindrance to modernization, supine before and complicit in the most extreme violations of democracy, human values, and, for that matter, socialism. Without a complete analysis of Russian labor history, freed not only from the old narratives and conventions, but also from the chronological boundaries of 1917, the history of the Revolutions will continue to rest on a combination of conjecture, outworn concepts, and several political partisanships. The participants in this collection and in the Wildman Group, by nature of their research priorities and efforts, suggest to the field that it is too early to close the book on the history of Russia's workers.

Michael Melancon
Auburn, AL

Alice K. Pate
Columbus, GA

March 2002

Index

Aksel'rod, P. B., 104, 109, 112, 115,116
Aleksandrovskii, V., 155, 159
Anarchists. See Parties.
Anarcho-Syndicalists. See Parties
Andreev, Leonid, 130
Arteli. See Workers' associations
Artillery Administration, Main, 180, 182–84, 201
   Bureau of, 188
   Conferences of (March and April 1917), 182, 184
August Block, 115

Badaev, A, 117
Baklanova, I. A., 185–186
Berdiaev, N. A., 69
Bibik, Aleksei, 127, 142, 148
Bloody Sunday, 98, 119, 120
Bolsheviks. See Parties
Broido, M. I., 103, 107
Bulgakov, S. N., Archpriest, 70
Bulkin, Fedor, 89, 142–143
Bureaucracy, State, 24, 29

Caucasus Delegation, 104–05, 107, 111
Central Industrial Region, 40, 26
Cherevanin, F. A., 106, 110, 190, 192

Child labor, 9–33
   age limitations, 14, 23–26, 27
   attitudes toward, 13, 24
   historiography, 10–11
   in agriculture, 12–13
   in England, 20
   in France, 20, 23,
   in industry, 10, 14, 16–23
   in mines, 10, 12, 14
   in state and manorial factories, 12, 14
   inquiries on, 18
   laws on, 13–16
   legislative proposals. See Legislation
   literature, 10
   public debates, 23–29, 32
   statistics, 10, 17–21, 30, 32
Child workers
   ages of, 17–20
   education of, 13, 24, 26
   health decline among, 21–23
   wages, 10, 15
   work related incidents, 21–23
   working hours, 26–27, 31
Childhood, 10, 131, 146
Chizhikov, Aleksei, 141, 146
Chkeidze, N, 117
Churikov, Ivan, 56, 59
Civil War, 69

M. Melancon, A. Pate, *New Labor History*, Bloomington, IN: Slavica, 2002

Contracted labor, 16, 24
Credo (Economist), 109

Denikin, A. I., General, 69
Dalin, D, 191
Dan, Fedor, 101–02, 104, 109, 111–13
Dostoevskii, F. M., 130, 152
Duma, 100, 121
 Elections, 107-16
 Fourth, 101, 115–17
 SD faction, 100–01, 107, 117–18

Economists, 97, 105, 110, 121
Economy, economic growth, 10, 16–17, 70, 80
Edinstvo (Unity), See workers
Education of factory children
 debates about, 24–27
 proposals concerning, 28–29
 in laws, 13, 30
Eight-hour day. See Workday limitations
Eley, Geoff, 163
Émigrés, 95, 97–99, 114, 116–17, 122
Engel, Barbara A., 42
Esaitis, E. G., 208, 214, 218, 220–21, 223–24, 227–31
Evangelical Christians, 54, 56

Factories
 Arsenal, 179–81, 183
 Baltic Ship Building, 85–86, 91, 180, 184–86
 Izhorsk, 80, 85, 180, 186
 Gergard Bobbin, 211, 215, 225
 Nevskii Ship Building, 58, 80, 84, 87–88, 186
 Putilov, 83, 187–88
 Sestroretsk, 87, 180, 182, 186
 Sokolovskaia Cotton Mill, 20, 22
 Trekhgornaiia Textile Mill, 39, 43–44
 Viliia Metal Works, 207, 211–18, 223, 227–29
Factory (Plant) Committees, 88, 90, 177–206 passim, 213–18
 activists of, 177
 All-Russian Conference, August 1917, 189, 196
 First Petrograd Conference, May-June 1917, 177, 183, 186, 188–97, 204
 organizers of (organizing bureau of), 182–89, 195
 State, 180–86
Factory inspectors, 30–31, 82, 173–176
 All-Russian Conference, June 1917, 170–71
Factory legislation. See Legislation
Factory schools
 debates about, 26, 27, 28, 29
 in legislative proposals, 27
Family, 10, 12, 13, 16, 24, 25, 26, 36, 78, 81
February Revolution, 177, 212, 215
Fedorov G., 190–91
First Russian Revolution. See Revolution of 1905–07
Folk culture, 130, 136, 144
Foucault, Michel, 162, 166

Gan'shin, Sergei, 147, 156
Gapon, G. A., 73, 75, 83

Gapon Assembly, 83
Galili, Ziva, 208
Garvi P., 113–14, 88
Gastev, Aleksei, 146, 159
Gender (relations), 146, 164–65, 174
Gessen, V. Iu., 11
Gippius, Z. N., 76
Glebov-Avilov, N., 190–92
Gol'denberg I. P., 100, 103, 113
Golgofsie Khristiane, 74
Golos Sotsial-Demokrata, 100–01, 108, 110–13
Gorky, Maxim, 10, 49, 145, 151, 184
Gorev B., 101–03, 114, 122

Haimson, Leopold, 96, 122, 167
Holy Synod, 71
    Procurator General, 65, 67, 71. See also Pobedonostsev K. P.
Hooliganism, 73, 140

Ignat'ev, P. N., Count, 25
Ignat'ev commission, 25, 27
Industrialists, 16, 24
    Associations of
      Council of Russian Industrialists, 29,25
      Manufacturing Council, Moscow Section of, 23, 24
      Moscow Association for the Support of Russian Industry, 31
      Petersburg Society of Factory and Mill Owners, 83
      Smolensk Society of Plant and Factory Owners, 208, 225–27

Industrialization, 12, 16, 69, 80, 93
Initiative groups, 107, 118–20
Intelligentsia, 26, 77, 88, 93, 109, 154, 156
Ivanovo-Voznesensk, 72

Joyce, Patrick, 172

Kanatchikov, Semen, 36, 40, 48, 49, 100, 107
Kankrin, E. F., Count, 15
Koenker, Diane, 41, 230
Kokovtsov, N. V., 31
Kokovtsov commission, 31–32. See also Law of 4 March 1906
Kornilov rebellion, 221, 231
Kotkin, Stephen, 209
Kozodavlev, O. P., 15
Kristeva, Julia, 147
Krugovaia poruka (collective responsibility), 93
Krupskaiia, N. K., 49
Kubikov, Ivan, 127, 133, 141, 143, 145, 156

Labor Arbitration Committees (Smolensk), 225–26
Labor Commissars, 226
Labor historiography, 77, 164
Labor unions. See Trade unions
Lasalle, Ferdinand, 144
Leiberov, L. P., 178
Legislation
    on factory labor, 13, 14, 15–16, 29–30, 31
    debates about, 23–29, 32
    impact on children's employment of, 32
    proposals on, 23, 25, 27, 29

regarding women workers, 30-31
Law of 1903 on Starosty, 82-87
Law of 4 March 1906, 95
Law on Sickness Insurance 1912, 121
Law of November 1917, 228
Lena Gold Field Massacre, 119
Lenin (Ul'ianov), V. I., 72, 77, 97, 99, 105-06, 109, 112-16, 118, 122, 190-92, 199, 205
Lermontov, Mikhail, 129-130
Levin, V. M., 180, 184, 187-89, 192-94, 202-04
Liashko, N., 152-54
Liquidationism. See parties
Literatory, 100, 103
Loginov, M. A., 141, 154, 159
Luch, 110, 119-21
L'vov-Rogachevskii, 148-49

Malinovskii R. V., 100, 107
Martov, I. O., 95, 97, 99, 110-13
Martynov, A. S., 101-03, 114
Mashirov, Aleksei, 146, 148, 152, 156
May Day, 119-20
Mensheviks. See Parties
Merezhkovskii, D. S., 74
Mezhraionka. See Parties
Milukov, P. N., 186
Ministry of Finance, 18, 23, 82
Ministry of Internal Affairs, 15, 82
Moscow, 13, 61, 141, 150

Nardinelli, Clark, 11
Naval Administration, 180, 184
    Conference of, 184

Factory committees, 187
Nechaev, Egor, 126, 136, 148, 150, 156
Nekrasov, N. A., 9, 10, 130, 152
Nekrasov, N. V., 167, 169
Nield, Keith, 161
Nikitin, Ivan, 130, 152

October Manifesto, 58
Old Believers, 45, 74
"Open Letter," 108-9
Orthodox Church, (Russian), 35, 38, 42, 45, 48, 65, 70, 72-74, 76, 129, 135
    influence on peasants, 65, 67, 68
    influence on Russian society, 65, 66
    influence on workers, 35, 37, 49, 50, 65-67, 70, 135
Ostroumov, S. S., 69
Otkhodniki. See Peasant migrants

Palmer, Bryan, 171-72
Pankratova, A. M., 91, 92
Parties
    Anarchists, 179, 211
    Anarcho-syndicalists, 196-97, 199-200
    Bolsheviks, 96, 99-100, 104, 106, 110, 116, 121, 148, 173, 185, 188, 191-93, 195-99, 203, 205, 207, 212, 216-18, 221, 226, 231-32
        Conciliators, 100, 111, 112, 120-21
        Otzovists (Recallists), 99, 111
    Bund, 103, 115, 210, 212

Mensheviks, 99, 100, 103–04, 106, 108, 110, 111, 114–16, 118, 120
   Liquidationism, Liquidator and Liquidationist Controversy, 95–97, 99–102, 103, 107–08, 111–12, 116–18, 121–22, 179–80, 186, 189, 191–93, 195–97, 199, 205, 207–08, 212, 219, 224, 226
   Organizational Committee, 115, 117, 119, 120
Mezhraionka (mezhraionets) 120, 196–97
RSDRP (Social-Democrats, SDs), 88, 96, 98, 100, 103, 112, 118, 122, 173, 200–01, 210
   Central Committee, 101, 102–03, 105, 117–18, 120
   Conferences: Fifth, 103–05; Sixth, 114–115
   Congresses: Fourth, 98, 99, 101; Second, 97, 105, 116
   Foreign Bureau, 105, 114
   Petersburg Committee (PK), 100, 101, 104, 107, 108, 120
   Plenums, 103, 111, 115
   Russian Bureau, 103–04, 113
Socialist-Revolutionaries (SR), 40, 88, 106, 119, 120, 180–81, 186, 189, 191–93, 195–97, 200–01, 205–06, 208, 212, 214, 219, 225–26
   Left, 195, 197, 226

Maximalists, 206
Party (*Partiinost'*), 99, 102
Pashkovtsy, 56
Paternalism, 39
Pavlovskii, Feodosii, 68
Peasant commune, 77, 78
Peasant migrants, 9, 14, 35, 42, 48, 49, 51, 66, 68, 78, 80
Peasants, 67, 77
   traditions of, 77, 78
Peskov, P. A. 30
Petersburg Spiritual Consistory, 46
Plekhanov, G. V., 95, 97, 108
Plekhanov Commission, 167–70, 173–75
Pobedonostsev, K. P., 71
Podvitskii V. V., 214
Population growth, 17
Potresov, A. N., 99, 109, 112
Praktiki, 95–96, 98, 100–03, 105–08, 110, 112
Prishvin, M. M., 75
Proletariat. See Workers
Provisional Government, 183, 191, 194, 199, 201, 218
   Commissars (Moscow, regional labor), 218
   Commissars (Smolensk), 208, 220, 225
   Ministry of Trade and Industry, 170
   Ministry of Transport, 167
Pushkin, A. S., 152–53

Rabochaia Gazeta, 118
Rancière, Jacque, 139
Rashin, A. G.,17
Rasputin, G. E., 75
Reed, Christopher, 206

Revolution of 1905–07, 35, 37, 46, 63, 66, 67, 77, 94, 96–97, 106, 136, 138, 149, 158
Revolutionary culture, 96, 106, 109, 110
Riazan', 13
Riazanov, D., 190, 192, 195
Rosenstein, M., 187–89, 191, 195

Samoilov, F. N., 72
Savin, Mikhail, 135, 145–46, 155
Scott, Joan, 171
Semenov, Mikhail, Bishop, 74
Senate, Imperial Russian, 13, 79
Shchetinin, A. G., 75
Shidlovskii Commission, 84, 86, 87
Shliapnikov, A., 189
Shur, S. P., 208–09, 218–22, 224, 226–27, 231
Shvarts, S. M., 121
Skobelev, M., 190, 194
Smidovich, P. G.,
Smith, Steven, 181, 199–201
Smolensk, 200, 207–32 passim
Smol'ianinov V. A., 208, 212, 215, 220–21, 223–25, 230–31
Social Democrats (SDs). See Parties
Socialism, 67, 70, 71, 72, 202–03
Socialist, 71, 116, 121–22
    Bloc, 212
    Left, 197, 213, 220
    Moderate, 208, 213, 219, 222, 232
    Right, 190
Socialist Revolutionaries (SRs). See Parties
Society for Religious and Moral Enlightenment (ORRP), 37, 50, 52
Soviet
    Council of National Economy
    Deputies, 72, 86, 87
    Petrograd,192
        Executive Committee, 169, 180, 195
    Smolensk, 219, 228, 230
    Provincial Executive Committee, 212, 215
    Sovnarkhoz, 230
St. Petersburg, 13, 23, 44, 46, 62, 95–96, 104, 109, 112, 115–16
Stalin, 116–18
Starosty, 84–92 passim
    elections of, 84, 85, 86, 87
    Law of 1903. See Legislation
    regulations on, 84, 85, 86
State and manorial factories, 12, 14, 16, 86
Imperial State Council, Imperial Russian, 25, 29
Stepanov, Z. V., 186, 196–99
Stolypin, P. A., 95, 106
Sverdlov, Ia. M., 191, 195–96, 205

Technical Society, Imperial Russian, 17, 28
    Commission for Technical Education of, 17, 19, 21, 28
Temperance Society, Aleksandr Nevskii, 52, 56
Thompson, E. P., 164
Trade unions, 83–84, 88, 95, 97, 99, 100, 106, 107, 110, 210, 126, 133–34, 140, 142, 147
    activists, 83, 100

All-Russian Metalworkers'
    Union, 223
  Central Bureau of, 100, 190,
    194
  Petersburg Metalworkers'
    Union, 89, 100, 118, 120-
    21, 126, 132, 142–43, 189
  Petersburg Printers' Union,
    89, 90–91, 144
  Smolensk Metalworkers'
    Union, 207–08, 210–11,
    213, 215–19, 222, 227
  Textile Workers, of, 100
  Trade Union Commission,
    103
Trotsky, L., 95, 111–14, 118, 165
Tsetlin, G. L., 228

Urbanization, 93

Valuev, P. A., Count, 27
Valuev committee, 27, 28
Vasilsftev, A., 187
Vladimir province
Voronkov, N., 178–82, 184–86,
    188–92 passim, 195,
    203–04
Vostorgov, I. I., 71
Vyborg District St. Petersburg,
    110–11, 186
Vyshnegradskii, I. A., 31

Wade, Rex, 206
Women, 130–34
Work day limitations, 181–82
    suggestions regarding, 23,
      25, 27–28
    in factory laws, 15–16, 29–31
Workers, (see Peasant migrants)
    activists (activism), 77, 82,
      96, 98, 106, 112, 116,
      120–22, 144, 156, 173,
      179
  apprenticeship of, 13–15
  associations (*arteli*, clubs,
      cooperatives, and *zemli-
      achestva*.) See also Fac-
      tory committees), 49, 79,
      80, 92, 95, 96, 97, 106,
      107, 110, 120
  atheism, 36, 37–38, 40,
      59, 66, 70, 72
  civic consciousness, 81–82,
      137, 204
  class consciousness, 66, 70,
      93, 130, 135–36, 138,
      148, 156–57, 204
  collectivism, 93, 135, 143,
      156, 175
  cult of man, 123-39
  cult of self (*lichnost'*), 123,
      139–44, 154
  cult of suffering, 128–36, 158,
      160
  drunkenness, 47, 51, 57, 59,
      91–92, 140–41, 143,
      146, 148
  education of, 72
  funeral practices, 39-40
  immorality, 51, 68, 72,
      140–42, 146
  individualism, 88, 144,
      149–50, 156
  intelligentsia, 148
  literacy among, 53–54
  morality of, 72, 123, 128–29,
      131, 137–38, 168
  movement, 77, 82, 84, 99,
      102, 109, 157, 178
    legal, 102, 107, 104, 110,
      111

illegal, 99, 101, 102, 104, 107, 110
participation in Bible readings, 53–55, 63
politization of, 66, 92
poverty, 13, 25, 41, 128, 151
prostitution, 133, 140–41
religiosity, 35–36, 39–40, 46, 48, 50, 52–54, 57–63, 66, 68–69, 71–72, 129, 145
temperance, 52
sexuality, 140
social life, 37, 128, 141
statistics, 17, 19, 20, 80
strikes, 15, 58, 72, 80, 83, 89, 119–20, 178, 207–30 passim
unity movement, 98, 101-02, 104–05, 108–10, 113, 116, 120–22
violence among, 92, 141, 151, 175
wages of, 15, 21, 26, 207, 220, 223, 230
wedding practices, 38, 40–42
Workers' control of industry, 93, 118, 183–85, 199–201, 203, 207
Soviet Nov. 1917 Decree on (see Legislation)
Workers' organizations. See also Trade Unions, Factory Committees and Workers' associations
influence of peasant tradition on, 41–42, 77
influence of the intelligentsia on, 77
Petersburg Assembly of Russian Factory Workers, 83
Strike Committees, 178, 179
Unemployed Council, 87, 92
Working conditions, 10, 21–22, 73, 98
World War I, 11, 32, 33, 122, 125

Zemliachestva. See Workers' associations
Zenkovskii, V. V., 66
Zhuk, 119
Zinoviev, G., 190–92, 205
Zubatov, S. V., 82
Zubatovist experiment, 82